Screening Cuba

Film Criticism as
Political Performance
during the Cold War

Hector Amaya

University of Illinois Press
Urbana, Chicago, and Springfield

Library of Congress Cataloging-in-Publication Data
Amaya, Hector.
Screening Cuba : film criticism as political
performance during the Cold War / by Hector Amaya.
    p.   cm.
Includes bibliographical references and index.
ISBN 978-0-252-03559-3 (cloth : alk. paper) —
ISBN 978-0-252-07748-7 (pbk. : alk. paper)
1. Motion pictures, Cuban—United States.
2. Motion pictures—Cuba—History—20th century.
3. Motion pictures—Political aspects—Cuba.
4. Film criticism—United States—History—20th century.
5. Film criticism—Cuba—History—20th century.
I. Title.
PN1993.5.C8A63   2010
791.43097291'09045—dc22   2010001599

Contents

Preface

Throughout my life I have claimed several political identities. The first one was leftism or socialism or communism. At the time, I was not quite clear on the difference. Growing up in Mexico, I needed to break with my traditional up-bringing and developed a taste for Canto Nuevo, a brand of political song that postrevolutionary Cuban musicians made famous in Latin America. I expressed my claim on leftist identity by learning to sing and play on my guitar music from Cuba. Later came film. Under the influence of lyrics by Silvio Rodríguez and movies by André Kieslowski and Tomás Gutierrez Alea, I became acquainted with a form of expression that helped me interpret the world around me, and I did just that. With strongly felt and well-rehearsed contempt, I criticized a society of oppression and injustice and applied the verses from the songs and dialogues from the films to interpret Mexico and the world.

Since that time, I have been interested in the cultural practices that people feel compelled to embrace to become proper political beings, in particular film viewing. Because most people go through their lives with a learned sense of what they have to do in order to be and seem political, I believe the practice of film viewing is often a type of public performance of political self-defi-nition. Take for instance Andrew Kopkind, who, on March 30, 1985, wrote for *The Nation* the following commentary about the Cuban film *Memories of Underdevelopment* (1968): "The persistence of *Memories* in the consciousness of a political generation is like the permanence of a sacred text in the culture of a sect. . . . The crowds that saw the movie that weekend at the Film Forum went to take part in a ritual that told them who they were or what they had been, which is not only a wonderful way to spend an hour in the dark but almost redeems the whole painful, extravagant and self-indulgent process of movie making" (377). Viewing this "sacred text" was a "ritual" that "the crowds" used to enact their identities and "sect" membership. Kopkind's interpretation of the film also identifies him as belonging to the "sect" not only for the caring way in which he wrote, but also because of the place where he published it, *The Nation*. Like in this example, the practice of film viewing, which is at the center of this project, relies on publicity and thus on community and institutions.

These are the things this book is about. But a book is more than a piece of writing. It is also a community artifact that signals the architecture of relationships, institutions, and, in my case, geographies. And so, while in the following pages this architecture is hidden in a performance of academic professionalism, here I present it to you as transparently as possible.

That I compare two cultural practices in two different nations comes naturally to me as an immigrant; the geographies of Mexico (my place of birth), Canada (my first immigrant home), and the USA (my present and my future) provide perhaps my deepest subjective voice, perhaps not mentioned enough in the book. These geographies are the standpoint from which I write, a transnational vantage point from which culture is rarely static and semiosis is fleeting. So, though I do not strongly signal this book's transnational roots, the reader should be warned. The book is about movement and transnational connections. I marvel at the power of culture to provide, however limited, a platform for mutuality. To love the same thing may not make us the same, but it brings us together. The Cuban films I write about are the objects of affection that connect, in disjointed timelines, the Cuban and American critics, all of this in the middle of the cold war.

If my life has been that of an immigrant, so is my academic formation and professionalization. From Universidad Autónoma Metropolitana, in that universe of a city we call "el de-efe," to the University of Calgary, to the University of Texas at Austin, things, ideas, professors, peers pile up. I am thankful to all and to the institutional support of my first professional home, Southwestern University, a remarkable place of learning and research in Texas. Last, I need to thank the University of Virginia and the Media Studies Department for assisting me in this project's last stages.

This book would not have been possible without the advice and support of many people. My gratitude goes to Janet Staiger, who walked with me every step of the way, acting as an invaluable guide in all matters. Thanks also to John Downing for his expert advice and political commitment. I also need to thank Kathleen Higgins, Mary Kearney, Michael Kackman, and Sonia Labrador-Rodriguez. The list of wonderful editors and expert commentators is long, but also necessary. I thank Chris Lucas, Avi Santo, Kyle Barnett, Dustin Harp, Mark Tremayne, Mary Grace Neville, Jay Baglia, Teena Gabrielson, Erika Berroth, and Katy Ross for lending me their editing skills, reading chapters of my work in an admirably expedient and professional fashion.

Two people read every page of this book, and my very special gratitude goes to them. Jennifer Petersen, my friend, colleague, and my wife, read every word and made the writing process not only humane but also joyful. Jennifer's theoretical expertise brought coherence to many of my ideas and propositions and she helped me polish the writing throughout. Denise Blum, a friend and mentor, read, edited, and expertly commented on the entire work. Her love for Cuba and for Cubans and her knowledge of the island exemplify reflexive scholarship, teaching the balance between knowledge production and ethics.

Finally, I wish to thank my parents, Mita and Hector, who are the real origin of the book and to whom this work is dedicated. They are the structure in my thought, my moral fiber, and my perseverance; whatever wisdom I may possess I have only borrowed from them. My siblings, Angelica, Macky, and Cesar, and their partners Eleazar, Ritchie (we miss you), and Mayra, also deserve my thanks for so patiently supporting my endeavors.

Introduction

The venue for the first Festival of Cuban Film in the United States was the Olympia Theatre in New York City where, from March 24 to April 2, 1972, seven feature films and fifteen documentaries, all of which had received international prizes and acclaim, would be exhibited for the first time in the United States. The event was noteworthy not only because it marked the debut of Cuban film in U.S. theaters, but also because it signaled a potential shift in the strained cultural exchanges between Cuba and the United States. According to the film critic of the *New York Times,* "the Festival promised to be 'the most important film retrospective of the year' " (Myerson 1973, 27).[1] Instead, it became the stage for deeply anti-Cuban sentiments by social, political, and governmental forces. The Cuban filmmakers were denied visas; the Olympia Theatre was stoned and threatened with bombs; and during the exhibit of the first and only film that was eventually shown (*Lucía* 1968, d. Humberto Solás), anti-Castro agents released white mice, interrupting the event and marking it with a sense of mockery. The next day, newspapers mentioned the disturbances caused by the mice but failed to mention that ambassadors from twenty-two nations attended the festival.

Although a number of the films later gained distribution in the United States, these events demonstrate how national animosities affected cultural exchange between the two nations. Yet, the events also show how *citizens* (involved in cultural activities) in both nations attempted, and often succeeded, at establishing cultural links, even if this required defying their own governments. I refer to citizenship in its social manifestations, as a composite of public behaviors that are socially interpreted as civic and political. On the American side, leftist individuals, intellectuals, and critics challenged the American government, embracing a counter-hegemonic style of citizenship. On the Cuban side, directors and officials tried to travel to New York to show postrevolutionary Cuban culture; in doing so, they were embracing a socialist-revolutionary style of citizenship that supported the Cuban government. These two styles of citizenship in cultural workers (directors, writers, film festival organizers, and critics) are a central theme in this book. Both are leftist, both are active, both are professional, and both embody a civics in which culture plays a central role.

This book examines and compares the critical reception of four Cuban films in Cuba and the United States. I propose that certain film criticism is civic public behavior and a way of performing citizenship when criticism is prompted by what is recognized as a "political film." In the following chapters, I show two ways of doing criticism that fitted two institutional structures and two discursive practices that fitted the different political and critical traditions of the United States and Cuba. The films are: *Memories of Underdevelopment* (1968), directed by Tomás Gutiérrez Alea; *Lucia* (1968), directed by Humberto Solás (both *Memories* and *Lucia* were released in the United States in the early 1970s); *One Way or Another* (1974), directed by Sara Gómez; and *Portrait of Teresa* (1979), directed by Pastor Vega. The period covered in my investigation roughly spans 1968 to 1985. These years in Cuba coincide with the first two decades of the revolution and the maturation of revolutionary cultural (film and criticism) practices. In the United States, this period is shaped by the political and cultural struggles of the 1960s and the politicization of foreign film consumption. For the Cuban cases, I concentrate on people (from here on, cultural workers) working for official cultural institutions (for example, ICAIC), magazines (for example, *Bohemia*), journals (for example, *Cine Cubano*), and newspapers (for example, *Granma*). For the United States, the cultural workers I analyze were also part of cultural institutions (for example, American Documentary Films [ADF]), magazines (for example, *The Nation*), journals (for example, *Cineaste*), and newspapers (for example, the *New York Times*), where political writing is not only permitted but also encouraged. These institutional venues are either centrist or leftist, which allows me to compare them with the leftist Cuban sites.

Although legal aspects of citizenship are important, in this book I make no attempt at theorizing Cuban and American legal aspects of citizenship. I remain at the level of the social and the cultural. At this level, citizenship is contingent, historically specific, and pluralistic. Different public behaviors are civic in different nations and political communities. Moreover, these behaviors are "learned" and their public performance is what specific political communities recognize as a "political identity" and "good citizenship." Although the political field is the source of many ideas about citizenship, all aspects of social life contribute to the understandings of citizenship. The cultural field is a prime contributor to citizenship, because it mediates between political lingo and structures, and popular ideas and the people. Because of the power associated with mediation, the cultural field is a place for debate and struggles over the meanings, and proper displays of, citizenship. It is thus never a unified field, but fragmented and rich.

Characteristics of the Study

From the 1960s to the 1980s, Cuba had roughly ten million people and the United States around 250 million. Cuba was organized politically and economically as a socialist nation with a centralized planned economy, a single leader, and a single official political party, the Cuban Communist Party (PCC). The United States, a symbol of capitalism, was also a symbol of democracy, with more than two centuries of a bipartisan, electoral system of government. Cuba's underdeveloped status and its Latin and African ancestry opposed the United States' developed Anglo-Saxon self-image. The list of differences between the nations could go on, and the obvious question is: if comparing assumes similarities, given that the differences between these nations are so stark, how can they be compared? This question is particularly relevant to social and cultural comparisons, because most social and cultural theories are built on the basic assumption that social, economic, historical, cultural, and political contexts determine societal phenomena. "Class," for instance, a basic unit of analysis for capitalist societies, has had a very different meaning in Cuba, where the leadership has tried to construct a classless society. Private ownership and capital, two key elements of Marxist theories of reification, ideology, and hegemony, are also manifested differently in the Cuban and U.S. contexts. Arguably, even the most basic notions of stratification in these nations may very well be incomparable. Yet, this study is built on the theoretical and methodological assumption that comparisons are not only possible but also reasonable. Certain similarities allow me to assume this. Both are nation-states partly defined by discourses of nation and citizenship. Both are societies that use culture to exercise social and political control.

Leftist, Marxist, and feminist identities and communities, though differently expressed, have existed in both nations. Finally, both nations have strong discourses linking culture, including film and criticism, to identity, politics, and ethics. All of these factors make some comparisons reasonable.

In the following chapters, I elaborate on four areas that are basic to the constitution of criticism and criticism's politicized mode of film reception. 1) The first is the institutional contexts, particularly as they relate to the political fields. Here, political criticism is constituted through social, organizational, and political coordinates, which determine criticism's institutional location. The site of political criticism also exists in three other cartographic dimensions. 2) Political criticism is determined by the contingent way cultural work becomes politicized. 3) Political criticism is also located in the map of ideas, theories, and discourses that explain criticism in relation to its purported social role, namely, to provide the proper understanding of politicized cultural texts. 4) Finally, political criticism has a place in the map of self-identities and is thus an expression of ideas about selfhood, politics, and public performances of citizenship. These four social maps come together in the practice of political criticism, and although each can help explain the other three, each has its own rules that are the result of specific histories, discourses, and practices. Following Erving Goffman (1959), I refer to "performance" as "all the activity of a given participant on a give occasion which serves to influence in any way any of the other participants" (15). In his theories on performance, social actors behave according to specific rules to have the desired effect on others. Criticism as political performance is a practice that obeys staging cues provided by social norms and historical contexts. The goal is not only to be political, but also to appear political.

Given the complexity of these four social maps, I heavily rely on secondary sources to draw the institutional and historical contexts. I am indebted to the work on Cuban film and culture of Michael Chanan, Julianne Burton, Paul Julian Smith, Ana López, Marvin D'Lugo, John Downing, and others. I add to these an emphasis on cultural policy, which is key to linking criticism to Cuban official cultural institutions. On the American side, I am indebted to the cultural historical works of Todd Gitlin, Michael Denning, Barbara Wilinsky, Arthur Marwick, Winifred D. Wandersee, and Andrew Ross, among others. I draw the other three areas of argumentation using primary and secondary research that includes archival evidence, reviews, articles, essays, interviews, cultural policies, aesthetic treaties, declarations of intent, and other historical evidence.

Theoretical Contexts

It is safe to say that Cuban film was experienced differently by Cuban and American critics. For Cuban cultural workers, the films' power to signify was an expansion of the social promises of the Cuban Revolution. For liberal and leftist American cultural workers, the same films were rendered meaningful by cold war discourses and by socialist, revolutionary, and antiestablishment values common among progressive Americans. Both sets of viewers experienced Cuban films as political, and to view them, to enjoy them, or to hate them was a way of being political, a way for these citizens to perform their respective political identities.

There is nothing random about properly performing a political identity. These performances are embedded in contingent social and discursive traditions, with their respective histories and sets of knowledge that serve to legitimize, explain, and reproduce political behavior. Voting, for instance, is a recognizable political behavior and a way of performing a political identity in the United States and Cuba. Political theories about democracy, psychology, and social behavior render it possible to argue that, in contemporary society, a person's politics can indeed be represented by a vote. Practices, discourses, and knowledge sets come together to give a political identity a discernable shape that can be identified and imitated. By extension, when I claim that this particular set of cultural workers enacted their political identities via film criticism, I am thus hypothesizing that there is nothing random about the way film reception relates to one's political identity. This book explores this hypothesis by examining the social and discursive traditions, sets of knowledge, and historical events that made the critical reception of these Cuban films performances of discrete political identities. In doing so, I am also claiming that the hermeneutic and textual processes involved in viewing, interpreting, and evaluating the films are part of the discernable shape of American and Cuban cultural workers.

I bring together theories of citizenship, film reception, institutions as cultural systems, and self-formation. Citizenship here is an identity, a political expression of the self, that is related to cultural policy and national discourses of civics and history. I use Toby Miller's ideas to bind citizenship to culture. Film reception theory is a historiographical and materialist approach to film history and theory, based on the work of Janet Staiger, that helps theorize the Cuban and American modes of critical film reception. I use the work of

Pierre Bourdieu on habitus and the field of cultural production to explain the structural behavior of the American and Cuban cultural systems. Finally, Michel Foucault's propositions on self-formation serve as a model to understand behavior, ethical and political dispositions, and the role these two have in an individual's sense of selfhood. Together, these frameworks offer a model for investigating structural issues (social, political, historical) as they shape politicized critical film reception, and also the role politicized film reception plays in the subject's sense of self.

Film reception theory is an approach to cinema formalized in the 1990s as a reaction to overtly textual approaches to film theory. In *Interpreting Films: Studies in the Historical Reception of American Cinema*, Staiger (1992) produces a theory of film reception that, shaped by materialist historiography, stresses "contextual factors rather than textual materials or reader psychologies" (xi). Though typical film theories have tended to pay exclusive attention to either textual or psychological factors surrounding the viewing/reading process, Staiger analyzes text and context in history, even historicizing the psychological makeup of viewers and the way this historicized psyche relates to material conditions.[2] Although contingency is thus central to reception, the social nature of viewing and its immersion in economic, cultural, and political structures tend to normalize it. Janet Staiger calls this normalization "modes of reception." These modes, some of which are central to this book, include techniques for interpretation, strategies for viewing, and the textual and contextual factors shaping reception (Staiger 1992; Staiger 2000). They are embedded in history, nationality, and, as I later show, belong to specific communities. With this in mind, I ask: *What makes modes of reception political?* In the next chapters, I answer this question by reference to different social and discursive processes including the following: political cultures of the time; modes of film production and exhibition; and sets of knowledge most responsible for defining film as political in the United States and Cuba.

Criticism is a professional activity and thus bound by institutional conventions, templates of professionalism, and an array of cultural, economic, social, and political expectations that define the particular role of the critic and of criticism at any given time in any given setting. A useful way of thinking through these complex set of variables is to draw attention to the structural nature of the cultural world. Bourdieu uses the term "field of cultural production" to talk about the structural properties linking a diverse array of institutions and peoples into a somehow coherent social system. Comprised by museums, artists, art schools, galleries, and the like, in contemporary societies, this field includes film production, exhibition, and distribution systems as well as the institutions that validate and legitimize work and membership. For Bourdieu, the field of culture occupies a subordinated position to the field of power (the system of power relations or the "ruling classes") (Johnson 1993, 15). The intellectual class that comprises the cultural field lacks economic and political power, and for that reason Bourdieu refers to it as a dominated segment of the dominant class. Holding the field together are the structural relations between its subfields (that is, criticism, film production) and the field's "habitus," which structure dispositions and practices within the field (Bourdieu 1993, 125). The habitus includes systems of cognitive and motivating structures that help agents act ethically. It governs thought, expression, and action while constituting the objective possibilities of freedom (Bourdieu 1990, 53). Moreover, because the habitus is not only objectified in social structures but also in the bodies and minds of individuals, it would be improper to talk about the social as subjecting the individual. Agents exist in positions from which they are constantly enacting and modifying the habitus, always structuring, always in sites of regulated freedom. In the next chapters, I explore the Cuban cultural field in which criticism was inscribed in relation to the formation of cultural institutions (for example, ICAIC, Casa de las Américas, and so forth), cultural policy, and intellectual and hermeneutic postrevolutionary traditions. I investigate the U.S. cultural field in which progressive criticism was inscribed in relation to the cultural transformations of the American sixties, political movements shaping progressive culture such as the women's movement and the New Left, and foreign film exhibition.

Different sets of conventions guided these cultural workers on how best to profess and perform a political identity. The bulk of these conventions relate to the historically specific ways in which citizenship, as an identity, is publicly expressed. These conventions dictate the type of work individuals must perform for themselves to appear properly political. What areas of the self will be seen as political depends on contingent traditions knowledge. For example, for an American feminist in the 1970s, these areas may include behavioral work for interacting with men and also intellectual work such as reading and discussing feminist texts. Because this work required specific techniques, knowledge sets, and calculated outcomes, Foucault called it "technologies of self."

Foucault states that technologies of the self "permit individuals to effect by their own means or with the help of others a certain number of operations on their own bodies and souls, thoughts, conduct, and way of being, so as to transform themselves in order to attain a certain state of happiness, purity, wisdom, perfection or immortality" (Foucault 1988, 18). Using technologies of the self, individuals address issues of personal identity, community, personal freedom, and historicity. They do so by embracing culturally specific ways of ethically taking care of themselves. This process of self-formation depends on reflection and on defining such reflection, and the actions ensued by it, as acts of contingent freedom. The individual does not create the technologies she/he will use to transform herself/himself, nor does she/he create the "utopian" form the self may be shaped after; a habitus provides both things. Nonetheless, at the individual level of analysis, technologies of self are not simply evidence of subjection; at the individual level of analysis, technologies of self are practices of contingent liberation, practices the individual takes toward the constitution of its freedom and completion. That is, Foucault uses technologies of the self to talk about the fact that ideology is not reflected in a straightforward fashion in the individual and that the relationship between social structures and individual practice is highly dynamic, prone to discontinuities and multiplicities (McNay 1992, 59). These technologies address the historically specific modes in which individuals come to understand themselves as subjects by providing individuals with the know-how to interpret and reflect on their own experiences. But besides providing techniques of hermeneutics, technologies of the self function, at the social and individual levels, to draw the boundaries of freedom and liberty because they ask the individual *actively* to seek methods for self-fashioning and propose a final shape or form for the self that in most instances fits the historical representation of a free man or a free woman (Foucault 1985, 50).

Foucault's approach allows me to talk about people, ways of being, and knowledge sets that I respect and consider progressive (feminist, leftist, and socialist), while acknowledging that they are and have been institutional, normative, and traditional. This may seem a paradox, but only if "freedom" and progressive politics are defined by reference to liberal ideas of freedom. In my work, freedom is contingent and historical, and thus I am interested in locating practices that we historically define as free.

With these ideas in mind, I track the elements of cultural work in Cuba and the United States that can be assembled into a technology of self that includes film reception practices. We can begin by stating that film viewing, interpretation, and enjoyment are social activities constituted in a habitus.

Because of this, and as discussed in most film theory, viewing is an activity bound by tradition; it is accumulated cultural capital that ensures the habitus's permanence. As with any other social practice, however, film viewing is not simply an expression of social structures but also an expression of the film viewer's ability to structure the system, to reflect on it, even if this reflection is incomplete and ideological. And just as film viewers exist "in sites of regulated freedom," film viewing is exercised in "relative autonomy with respect to external determinations of the immediate present" (Bourdieu 1990, 56).

Returning to Foucault, I argue, and this book demonstrates, that technologies of self are linked to Cuban cinema in that they have historically acted as mediating systems that structure the critical reception practices of American and Cuban cultural workers. In these cases, film reception has become a part of technologies of self, for it became an operation geared toward the transformation or reconstitution of cultural workers in order to attain a specific type of public selfhood and citizenship (Foucault 1988, 18). The revolutionary Cuban society and feminist and leftist communities in the United States typically required that their members should try to become specific types of individuals, selves, and citizens. Members of these communities who were also cultural workers (film critics, academics, and essayists) were also expected to master specific hermeneutic techniques that would constitute the community as a habitus. This is particularly clear in the Cuban case. Part of this clarity was the result of a certain harmony that existed between the discourses of citizenship, individuality, and culture. Those interested in becoming cultural workers were also expected to be members of the political vanguard and, accordingly, were expected to embrace cultural policies and the theoretical definitions that could further these policies. Though contradictions and ambiguities existed, these were minimal, particularly within institutional settings. Moreover, hegemonic ideas of ideal citizenship were common in Cuba, and the model of the "New Man," as in other socialist nations, served as a culturally accepted utopian form for the public self. To publicly display the characteristics of the "New Man" was a generally accepted value.

Given the complex and ambiguous positions feminism and leftism occupy in the American social structure, the U.S. case is harder to make. Perhaps the most obvious reasons are that feminism and leftism are discursively and theoretically constructed on the negation of hegemonic definitions of citizenry and on an identity bolted to the notion of cultural independence. This liberal ground cannot easily be offset by the inherent antihumanism of contemporary leftisms and feminisms, and permeates the discourse of individuality and politics. To be a cultural worker is, at best, to be free and to make use of the cultural freedoms granted by the U.S. Constitution. Most American cultural workers are also likely to reject the idea that they must share the same hermeneutic techniques to interpret film. Moreover, the relative homogeneity of Cuban cultural production was related to the fact that cultural work was considered valuable because it could foster a better society. The relative heterogeneity of American cultural work goes hand and hand with the notion that the value of cultural work is its originality, which can foster social and political pluralism.

Of course, heterogeneity and pluralism are relative terms. In America, professionalism required specific types of education as well as the ability to work within a limited set of theoretical perspectives. Moreover, class, race, and gender played significant roles in shaping the community of cultural workers. Regarding accepted knowledge pools, during the 1960s and 1970s, for instance, auteur theory became a common framework for film interpretation, particularly in liberal media catering to educated, upper-middle-class readers, such as *The New Yorker*. Feminism and Marxism were also common, though they were found in more specialized media such as *Ms.* and *Cineaste*. These theoretical perspectives gave way to a variety of interpretations of the Cuban films, but a few ways of seeing politics common among feminist and leftist writers produced consistencies, most of which centered on Cuba's system of politics and the writers' assumptions of it. Either paralleling Cuba to absolutism or to anticapitalism, American writers showed a strong tendency to view the films through cold war hermeneutics and to evaluate them accordingly. In addition, writers showed a tendency to use stereotypical ideas (read, strong knowledge pools) about Latin America and Cuba and with these, wrote racialized, eroticized, and gendered interpretations of the films.

The point is not only that American cultural workers showed consistencies, but that the consistencies, placed beside the historical ways of being political, are evidence of a set of normalized hermeneutic practices used to receive the films. These practices, in turn, clue us into the political standpoint of the cultural workers, and into the way historical political communities enacted their identities through film reception. As with the Cubans, to write about Cuban political film—in media important to specific political habitus—was to perform an identity, and to use this performance as a ritual of membership. To have that effect, the authorial practices needed to be traditional, disciplined, and technological.

As discussed, the construction or maintenance of citizenship is self-formative and evidence of an individual's desire to attain or maintain a specific type of self. In the Cuban and American cases, writing on Cuban film became self-formation also because writers used their professions to show the ways their reason (how to evaluate and interpret a film) and senses (especially sight and hearing) were subject to ethical monitoring. Though embedded in specific traditions of thinking and seeing, these practices of writing were also emblems of personal liberty. Both set of writers produced cultural work that replicated, reproduced, and sustained hegemonic ideas of freedom in their respective communities. Moreover, through their writing, these cultural workers illuminated the specific and contingent relation of their position within institutions—positions of subjection—to freedom, suggesting the importance of this ambivalence to the practice of freedom.

Conclusion and Outline

The usefulness of understanding film critical reception as part of technologies of self is that viewing practices become interlinked to political and identity practices. Such an approach sheds light on the American and Cuban cultural systems, for it identifies key locations for performance of identity within the system. In particular, the approach illuminates the location of film criticism in the cultural field and the importance of the epistemological and aesthetic underpinning of such cultural work. My approach also calculates the importance the field of culture has for the political and hermeneutic lives of those that inhabit it. Moreover, and central to my goal, is that this approach allows me to see disciplining practices within progressive frameworks, something that some may wrongly see as a paradox.

Mine is a cultural studies approach that treats institutions as social, cultural, and political organizations peopled by historically constituted subjects, selves, and agents. Any study trying to understand production is defined as a political economy study, and, by that definition, the bulk of this book is also a political economic study of criticism in Cuba and the United States. But instead of framing production in terms of economics and market logic, I theorize it in terms of politics, cultural policies, knowledge sets, and social ways of defining selfhood. Although I believe, like most media and film scholars, that in the current moment of neoliberalism, understanding capitalism is a key political project, I do not think that every analysis of production must be done using the market paradigm. Political economy should also be concerned with laws, government, and power in its broadest sense. To reduce political economic inquiries to economics is to forget that the power of commodities is not only dependent on the rules of capitalism. Political criticism speaks to power not simply because it is human labor, but also because criticism is part of the rhetorical arsenal of political and social structures, and it is produced to fit that role.

Section I includes four chapters that explore the contexts of critical reception in Cuba and in the United States. In chapter 1 I historicize the development of the postrevolutionary Cuban field of cultural production, paying special attention to cinema and its relationships to citizenship. In chapter 2 I discuss seven areas of debate that shaped cultural policy and created organized sets of knowledge that informed many decisions regarding culture. In general, these discourses address different ways of politicizing culture. In chapter 3 I investigate social and political contexts to the U.S. critical reception of the Cuban films. In particular, I explore how the sixties provided the political rationale to make criticism a practice of dissent. I also argue that changes in the structures of the cultural and political fields have given way to increasingly complex ideas of citizenship in the United States. Among these changes are the increasing exhibition and distribution of foreign films during the 1950s and 1960s, the development of university culture, 1960s social movements, the popularity of television and television news, and the mainstreaming of political leftisms. In chapter 4 I examine specific sets of knowledge and discourses available to liberal cultural workers in the 1970s and 1980s, particularly as these relate to political, foreign, and Cuban films. I pay particular attention to cold war ideologies in American culture and the popularization of leftist and feminist interpretive tactics.

Section II includes four case studies of critical reception in United States and Cuba to *Memories of Underdevelopment* (1968, Alea), *Lucia* (1968, Solás), *One Way or Another* (1974, Gómez), and *Portrait of Teresa* (1979, Vega). These chapters examine at length the official reception of these Cuban films in Cuba and the leftist, feminist, reception in the United States. For Cuba, my primary evidence consists of reviews, essays, and commentaries in official cultural and journalistic media from Cuba (for example, *Cine Cubano, Casa de las Américas, Bohemia, Revolución y Cultura, Granma, Unión, Adelante,* and *Mujeres*). My findings include interpretive consistencies that support the notion of a revolutionary hermeneutics, and that prove that criticism was a type of civic performance that cultural workers undertook to become, or at least be seen as, proper revolutionary citizens. For the United States, I use evidence coming from liberal (for example, the *New York Times,* the *Los Angeles Times,* the *Washington Post*), leftist (for example, *The Nation, The New Republic*), and feminist media outlets (for example, *Ms.*). The evidence also includes a fair number of academic sources, because academics have been one of the main groups interested in Cuban film.

In the conclusion, I analyze this evidence in relation to cultural institutions and the location of the cultural worker within the grids of culture and power, as this location is manifested in discourse. The evidence is then weighed in relation to issues of technologies of self, the field of cultural production, and ideas about politics. My findings include interpretive consistencies that support the notion of liberal/leftist hermeneutics, and that prove that criticism was a type of civic performance that cultural workers undertook in order to become, or at least be seen as, proper progressive citizens.

Each chapter brings attention to how political identities are evidenced in the social act of film interpretation and evaluation. Moreover, comparing such reception and political settings is expected to illustrate the contingency of modalities of reception and politicized interpretation, as well as their ambiguous relation to normativity. As I show, although Cuban reception of these films may be normative, the influence of civic goals in private lives defined their interpreting activities as important for the progress of the revolution and for constituting themselves as cultural vanguards. United States cultural workers, however, used the interpretation of Cuban films to reflect on their cultural locations and to politicize them. Such a style of interpreting, I argue, attempted to assert the cultural workers' independence from the field of power while aligning with it. Finally, I hope to show how the different ways of using politics to interpret Cuban film signaled a difference in the definitions of political selfhood between Cuba and the United States.

PART I

Staging Film Criticism
The Cuban and American
Historical and Political
Backgrounds

Chapter 1

Cuban Culture, Institutions, Policies, and Citizens

In 1955, Italian neorealism entered full force in the political culture of Cuba. In that year, the young filmmaker Julio García Espinosa directed *El Megano,* a documentary that denounced the living conditions of charcoal burners in the Zapata Swamps region. The film gained immediate fame when Cuba's president, Fulgencio Batista, decided to seize it right after its first showing at the University of Havana. Espinosa was interrogated and set free only when he promised to bring the film to the authorities. Surrounded by a strong and independent filmmaking community organized around Nuestro Tiempo (a social and artistic group that organized cine-clubs, film cycles, and a cultural magazine) and that included Alfredo Guevara, José Massip, Santiago Álvarez, and Tomás Gutiérrez Alea, Espinosa managed to make a copy and take one print to the police (Chanan 2004, 108–11).

Like Alea and other founders of the New Latin American Cinema (NLAC), Espinosa had studied film in Italy in the renowned Centro Sperimentale di Roma, where he learned the neorealist style and to express the relationship of politics and art from a Marxist perspective. His way of seeing filmmaking was common among a type of intelligentsia that in Latin America and within Cuba had grown distant from the politics of market capital and its system of intranational and international domination, and was attracted to a variety of Marxisms and socialisms. In England, the Labour Party came to power in 1945; Mao triumphed in China in 1949, and the Korean War began the following year; the civil rights movement was at full force in the 1950s. Each event catalyzed intellectual communities around the world and produced deep separations between those on the right and those on the left (Daniels 1994; Gittlin 1987, 21–60). The first wave of Cuban revolutionary cultural workers came from these intellectual and political contexts. However, as Michael Chanan (2004) notices, they were also heavily influenced by Cuba's political culture, history, and the unusual set of circumstances that surrounded Cuba's transition to socialism/communism from capitalism.

It is important to note that at the same time that the Cuban Revolution was changing the film habitus, Cuban filmmakers were participating in the formation of the NLAC, a leftist pan–Latin American film movement. Most of the aesthetic ideas that circulated in Cuba were thus common to the NLAC, though Cubans were the only filmmakers capable of incorporating these calls for aesthetic transformation (in the name of social justice) to a whole national film system. The working conditions of filmmakers like Fernando Birri in Argentina or Glauber Rocha in Brazil were very different. In the spirit of being faithful to that difference, I shy away from generalizing the Cuban reality to the reality of other NLAC practices.

In this chapter I briefly historicize Cuba's cultural transformation since the revolution, its cultural institutions, and its intellectual life. These social spaces frame critical reception and constitute locales for the performance of citizenship. My account bridges the gap between history and institutions by discursively analyzing intellectual debates on culture, politics, and cultural policy. I examine how structural properties of culture developed alongside ways of thinking about culture. I argue that official ideas about culture helped constitute aesthetic and hermeneutic frameworks that cultural workers used to interpret, evaluate, and understand cultural texts, including cinema. Because these frameworks became common at the same time that postrevolutionary political arrangements were giving way to a new political culture, applying the frameworks became a way of performing a new style of being a citizen.

The films under consideration were released from 1968 (*Lucia* and *Memories of Underdevelopment*) to 1979 (*Portrait of Teresa*). Thus, I look at the span between 1959, the beginning of the revolution, to the early 1980s. This period of Cuban cultural history is particularly important because it includes two key epochs. From 1959 to the end of the 1960s, the Cuban cultural milieu experimented with a fast pace of change and development that can be interpreted as a cultural revolution. During this time, high idealism and the dream of communism marked a process in which culture became increasingly politicized and utilized to effect social change in Cuban society. From 1970 to 1985, a more somber epoch, the Cuban cultural milieu became increasingly institutionalized and centralized, invested in the realities of Soviet-style socialism. Throughout, Cuban cultural workers came together as a hermeneutic community of differing cohesion, constituted by a habitus that legitimized some cultural practices (including criticism) while precluding others. What was to be sponsored or not often depended on pressures from the field of power, which in Cuba included the central government, particularly Fidel Castro, and the Cuban Communist Party (Partido Comunista Cubano — PCC), and/or internal pressures related to conflicting cultural traditions and understandings on how to carry on broad institutional goals, such as the development of *conciencia* (the term roughly translates as social consciousness that motivates social action) in the general population. Cuban cultural workers embraced a revolutionary hermeneutics that could help them negotiate these and other internal and external pressures. This revolutionary hermeneutics attempted to apply Marxist aesthetic principles to cultural production and evaluation as ways of responding to the requirements of the revolutionary government and to existing cultural traditions.

Actors motivated by historically specific reasons undertake cultural activities. Though some of the reasons for actions may not be conscious, the important emphasis the revolution placed on the construction of the New Man, which translated as an emphasis on the crafting of a proper public self, suggests that being able to justify actions and decisions based on revolutionary morality often determined the likeliness of actions. I do not believe that cultural workers' actions (for example, criticism) were motivated solely by theoretical, administrative, or political principles. However, I believe that cultural workers often used these principles to legitimize their actions and that this "style" of being public afforded them a proper stylistics of public selfhood. Moreover, because these ways of rationalizing social actions became organized sets of knowledge, following Michel Foucault, I will understand these "knowledges" and these actions as comprising technologies of public selfhood that historically situated individuals used in Cuba to become good citizens in the eyes of government, society, and themselves.

The chapter is organized chronologically around a number of events and cultural policies that determined Cuban cultural life, which I roughly split into three epochs: 1959–61, the beginning of the cultural revolution; 1960–70, cultural experimentation and idealism; and 1970–85, institutionalization and socialism. I emphasize ideas about culture endorsed by cultural workers. By cultural workers I am not only referring to professional critics but also to designers, editors, journalists, artists, writers, filmmakers, academics, cultural critics, film critics, film academics, and filmmakers, all of whom are, at times, involved in criticism. This strategy allows me to link the institutions of film-making and cultural criticism to the larger category of cultural institutions.

1959–61: The Beginning of a Cultural Revolution

Cuba's struggle to build an independent nation had shaped the experience of being a cultural worker since the nineteenth century (Chanan 2004, 56–114). In particular, Cubans had to endure the bullying presence of the United States in Cuba's economic, social, political, and cultural affairs, highlighted by the American occupation of Cuba from 1898 to 1902 and the institution of the Platt Amendment (Pérez-Stable 1993, 37). The necessity to fend off U.S. influence, invasions, military pressures, and economic coercions engendered a modernity based on the tension between a pro-American oligarchy and a counter-hegemonic intellectual and popular base that defined itself, and its habitus, in terms of radicalization, antiimperialism, and, as the century advanced, socialism. The fall of General Fulgencio Batista in 1958 presented an opportunity for political dissidents, intellectuals, and a young leadership to put into practice the ideas and ideals that had been conceived over years of political dissolution and/or coercion.

The triumph of the Cuban Revolution on January 1, 1959, began a phase of intense nationalism and radical populism that ended with the failed invasion, on April 17, 1961, of the Bay of Pigs by 1,500 exiles sponsored by the CIA. During these important months, the Cuban leadership set the basis for future social, political, and economic transformations. The regime established an agrarian policy that expropriated North American property and subsidized the cost of medicine, electricity, telephone, and rent. They tried to establish trade relations with, among others, the United States, Japan, Egypt, India, and the Soviet Union. Meanwhile, with the U.S. government–sponsored attacks multiplying during 1960 and 1961, the Cuban leadership could do little to stop the polarization of Cuban society as well as its catalization. In fact, the Cuban leadership gained strength and popular support thanks to the U.S.-sponsored violent events of these years and consolidated its nationalist, liberatory, and antiimperialist character. This period culminated with the Bay of Pigs invasion. The eve of the invasion, Castro declared the socialist character of the revolution.

The changes engendered by the revolution included a radical restructuring of the field of culture and a rearticulation of citizenship to cultural production. In particular, changes affecting intellectuals began almost immediately. The reorganization relied on already existing revolutionary cultural cliques to organize early cultural activities. Within these groups, leadership was given to those who either had participated in the guerrilla movement or who had been part of the communist parties in the past. Filmmakers who had been organized around Nuestro Tiempo, for instance, became central to the Cuban film institute. Alfredo Guevara became its leader, and other members of Nuestro Tiempo such as Massip, Álvarez, Alea, and Espinosa became central figures. Carlos Franqui, a revolutionary who organized the radical newspaper *Revolución* in 1956, was given power and resources to turn it into the official newspaper of the revolutionary government. Alea, Álvarez, Espinosa, and Massip were given funds and institutional support to make films (Chanan 2004, 108–14). Alejo Carpentier, the prominent novelist, was given the reins of the Dirección de Cultura. Haydée Santamaría, wife of the minister of education at the time, Armando Hart, and part of the 26th of July movement that attacked the Moncada barracks in 1953, became the head of Casa de las Américas (Cabrera Infante 1994, 68, 71). Nicolas Guillén, a laureate poet and member since the 1920s of the Communist Party, was elected president of the Unión de Escritores y Artistas de Cuba (UNEAC) in 1961. Given the fact that no ministry of culture existed during the first decade and a half of the revolution, all of these institutions (together with a handful more) became key to the cultural formation of the new Cuba. Significantly, *Revolución* became *Granma*, the official newspaper of the Cuban government.

Conversely, those who did not belong to revolutionary cliques, and belonged to cultural organizations and corporations that worked alongside the Batista regime, were often taken out of the revolutionary cultural field. For instance, a purge in 1959 of non-Castroist professors at the University of Havana replaced nearly 80 percent of the faculty with new professors that supported the new leadership (Reed 1991, 40). During 1959 and 1960, the dailies *Alerta, Pueblo, Ataja, Prensa Libre, Diario de la Marina*, Radio Mambí, the CMQ television network, and the magazines *Bohemia* and *Carteles* were either closed or nationalized, which meant that their editorial staffs were fired, intellectuals and technicians supportive of the government took the installations, and the Republic of Cuba assumed ownership (46–52).

With the formation and disciplining of cultural institutions also began the institution of cultural policies and their effect on the cultural habitus. The first revolutionary cultural policy was Law 169 of the Council of Ministers of the Cuban Republic (Ley No. 169 del Consejo de Ministros de la República de Cuba), issued on March 24, 1959, which established ICAIC, the first cultural institution of the revolutionary government ("Creación del Instituto" 1987, 7–10). According to this legislation, ICAIC would control filmic production and distribution in internal and external markets, prepare technicians and filmmakers, and administer studios, laboratories, and any other infrastructure related to film production and distribution. The harnessing of all of these administrative, regulatory, educative, and promotional activities under one institution attempted to regulate what was perceived to be the most powerful ideological tool of its time: film.

Beside laying down administrative roles for ICAIC, which has structured the cultural subfield of cinema to this day, Law 169 set a discursive primer for thinking about film and art (indeed, the ideas of this law would affect most cultural work) in revolutionary Cuba. The law states: "Because film is an art. Because cinema constitutes, due to its characteristics, an instrument of opinions that forms individual and collective consciousness and can contribute to deepen and purify the revolutionary spirit and sustain its creative impulse" (7). Film must remain free from the coercion of the market and achieve its potential as a tool of education, reason, and national pride. This law had profound effects on the habitus of the cultural field, for it established cinema as a set of activities (acting, scripting, directing, promoting, and reviewing) of extreme social and political importance. Reasonably, those involved in cinema, and culture, would have to take cinema's importance into consideration and reflect on its social and political potential.

Law 169, issued only three months after the triumph of the revolution, introduced areas of debate that became central to cultural reflection in the following decades: 1) What is the role of the intellectual in a communist/ socialist society? According to Law 169, the role of the intellectual was to educate the people using film's ideological potential. This question engendered debates about the relation of the intellectual to the revolution, the relationship between the artist and his/her work, and the definition of intellectual labor in relation to revolutionary praxis. 2) What works can be considered revolutionary film, literature, or art? According to Law 169, revolutionary cultural work should be able to transform collective consciousness and deepen the revolutionary spirit. Any work deemed incapable of doing either could not be considered revolutionary work. 3) What are the proper objects of filmic and artistic reflection? These objects would be those that have the potential to educate the people. To implement this idea, it would be necessary to establish a pedagogy based on aesthetics. (These principles and ideas are discussed in the following chapter.) The debates Law 169 made relevant suggest that the writers of this law were more than merely acquainted with modernist aesthetics and, as I show in the following chapter, that cultural debates in Cuba were largely centered on Marxian thought even before the official embracing of socialism in 1961.

A cultural field, like Pierre Bourdieu argues about the French field of cultural production, depends on aesthetic ideas that can help explain, legitimate, and value actions within the field and give distinction to those that embody them. In this, the Cuban cultural field resembled the French. Indeed, developing socialist/communist aesthetic ideas was a task that cultural leaders took with great conviction early on. This was already evidenced in Law 169, but also in the immediate aesthetic turn taken by cultural magazines such as *Cine Cubano* and *Casa de las Américas* (*Casa* from here on), both initiated in 1960. Though *Cine Cubano* carried essays about filmic technique and film reviews, each number introduced new and complex ideas about filmic aesthetics, most of these under the general umbrella of Marxist aesthetics.[1] Highly theoretical interviews with directors like Joris Ivens, Chris Marker, Tony Richardson, Agnès Vajda, to mention some, during the first five years, were supported with essays about Brecht, Lukács, Eisenstein, Alea, and, ICAIC's president and chief editor of the journal, Alfredo Guevara. Similarly, *Casa*, which was created with the goal of showcasing revolutionary literature, effectively hosted ongoing debates about revolutionary aesthetics that included essays on Marxist aesthetics, Brecht, Lukács, Paul Baran, Adolfo Sánchez Vázquez, Louis Althusser, Frantz Fanon, and Lucien Goldmann, to name a few.

Given the multiple roles that cultural institutions played in Cuba, stressing thinking about aesthetics is not surprising. A proper aesthetics was required to discriminate, or legitimize the discrimination, among works. An aesthetics would be used when it came time to select which films would be produced, which books would be published and promoted, which painters would be exhibited, which plays would be performed (Dopico 1989). This was particularly important in the context of a film industry lacking economic funds. Moreover, embodying the "right" aesthetics gave the cultural worker distinction. The complexity of issues of aesthetics and their relevance to criticism merits its own discussion and is undertaken in the following chapter.

1961–70: The Sixties, or Cultural Experimentation and Idealism

On April 16, 1961, Fidel Castro declared in an impassioned speech the socialist character of the revolution. The next day, an anti-Castro military force supported by the U.S. government invaded the Bay of Pigs (Playa Girón). Within seventy-two hours, the Cubans halted the invasion. During the following months, the Cuban government proceeded with the implementation of social, political, and economic reforms that profoundly altered the populist and nationalist character of the revolution. In a gradual manner that culminated in the late 1960s, the Cuban government nationalized the means of production, and changed, or at least tried to change, the relation between citizens and economic production. Instead of being driven by material desire, citizens were encouraged to increase production and to exercise creative thinking based on moral incentives. To effect this change, the revolution required the political commitment and expertise of all intellectuals and cultural workers. Not surprisingly, the decade saw a rich variety of institutional initiatives aiming to fulfill these ambitious cultural transformation goals.

Structural changes went hand in hand with social and cultural changes. While an increased reliance on morality affected the economy, the increasing importance of ethical and political public behavior changed social and political life. People's participation in revolutionary tasks and the prestige this participation carried gave political public actions ethical import. For instance, 200,000 volunteers and teachers carried on a Literacy Campaign in 1961 that harnessed the masses into an educational action and mass media to the goal of framing the campaign and each of its participants in heroic, revolutionary, clothes. Radio, television, and newspapers made heroes of the volunteers by defining their actions "noble" because they replicated the heroism of the revolutionary armed struggle. Aside from mass-mobilization campaigns, political organizations multiplied, gaining legitimacy on moral grounds: the Committees for the Defense of the Revolution (CDR), which attempted to protect the nation from any enemy, reached 800,000 members by 1961; the Central Organization of Cuban Trade Unions (CTC), which sought to remedy labor injustices, became a powerful political force in the early

1960s (Bengelsdorf 1994, 86; Pérez-Stable 1993, 99). Paralleling the quick development of political and labor organizations, the Federation of Cuban Women (Federación de Mujeres Cubanas—FMC), which pursued policy and social changes affecting women in the areas of health, labor, and education, had 376,000 members by 1962.

The social rewards of participating in these activities, mobilizations, and organizations were related to prestige. However, also, over time, these rewards stratified economic resources by making those participants in revolutionary activities more likely to be given beneficial employment, advancement, professional training, advanced schooling, and other economic perks that were available in specific labor settings (access to cars, permits to travel, and so forth). As the decade progressed, it became clearer that good citizenship would be rewarded and that bad citizenship would be punished. For instance, in 1965, the government organized the notorious Military Units to Aid Production (UMAP camps) in which dissidents, homosexuals, and other types of "deviant" citizens were interned. According to Reed (1991), around 34,000 people were confined in these camps at different times. Though officially disbanded in 1966, the UMAP camps operated until the end of the 1960s (82–85).

Cultural Policing and "Palabras a los Intelectuales"

Culturally, the 1960s were years of relative freedom, high idealism, and institutional experimentation. But this freedom was given character partly by an infamous case of censorship and the cultural policies that ensued. Issues of intellectual responsibility and accountability, freedom of expression, proper revolutionary behavior, and the policing of culture came to the fore as a result of the release and censorship of the documentary film *P.M.* in early 1961. There are several and very different accounts of these events from highly regarded sources. Here, I have tried to present only the briefest version.[2]

P.M., directed by Sabá Cabrera Infante and Orlando Jiménez Leal, was a fifteen-minute documentary, filmed in a "free cinema" style, dealing with the nightlife of Havana that included blacks and mulattos in a cabaret drinking and dancing rumba.[3] Wanting to show it to general audiences, the filmmakers sent it to the Review Commission (Comisión Revisora), under ICAIC, for approval (Chanan 2004, 133). To some within ICAIC, including Alfredo Guevara, its president, the documentary represented Afro-Cuban culture in roles associated with imperialist oppression. Despite protests by Almendros and Guillermo Cabrera Infante (among many), the Review Commission judged *P.M.*

aesthetically and politically irresponsible, refused to approve it, and seized the copy they received (Cabrera 1994, 66–67). The film's restricted circulation, soon after its first showing, gave way to a series of meetings and statements that attempted to clear the air and clarify the position of ICAIC and the Cuban government in relation to cultural boundaries. The results were mixed, for they clarified some issues but made other issues murkier. This first and influential event of cultural policing culminated in June 30, 1961, when Fidel Castro spoke to the intellectual community at Havana's National Library. In this speech, known as "Words to the Intellectuals" ("Palabras a los Intelectuales"),[4] Castro (1987) laid out what would become the most important themes and issues surrounding art, literature, and film in Cuba (23–42).

As in other instances of policing, these events related to processes of restructuring within the cultural field (Chanan 2004, 138), but were also discussed publicly in terms of aesthetics. Regarding the trajectory of the cultural field, divisions among intellectuals that existed *before* 1959 were re-created in the new cultural milieu. Notably, Franqui, who did not favor those communists who had not participated in the armed struggle, openly disliked Alfredo Guevara. Franqui had put himself at risk organizing *Revolución* in 1956 as an underground paper that gave voice to the radical revolutionary guerrilla 26th of July movement (for a different account, see Chanan 2004, 123). The newspaper became, after the triumph of the revolution, the most important newspaper in Cuba and an institution antagonistic to the film institute headed by Alfredo Guevara (Cabrera 1994, 64; Chanan 2004, 124). This newspaper produced *Lunes de Revolución,* a cultural supplement published every Monday by intellectuals who, like Heberto Padilla, Pablo Armando Fernández, Edith García Buchacha, Sabá Cabrera Infante, and Guillermo Cabrera Infante, understood the revolution as an opportunity for intellectual expansion, freedom of expression, and formal experimentation (Menton 1975, 125–29). Until its dissolution in 1961, *Lunes,* with a circulation that reached almost 200,000 copies, printed articles on Marxism, leftist classics, Cuban history, the writings of Castro and Ernesto "Che" Guevara, and a wide array of articles about art. Jean Paul Sartre and Simone de Beauvoir had been so impressed by the magazine that they commented, in their visits to Cuba, that they had found ordinary Cubans more knowledgeable about avant-garde art than a good many Frenchmen (K. S. Karol in Menton 1975, 128).

In addition to disliking Franqui, Alfredo Guevara also opposed the experimental and apolitical aesthetic positions of *Lunes.* He believed that change in cinematic form had to be gradual because people's taste was trained by nonexperimental dominant formal techniques; the new cinema, he proposed, had the responsibility of appealing to the taste of the people, and thus it had the obligation to use nonexperimental forms (Menton 1975, 100). *Lunes* embraced a different definition of revolutionary art, and, according to ICAIC, this resulted in the improper selection of an aesthetic treatment and theme. A proper aesthetics, according to Law 169, would deepen the revolutionary spirit. A proper theme would educate the people. *P.M.* arguably challenged these two ideas and the cultural police had to act (Chanan 2004, 136).

Castro responded to the events with his famous speech "Palabras" that, following the tradition of the Surrealist Manifesto written by Diego Rivera, Andre Bretón, and Leon Trosky ("Manifesto: Towards a Free Revolutionary Art," 1938), laid down principles that cultural production would have to follow if it was to be considered "proper" to the revolution (Chanan 2004, 139; Menton 1975, 105–6). In this speech Castro states the working principle for cultural production and cultural policy in Cuba: "Within the revolution everything, against the revolution nothing" ("Dentro la revolución todo, contra la revolución nada"). After "Palabras," *Lunes de Revolución* disappeared, and soon afterward the Unión de Escritores y Artistas de Cuba (UNEAC), a government-sponsored institution, was organized to bring together writers and artists. Like other institutions, UNEAC aimed to regulate that which it organized.

"Palabras" introduced a number of ideas that became important in the cultural habitus and central to the practice of criticism. "Palabras" was built on a complex discursive structure that made official some logical connections and discursive boundaries and that left other areas full of ambiguities. Take for instance the idea of "the vanguard." "Palabras" occurred only two months after the Bay of Pigs invasion and after the declaration of a socialist revolution. As a socialist notion, the vanguard contained logical contradictions that were already present in "Palabras." According to Castro, the vanguard had to act as the redeemer of the masses; yet, because the masses represented both the purity of labor and, through their will, the legitimation of the regime, the masses would also have to redeem the vanguard. So, Castro stated that the revolutionary must be focused on the redemption of the people but should also cater to their (social) goals and (aesthetic) necessities: "The prism through which we analyze everything is this: to us, good will be what is good to them (the people); to us, it will be noble, beautiful and useful that which is noble, useful and beautiful to them" (translated by the author from Castro 1961, 8). The populist tenor of the paragraph cannot hide the epistemological challenge that Castro and other revolutionaries would have to solve: how can the vanguard know what is beautiful, useful, noble, and good to the people? And how can the vanguard separate that which is good and beautiful to the people from that which must be redeemed? These questions have been central to Marxist aesthetics and politics and replicate the debates, in aesthetics, between popular culture and the avant-garde, and in political Marxist theory, between objective and subjective conditions for social transformation.[5] The Cuban case offers an instantiation of the questions and an attempt to reconcile theoretical answers with institutional practices.

At the center of Castro's argument was the idea that in revolutionary ideology, the potentially discrete categories of the revolution, the nation, and the people were structured in systems of equivalences. Castro mentioned these halfway through his speech: "Against the Revolution nothing, because the Revolution has its rights and its first right is the right to exist and against the Revolution's right to be and to exist, no one should stand. Because the Revolution involves the interests of the people, because the Revolution signifies the interests of the whole Nation" (28). This statement depends on the notion that the revolution "signified" the nation. This relation of signification depended on a discursive context where the revolution signified the nation because only the revolution could break the people's oppression and their alienation from who they really were (Chanan 2004, 395). *Casa* stated the same idea in its opening issue in 1960 as follows: "The people are an unknown force; the people, that ignoring false patience or self-serving resignation, are, finally, creators of the environment where man is produced" ("Como Haremos" 1960, 3). Conceiving of the people as alienated, a common move in Marxist discourses, partly reconciled the contradiction that the vanguard would have to lead the people, yet the vanguard's inspiration would be the people.

For criticism, these ideas are important because they established the need for a revolutionary hermeneutics. The revolution required the active interpretation of the people's reality in order to separate that which is pure and noble, using Castro's words, from that which is alienated. Indeed, the legitimacy of the revolution, which was dependent on the revolution's ability to break the people's oppression, had to rely, at all times, on hermeneutic tasks carried on by the political and the cultural vanguard. This hermeneutic principle established the parameters of dialogue among artists, filmmakers, and Castro.

Creative freedom, the signature characteristic of the prerevolutionary artist, was questioned because the concept was shown to be ahistorical; it was a concept that produced a diffused semantic that was potentially excessive and thus dangerous. Hence, and contrary to the North American liberal tradition, creative freedom was not defined as an inalienable individual right but as a cultural concept that, in its extreme expression, could only be supported by a bourgeois regime. The new Cuban freedom depended on the cultural context, on the subject, and on the social landscape, and freedom ceased to be an important marker of artistic and intellectual production. Instead, in the cultural Cuban habitus, the revolutionary cultural worker embraced a revolutionary hermeneutics, which applied a revolutionary aesthetics, as his/her new and complex task.

Although "Palabras" provided some of the parameters that would guide cultural production and cultural policy in the following years, it cannot, strictly speaking, be called policy. Instead, the speech played the role of an ethical and political framework that would be followed and debated within cultural institutions; the results of these debates would inform actual policy. Indeed, the speech justified the activities of the Cuban film institute, and it was thus a defense of already existing cultural policies. The speech was also a reworking of Cuba's main cultural themes and thus framed aesthetic discussions from then onward: the role of the intellectual, or vanguard as it would also be called, in a communist/socialist society continued to be the using of ideological tools for the education of the people. Yet, the vanguard was asked to learn revolutionary values *from* the people. Ideally, this process of mutual education would result in different things for each group: through it, the people would acquire *conciencia:* exercising it, the vanguard would acquire a revolutionary hermeneutics and aesthetics.

Reorganization of the Cultural Field

Besides the ideological parameters that "Palabras" set for culture and art, the speech marked a reorganization of the cultural field. The disbanding of *Lunes* placed a number of Cuba's best literary and filmic talents into positions from which they could exert little cultural influence. Guillermo Cabrera Infante was sent to Brussels as a cultural attaché, and his brother Sabá was sent to Madrid. Jimenéz went as a cameraman to Channel 2. Almendros defected. The exception was Antón Arrufat, who was called by Santamaria to *Casa,* where he was instrumental in making that journal one of the best in Latin America

(Cabrera 1994, 52–72). In addition, "Palabras" was immediately followed by the organization of the First Congress of Writers and Artists in 1961 and, during the Congress, a brand new institution responsible for and to the literary field of cultural production: The Union of Cuban Writers and Artists (Unión de Escritores y Artistas de Cuba, UNEAC).

UNEAC's first president, from 1961 to 1986, was Nicolás Guillén, who, though belonging to an early generation of intellectuals, became Cuba's national poet and exemplar to all revolutionaries. A member of the Communist Party since 1934, and with ample national and international fame and recognition, Guillén was a selection suited to mediate the theoretical and political debates of the literary community.[6] Though the general goal of UNEAC was to establish "links between Cuban artists and writers and [artists and writers] from socialist and non-socialist countries," the institution also had the goals of linking artistic work to revolutionary objectives, organizing discussion on literature and artistic creation, and encouraging new talent through literary competitions and artistic exhibit (Cabrera 1994, 52–57; Otero 1972, 37). In following these goals, UNEAC became key to the constitution of standards of value (which implied the mediation between aesthetic and political concerns). In addition, UNEAC influenced the general field of culture by publishing an art bulletin and two literary magazines, one of which remained influential for decades, *La Gaceta de Cuba*.

The reorganization of people within institutions and the creation of new institutions also meant the rehierarchization of theoretical positions, ideologies, and practices within the habitus. The ideological success of Alfredo Guevara over *Lunes* meant that ICAIC would gain even more prominence in the nascent Cuban cultural field. Moreover, UNEAC, together with *Casa*, profoundly influenced the literary and theoretical fields in Cuba. These cultural institutions controlled publishing, production, distribution, and promotion of art, literature, and film. Aside from UNEAC's sponsored journals and magazines, *Cine Cubano* (ICAIC's journal), and *Casa,* I should mention at least *Granma, La Gaceta de Cuba, Revolución y Cultura,* and *El Caimán Barbudo*. Together these institutional spaces crafted a relatively solid ideological front that shaped Cuba for decades and that would make culture and criticism an eminently political activity. The leaders generally sponsored ideas and cultural products that could politically exist "within the revolution." However, the areas of debate also continued within the revolution and existed as agonistic spaces where theoretical divisions could exist and where questions of taste and theory could be debated.

Although formal experimentation was partly at issue in "Palabras," during the following months the two Guevaras, Alfredo and Che, came to its defense. Criticizing the Consejo Nacional de Cultura (National Council for Culture, CNC) and UNEAC's early aesthetic populism, Alfredo Guevara argued that no one would benefit from reducing the complexity and substance of the artwork as a result of communicating to the masses. Backtracking from his position regarding *P.M.,* Afredo Guevara (n.d.) defended the young filmmakers' need to experiment with form (132). Similarly, in a celebrated letter titled "Socialism and Man in Cuba" ("El Socialismo y el Hombre en Cuba"), Che Guevara (1988, 133) encouraged cultural workers to pursue artistic investigations and reprimanded those in power for stifling culture by imposing socialist realism in a doctrinaire fashion.

During these years, the filmmaking community continued with formal experimentation, particularly in short film production. Though ICAIC began with personnel influenced by Italian neorealism, directors Giral, Alea, Solás, Fernando Villaverde, and Fausto Canel produced experimental work also influenced by the French New Wave (Chanan 2004, 164). The literary world, though shaken by the government's actions regarding *Lunes,* by 1965 regained its former vitality (Menton 1975, 130–34). Yet it would be a mistake to think that the only factors affecting the cultural field were cultural policy and policing. Ana López (1993b) notes that many cultural workers left Cuba from 1965 to 1968, shortly after the formation of the Central Committee of the Communist Party and the UMAP camps (53–55), thus reminding us of the profound effect the political field had on all Cubans, including cultural workers.

For the cultural field in general, the successes of the decade were significant. By the early 1970s, the size, international importance, and reach of the Cuban cultural field had multiplied. Literacy had reached levels higher than those of some first-world nations. The number of theater groups went from one in 1958 to thirteen in 1970. Museums went from six to thirty. Publishing, almost nonexistent before the revolution, became a thriving industry. Books per capita went from 0.6 in 1958 to 4.1 in 1975. Mobile cinemas performed more than 1.5 million screenings by the mid-1970s. By 1968, ICAIC had produced 44 features, 204 documentaries, 435 newsreels, 77 educational films, and 49 animated films (Otero 1972). The legacies of the first decade would have been as significant as its accomplishments had it not been for the cases of censorship and cultural repression, including the now famous

Padilla case, that tarnished Cuba's cultural reputation inside and outside the country.

Heberto Padilla was a novelist and poet originally affiliated with *Lunes*. In 1967, Padilla found himself working with the newspaper *Granma*, when he was invited by *El Caimán Barbudo* to write a critique of a novel written by Otero, the vice president of the CNC. Padilla's dislike for Otero's novel and his praise for *Tres Tristes Tigres,* a novel by Guillermo Cabrera Infante from *Lunes* and then in exile, put Padilla in trouble (Chanan 2004, 313). In October 1968 his collection of poems *Fuera del Juego* (*Out of Play* or *Offside*) won a national prize from UNEAC. In spite of this, UNEAC published the book with a disapproving introduction, and later, during November and December 1968, several articles criticizing him and his work appeared in *Verde Olivo,* a journal of the armed forces. He later lost his job at *Granma* (Chanan 2004, 312–14; Matthews 1975, 321; Menton 1975, 134–49; Bennedeti 1971, 7–32).

A debate of international proportions continued during the months to follow. Julio Cortázar, the renowned Argentinean writer, defended Padilla with no success. Other criticisms came from Chile, Mexico, and France (Menton 1975, 143). On March 20, 1971, Padilla was arrested and jailed for twenty-eight days (Chanan 2004, 312). He was released after writing a letter confessing wrongdoing. By then, the cultural climate in Cuba had changed and Cuba's international cultural appeal had dwindled.

1970–85: Institutionalization and Cultural Accountability

Since early in the revolutionary period, the leadership understood that the island's reliance on monoculture (sugar) was risky and attempted to diversify, though with poor results (Mesa-Lago 1977, 5). The USSR, however, began providing training and technical support for diversification and, in addition, bought the Cuban sugar. The Missile Crisis cooled off this relationship, and afterward, the Cubans, led by Che Guevara, attempted to adopt Maoist principles of economic development (one of which I have commented on already as the push to produce a New Man) that included voluntary work during the sugar harvest (6).[7] Throughout these years, the Cuban leadership moved away from the Soviets to the point that when the Prague Spring process began in 1967, the Cuban press gave it mixed reviews. However, by then the economy was in trouble and, later that same year, when Che Guevara died, the process of independence from the USSR crumbled (Mesa-Lago 1977, 8). In 1968, the

Soviets gave an ultimatum to Cuba threatening the country with halting the purchase of its sugar. This forced Cuba to maintain a pro-Soviet line, which meant supporting the Soviet invasion of Czechoslovakia in 1968. From 1970 until the mid-1980s, Cuba underwent a process of institutionalization that affected social relations, conceptions of citizenship, and public behavior. To some, the communist revolution had ended (Pérez-Stable 1993, 122).

During the 1970s the Cuban leadership redesigned their style of government, centralizing power in the Cuban Communist Party and instituting Soviet models of political and economic organization (Pérez-Stable 1993, 99). Alongside centralization, the Organs of Popular Power (OPP) decentralized power by spreading some administrative and economic decisions to municipalities. The Economic Management and Planning System (SDPE) instituted in the mid-1970s, with its emphasis on production, profit, and self-finance, was the "antithesis" of economic guidelines of the 1960s. The SDPE incrementally increased the average salary and improved the quality of goods. It also slowed the entrance of women into the labor force. In 1976, and to the dismay of the Cuban Federation of Women (Federación de Mujeres Cubanas, FMC), the Labor Ministry passed policies that banned women from three hundred job categories. Ironically, that same year, the Cuban government instituted the Family Code, a feminist-inspired law, that attempted to regulate the private behavior of men and stipulated equality of the sexes at work and at home. These measures were attempts to alleviate the unjust burden placed on women by a society in which they were expected to be part of the labor force and in a culture where machismo made women responsible for child rearing and home labor (139–42).

Cultural Normativity

Alongside the Sovietization of the economy came a reevaluation of the role of culture in society. This is more patent in the aftermath of the Padilla case, which brought an international intellectual debate about cultural freedoms in Cuba. On the Cuban side were official cultural workers of diverse affiliation who published declarations expressing their support for the revolution and who almost unanimously sided with the actions of UNEAC, Casa, and the Cuban government regarding Padilla. Fear was apparent and, as Reed (1991) argues, justified. Also apparent was the acceptance of understanding the value of cultural work and the cultural worker in terms of political signifiers. Responding to the criticism of international intellectuals over the handling of Padilla, these forty-nine cultural workers, which included writers, film-makers, poets, essayists, and cultural administrators, wrote a letter restating the political value of culture, and concluded: "Our people . . . are the makers of their simply and radically human, revolutionary, culture" (Cuban Cultural Workers 1971, 146–47). Those working at Casa, ICAIC, and UNEAC issued similar declarations. In these declarations, individual freedom of expression was valued less than the people's freedom of expression. Because the revolution was the medium the people used to express themselves, protecting the revolution was more important than protecting individual freedoms ("Declaración de la Casa de las Américas" 1971, 147–49; "Declaración de los Cineastas Cubanos" 1971, 149–52; "Declaración de la Unión de Escritores y Artistas de Cuba" 1971, 153–54).

This reevaluation of the role of culture in society largely happened, as had been the case after "Palabras," in a supervised space organized by the Cuban government (Chanan 2004, 397). In May 1971, only weeks after Padilla's imprisonment, cultural and educational organizations came together in the First National Congress of Education and Culture (Primer Congreso Nacional de Educación y Cultura). The joint declaration by the Congress left no doubt that it was organized partly as a place for discussing the Padilla case and the international criticisms issued by leftist intellectuals. Responding to criticisms by the likes of de Beauvoir, Cortazar, Marguerite Duras, Carlos Fuentes, and Sartre, who had labeled the revolution repressive and even Stalinist, the declaration called these leftists intellectuals "petit bourgeois" and "pseudo-leftists" who had used the Cuban Revolution as a means of gaining access and prestige in third world nations. The declaration defined the foreign intellectuals as the harbingers of a new political and cultural colonization that attempted to undermine Cuba's cultural sovereignty by dehistoricizing freedom of expression ("Declaración del Primer Congreso de Educación y Cultura"1987 [1971]), 212). Speaking against the ideas of natural rights and freedoms that supported liberalist *and* colonialist ideologies, the Cuban intellectuals referenced the many ways and times in which ideas of natural rights and freedoms had been used against Cuba. Spanish culture and, later, American-controlled media, Juan Marinello argued, have used liberal ideas of freedom to naturalize their oppression of Cuban society (Marinello 1987, 216). Supporting the Cubans' case were historically known facts such as the way Hearst and Pulitzer manipulated the press to legitimize American intervention in Cuba's war of independence against Spain in 1898 and the control of the Cuban press by U.S.-sponsored Cuban governments prior to 1959.

For these Cubans, to defend freedom of expression as a transcendental value, as they argued foreign intellectuals did, was to be blind to history and mistakenly place freedom of expression atop any other freedoms. Using this theoretical position may have been a way some Cuban intellectuals, without choice, rationalized state coercion, but the position is far from absurd. In fact, its political and epistemological underpinnings can be traced back to Marx and, more recently, to Althusser. Marx criticized American- and French-influenced ideas of civil society because they conceived of civil society as a space for the preservation of the rights and freedoms of individuals-as-monads ("egotistic man"), sacrificing the political character of society and of man. The "rights of man," among which Marx placed freedom of expression, pertain only to private interests, natural necessities, and property, curtailing the constitution of community and political association. According to Marx, the rights and freedoms of man can result in human emancipation only when human beings used them to establish community and, thus, assumed these rights and freedoms in their full political potential (Marx 1978, 41–46). Althusser, whose work was printed in Cuba since the mid-1960s, also criticized the status of liberal conceptions of individuality. He argued that freedom, and the humanist "philosophy" in which freedom was couched, were ideologies invested in the reconstitution of power structures (Althusser 1969, 229). Implied in Marx's and Althusser's ideas is the position that the well-being of society cannot be held hostage to any one freedom. Any freedom is part of a system of freedoms, and it is from the survival of the system that any given freedom can become beneficial to society and individuals. Moreover, understanding freedoms as being part of a system redefines them, because a system always places limits on its single elements. In addition, only within the system can these freedoms be defined and have a social character. Outside the system, any freedom becomes transcendental and, arguably, asocial.

The discursive construction of "freedom" in this epoch is consistent with the way Castro used freedom in "Palabras" and a theoretically viable option for treating freedom as dispensable in narratives of selfhood. Castro argued that creative freedom was ahistorical and had to be subsumed to the security needs of the revolution. The Congress defined cultural freedom as contingent and not a natural right and, agreeing with Marx and Althusser, assumed freedom's ideological character and challenged its ahistoricity. Ironically, freedom was defined as historical, yet it continued being a tool of the power structure. The PCC, Castro, and the cultural vanguard reserved themselves the right to define when history would have to trump freedom.

As in "Palabras," the criticisms of foreign intellectuals were seen as attacks on Cuba's sovereignty and thus as threats to the nation. Like in "Palabras," framing the problem (accusations) in terms of colonization attempted to rebuild the ideological boundaries of the revolution. But unlike in "Palabras," the new border was placed tighter around the ideological values of central government. Outside these boundaries were not only the values of the "imperialist" foe, but also some types of leftist politics and, by extension, leftist aesthetics. The Congress redefined the famed sentence "within the Revolution, everything; against the Revolution, nothing." While in the 1960s the question of what was within the revolution was open, it normally incorporated any and all types of Marxist aesthetics, be it Sartre's, Althusser's, Lenin's, or Brecht's. During the 1970s and 1980s, some Marxisms would not be seen as within the revolution, and an increasing intellectual and expressive conservatism began.

Ironically, the Padilla case and the challenges to Cuba's cultural freedom of the late 1960s roughly coincided with the film community's coming of age. While the inept handling of Padilla by cultural institutions and by the abusive involvement of the Cuban government shook the literary world, *Lucia* and *Memories of Underdevelopment* were gaining international acclaim. Not surprisingly, in 1972, when Otero published a report on Cuban cultural policy for UNESCO, he dedicated three times more space to ICAIC than to UNEAC and Casa together. Embarrassment aside, the successes of Cuban film did not need to be defended (Otero 1972).

Women and the Revolution

While cultural expression, freedom, and institutionalization demarcated the realm of the permissible, the cultural field also saw an increase in the public discussion of sex and gender. Since 1959 the "woman's question" had reached public forums chiefly through debates on the economy of gender, the inclusion of women in labor, and the role of women in the revolutionary wars. Outside these areas there was remarkably little discussion about gender and sex. A quick survey of mainstream, intellectual, and cultural media reveals that during the 1960s discussions of these issues were found in popular newspapers and magazines, particularly in the magazine *Mujeres*. Sex and gender became the object of intellectual cultural commentary in specialized cultural journals until the beginning of the 1970s. *Casa* included several articles on women's liberation in its March-June 1971 issue. *Revolución y Cultura* did the same in October 1974. These academic interventions in the issue continued looking at women in terms of the economy and the revolution, but new concerns about the culture of gender became a central aspect of public debate and cultural expression during the mid-1970s.

The Cuban Revolution had always made women a priority. Because of the efforts of the Cuban leadership and the Federation of Cuban Women (Federación de Mujeres Cubanas—FMC) directed by Vilma Espín (wife of Raul Castro), women integrated into the labor force in larger numbers since the 1960s and increasingly in nontraditional jobs. By 1981, almost one-third of university graduates with geology, mining, metallurgy, and construction degrees, and almost one-fifth of those graduating with electronics degrees, were women. By the mid-1980s, women comprised around two-thirds of the incoming students in law and medical professions (Leiner 1994, 64–65).

To implement and legitimize, theoretically and ideologically, these profound changes in society, the Cuban government and the FMC had approached the "woman's question" from a socialist perspective mainly influenced by Friedrich Engels. Like Engels, the hegemonic view of the woman question in Cuba asserted that women's oppression was the result of economic oppression engendered by capitalism, and that women's freedom could only come as the result of the abolition of private property and the class system. In an article published in 1971 in *Casa,* Isabel Larguia and John Dumoulin contended that sexual liberation was illusory freedom because only in a classless society could individuals overcome alienation. Criticizing all types of classes, Larguia and Dumoulin advocated for the elimination of most markers of femininity, given that these were seen as complicit with capitalism and patriarchy (Larguia and Dumoulin 1971, 47). Yet, neither Larguia and Dumoulin's article nor any of the articles published in *Casa* or, three years later, in *Revolución y Cultura,* criticized men's markers of identity, despite being obviously patriarchal and eminently related to capitalism. The problem of women was not men but capitalism. Engels's materialist and economicist view of gender became the theoretical basis that legitimated the FMC's institutional actions, goals, and orientations. As a consequence of these theoretical positions, the FMC and the PCC favored policies that would bring women into the workforce as equals to men, and that would provide socialized help to women in the areas of child care and sex education (Stubbs 1994, 192).

The successes in education and labor did not translate into an egalitarian social environment and, by 1974, the FMC began readdressing women's issues in terms of the social and cultural relationships between men and women. In

1974, during the Second FMC Congress, PCC leaders Blas Roca and Antonio Pérez discussed male attitudes about women and officially criticized machismo. Castro's closing remarks condemned the Cuban tendency to produce organizations centered on men, and he used the phrase "revolution within the revolution" (not in reference to Gloria Steinem's book) to signal the need to change the way gender differences produced gendered institutions and inequalities even within the revolution. Continuing with a push for developing a series of ideas that could be the basis for new legislation, the FMC produced the "Thesis on the Full Exercise of Women's Equality" (1975), delivered to PCC members during the First Congress of the Cuban Communist Party (PCC). In addition, in 1974–75 the FMC drafted the Family Code. The FMC's legal incursions in the juridical structure were successful, and they provided the basis for legislation that would account for women's issues in a socialist society (201).

The Cuban Family Code became law on March 8, 1975, International Women's Day. As a legal prescription for equality within the home, it was enacted to strengthen the Cuban family based on respect between sexes. Articles 27 and 28 were controversial because they prescribed shared housework and responsibilities in the home (201). Equality within the home became a legal right of women, blurring further the older lines between the private and the public (Lutjens 1994, 369). Also controversial, though for quite different reasons, was the emphasis that the Family Code placed on the nuclear family. This was seen as an attempt to prescribe white middle-class family values in a population where alternative family arrangements were common. In particular, Afro-Cuban populations, with a high percentage of single parents, particularly women, were seen as targets of this normalizing law.

Though the Family Code was not an enforceable law, it became a tool that educators and cultural workers used to try to shape a new system of sexual equality. As Debra Evenson explains, "the adoption of the Family Code and the continuing discussion it fostered has altered the way Cubans view domestic relations. Although men did not help with the laundry and cooking immediately . . . the message was clear that the correct, revolutionary thing to do is to share the housework" (Evenson quoted in Leiner 1994, 67). Attaching revolutionary value to gendered behavior became a way of transforming sex relations. It also became a way of transforming sexuality by framing sex education as political formation. Also since the mid-1970s, the FMC began lobbying for more sex education that would cover not only questions of female hygiene and pregnancy but also teen sexuality, virginity, and STDs. Though machismo and homophobia curtailed the value of some efforts (for instance, limiting the teaching on the use of condoms), sex education became widespread (67–68). By making public the private, and by attaching revolutionary value to sexual and gender ethics, the FMC and the PCC attempted, with some success, to craft a new ideology of gender that accounted for Cuba's historical specificity and worked for women's economic and social equality.

Because all of the films that will be discussed in the next chapters deal specifically with gender, more discussion regarding gender is reserved for those chapters. Suffice it to say that some cultural institutions have abided by tolerant ideas about gender and sexuality, while others have not. Despite general social intolerance of homosexuality, some public figures, such as Antón Arrufat, chief editor of *Casa,* Virgilio Piñera, celebrated poet, and Alfredo Guevara were able to negotiate their sexual orientation without compromising their status within the revolution. Sadly, others, such as Calvert Casey and Reynaldo Arenas, were not so fortunate (Cabrera 1994). Both were persecuted inside Cuba until they left the island.

Women in ICAIC had a different story. Though, officially, ICAIC functioned under the principle of sexual equality, only one woman, Sara Gómez, was able to produce a feature film in the period between 1959 and 1985. Whether the result of discriminatory practices or simply chance, ICAIC had been largely a male institution. Moreover, as far as I am aware, though other industries established affirmative-action-type policies to increase the representation of women within their ranks, no serious effort to increase women's representation in the film industry by ICAIC has existed (Aspinall 1983, 74–77). For instance, Julianne Burton reports that in 1974–75 ICAIC tried to inject new blood into the institution and "took a score of university graduates (the vast majority women) for training as 'analistas,' using them as apprentices in all sectors of the production process from script research to assistant production." Yet, she continues, to move from assistant to documentarian (most ICAIC directors started as this) is extremely difficult and takes a long time, thus slowing or making impossible injecting these women in the actual directing group (Chanan 1985, 137). Michael Chanan reports that half of the new documentary directors in 1984 were women, yet, as far as I know, no features by women have been released (1985, 292; 2004, 364). Women filmmakers do exist; they just do not have the chance of directing features. For instance, Rebecca Chávez, Marisol Trujillo, Belkis Vega, and Mayra Vilaris have worked as directors since the late 1970s and together have produced dozens of shorts, documentaries, and educational films (Anderson and Gold 1992, 18).

Cultural Institutionalization

In 1975, the First National Congress of the PCC was the forum for the FMC's theses about women in society. The Congress also marked the continuation of the institutionalization of culture. The process of centralization that had been occurring in the economy, politics, and government reached the cultural field and was made policy in the "Central Briefing to the First Congress of the PCC" ("Informe Central al I Congreso del Partido Comunista de Cuba") and the "Thesis 'About artistic and literary culture' " (1st Congreso del Partido Comunista de Cuba) presented to the Congress. These documents outlined the PCC's ideological program for literature and art (this included media). The "Central Briefing" celebrated the cultural development of Cuba since 1959 ("Informe Central" 1982, 59–65). The "Thesis" described the ways in which cultural policy, aesthetic ideas, and revolutionary goals had joined forces in the effort to transform Cuba into a proper socialist humanist state and Cubans into proper citizens of such a state ("I Congreso del Partido Comunista de Cuba" 1982, 72–74).

The "Thesis" was a document designed to fulfill several goals: First, by making reference to "Palabras," the First Congress of UNEAC (1961), and the First Congress of Education and Culture (1971), it placed itself as continuing the policy traditions instituted in these forums. The second goal of the document legitimized the habitus by defending the actions cultural institutions and government had taken with regard to the policing of culture. This defense was staged by appealing to aesthetic principles that resembled those of "Palabras." However, some differences are important to mention. In "Palabras," Castro stated the belief that revolutionary artists would produce revolutionary art. The "Thesis" was less naïve about ideology. Partly because of the Padilla case and the amount of leftist literature and aesthetics that Cuban cultural institutions were afterward forced to see suspiciously, "Thesis" suggested that art might embody bourgeois ideology in subtle ways; thus, it asked cultural workers to be vigilant of the manners in which their own art could embody imperialist ideologies (71).

A more significant difference between "Palabras" and "Thesis" had to do with the latter document's different levels of trust of the Cuban people. While "Palabras" asked cultural workers to reflect on the people in order to learn the goals of socialism (Castro stated: "to us, good will be what is good to [the people]; to us, it will be noble, beautiful and useful that which is noble, useful and beautiful to them"), the "Thesis" asked cultural workers to reflect on socialism: "The best source of originality in artistic production, based on our conditions, is found in the essence of socialism." This is not a small difference because it signaled a shift in the types of logics that would be used to justify cultural work production and aesthetic value judgments. Instead of being inspired and educated, in praxis, by the people, the worker, and the peasant, cultural workers were asked to reflect on socialism, its teachings, and its dogmas. Moreover, the "Thesis" asserted that the most vital aspect of socialism was the scientific certainty on a person's perfectibility, implying that reflecting on socialism meant reflecting on the transformation and transformability of the people. This signals a change in the way the PCC understood the relationship between cultural workers (and the cultural institutions they represented) and the people. Instead of following the people's tastes and values and learning from them, cultural workers were asked to see the people as the raw material from which socialism could be built. Therefore, I argue, though the revolutionary hermeneutics of the 1960s was evidently optimistic about the role the people could play in redeeming cultural workers from their latent capitalistic tendencies, the revolutionary hermeneutics of the mid-1970s placed more emphasis on a centralized version of "the noble, the beautiful and the useful." Instead of being led by the people, cultural workers were asked to follow socialism and to abide by an elitist and centralist ethics of social responsibility.

Institutionalization and centralism continued in 1976 with the promulgation of the *Constitution of the Republic of Cuba* (*Constitución de la República de Cuba*), which included a chapter dedicated to culture and education, and, in the same year, with the formation of the Ministry of Culture, headed by Armando Hart Dávalos. Hart was a seasoned cultural administrator who had been in charge throughout the 1960s of the Ministry of Education when the ministry included the Cultural Directorate (Dirección de Cultura) and was thus responsible for administering culture. Like Alfredo Guevara, head of ICAIC, Hart had strong and prolific opinions on the topics of cultural policy, opinions that were made permanent in speeches, essays, and books on culture in a revolutionary society. His views shaped the role the Ministry of Culture would play in the Cuban cultural field by establishing administrative parameters to the relationship between cultural workers and the material basis and resources of the ministry (Hart Dávalos 1984).

To this day, the ministry has the general goals of administering economic, material, technologic, pedagogic, and human resources related to the field of culture. In particular, the ministry organizes artistic education, at all educational levels, promotes culture (for example, organization of cultural events, advertising of cultural works), and oversees cultural corporations (for example, recording studios, publishing) and institutions (for example, ICAIC, Casa, UNEAC). According to Hart, the general objectives of the ministry were to set up a cultural infrastructure capable of, on the one hand, making the Cuban people participants in the production and enjoyment of culture and, on the other hand, developing individual talent (Hart Dávalos 1987, 116).

Echoing Castro and Guillén, Hart believed that revolutionary culture could be produced only through a revolutionary hermeneutics capable of showing cultural workers the needs and desires of the Cuban people (124). Thus, the ministry encouraged the participation of professional cultural workers (in particular artists, filmmakers, and writers) in amateur organizations by creating structural links between mass-cultural organizations and professional cultural organizations. In addition, in the ministry, artistic quality was understood not simply as the result of the artwork's intrinsic aesthetic characteristics. The work's sociality and the workers' social role were also determinants of quality. To Hart, the cultural worker's product depended on talent and creative capacity as well as on professionalism and technical proficiency, but in addition, the quality of the work depended on the social esteem the artist inspired in the people and on the contact the artist had with her/his community (124).

Hart's ideas created a normative definition of cultural work and cultural workers that, though inspired by ideas from the beginning of the revolution, shifted the phenomenological and epistemological role that the masses would play in the subjectivities of cultural workers. Though in the 1960s the masses were seen as having the potential to redeem the artist from the bourgeois past, from the 1970s onward the masses were seen simply as the artist's inspiration and audience.

Conclusion

Reviewing the Cuban cultural field from 1959 to the 1980s reveals a series of shifts regarding cultural policy and normative ideas about cultural communities, cultural workers, and citizenship. Discursively, the invasion of the Bay of Pigs gave the cultural leadership the opportunity to emphasize national security as a key element of proper civic behavior and cultural production. Soon after, "within the Revolution, everything; against the Revolution, nothing" became an ethical and aesthetic map that some cultural workers would have to draw, and most cultural workers would have to follow. Helping draw this ethical and aesthetic map was a revolutionary hermeneutics that the cultural vanguard used to take advantage of the social and ideological value of cultural work and cultural policy. The goal of government was the revolution's survival. This could only be guaranteed when each Cuban became a revolutionary; thus, the transformation of the Cuban people into revolutionary citizens was a key task of the revolutionary hermeneutics.

The centralization and institutionalization of the 1970s transformed these revolutionary hermeneutics. During the 1960s, the revolutionary hermeneutics was optimistic of the role the people could play in leading cultural workers toward a popular and transformative aesthetics. The revolutionary hermeneutics of the mid-1970s placed more emphasis on a centralized articulation of aesthetic and ideological values. Instead of being led by the people and being asked to emulate the values of peasants and laborers, cultural workers were asked to follow socialist precepts and to abide by an elitist and centralist ethics of social responsibility.

Implied in this shift is a change of ideas about the need to provide the cultural workers with social experiences that could change their subjectivities. In the 1960s, it was common to think of the cultural worker as occupying a partly alienated subject position. Given that capitalist and/or imperialist institutions and ideas formed most workers, the first generation of cultural workers was seen as, unavoidably and at times unintentionally, complicit with the preservation of prerevolutionary values. Accordingly, and despite being asked to assume vanguard positions, cultural workers were expected, at least theoretically, to transform themselves from bourgeois intellectuals to revolutionary vanguards and citizens. In order to accomplish this change, they were asked to embrace a revolutionary hermeneutics that could help them "see" the world anew and to see it in accordance with the needs and desires of the Cuban masses, the *raison d'etre* for the Cuban Revolution. Crafting this hermeneutics could not be accomplished using theory or aesthetic experimentation. Cultural workers would have to do more; they would have to interact with the people, learn their ways, tastes, values, and needs and from these interactions they would be able to outfit a new dealienated subjectivity, see the world anew, and produce truly revolutionary culture. Moreover, they would have to learn to narrativize their work and their social value without reference to freedom and autonomy. Their distinction would more likely be based on ideas of civic responsibility and political glory. To be a true revolutionary artist, the narrative would say, one needs to embrace the power of art to ideologically shape the viewer, the audience, and/or the reader.

The institutionalization process of the 1970s placed Soviet-influenced socialist doctrine at the center of the revolutionary hermeneutics, in a sense replacing "the people." In this new system of ideas, the people no longer embodied the goals of the revolution; instead, socialist theory and dogma provided these goals, and the people became the targets of culture, the material that socialism would use to fuel the revolution.

Although cultural workers used hermeneutic techniques to negotiate their position in the social grid, to show compliance with the government's rules, and to justify their actions to themselves, these revolutionary hermeneutic techniques did not simply appear. They had to be developed from specific sets of knowledge. After 1959, several important debates occupied most of the discussions about culture and art, and these developed knowledge traditions proper to the epoch. These debates were about the following: the role of the intellectual in a communist/socialist society; the definition of works that can be considered revolutionary film, literature, or art; the proper objects of filmic and artistic reflection; and the policing of cultural products. In the following chapter, I investigate the way these topics were discussed in Cuba from 1959 to 1985. These debates are key to understanding the articulation of citizenship to culture, because they provided rationales that could be used publicly to legitimize action and practice. They gave political meaning to cultural work and blurred the line between culture and civics.

Chapter 2

The Cuban Revolutionary Hermeneutics

Criticism and Citizenship

U.S. film dominated Cuban screens before 1959. This changed with the advent of the revolution. With Cuba moving away from capitalism and from American cultural products, Cuban movie theaters, to great box-office success, began substituting Hollywood fare with films from other nations and their own (Halperini 1976, 196). On December 12, 1963, the newspaper *Hoy*, which was considered the official organ of the Cuban Communist Party (PCC) and was headed at the time by Blas Roca, published a critique of Fellini's *La Dolce Vita* (1960) that argued that the film could not be considered wholesome entertainment for the Cuban working class. A scant reply signed by ten Cuban directors affiliated with the Instituto Cubano de Artes e Industria Cinematográficos (ICAIC) and Alfredo Guevara was printed in the newspaper *Revolución*. The reply compared the position of *Hoy* with the censoring activities of the Hayes Code in the United States and the Catholic Church around the world (195). Despite the high rank that Roca enjoyed in the PCC, Fidel Castro supported ICAIC's position.

Regardless of their differing positions on *La Dolce Vita*, *Hoy* and ICAIC were two cultural institutions that embraced and championed politicized culture. For those working in these areas of officialdom, the overall goal of film, and of all culture, was to shape the Cuban people into revolutionary citizens. The leadership of *Hoy* and ICAIC disagreed, however, in their understanding of the best means by which such an ambitious task could be accomplished. Their theoretical positions about the role film played in a revolutionary society made their opinions irreconcilable. Pierre Bourdieu comments regarding the French context: "Specifically aesthetic conflicts about the legitimate vision of the world—in the last resort, about what deserves to be represented and the right way to represent it—are political conflicts . . . for the power to impose the dominant definition of reality" (Bourdieu 1993, 101). With Bourdieu, I believe that issues of aesthetics important to Cubans during the period 1960 to 1985 give unique insight into criticism and the way criticism is part of politics.

Cuba's particular history and way of organizing cultural institutions is distinctive, and so are the discourses on culture. Like in American and Western societies, the distinctive set of discourses used in the Cuban cultural field determined a "lifestyle," a habitus, where criticism and film reception fitted within specific technologies of selfhood (more on this later in the next chapter). Moreover, these discursive spaces shed light on the phenomenological and hermeneutic relationship between films and historically situated official readers and were clues to the power relations in which these readers and the films were immersed. Finally, these spaces helped form specific, politically situated ways of knowing the world and of interpreting culture; the ideas they engendered were used to place limits on the community of cultural workers. For these reasons, ideas about culture and aesthetics can illuminate how cultural workers negotiated self-understanding and how they brokered for positions within the field.

In this chapter, I examine seven discourses that deeply influenced the cultural field in general and criticism in particular. These discourses were particularly important because they related to freedom and agency and included definitions of selfhood and individuality based on social practices. That is, they helped individuals evaluate cultural work by providing aesthetic, epistemological, and ethical frameworks. More important, they established that performing such evaluations would bring each individual closer to becoming a new person and a proper citizen.

The Politicization of Cultural Work and Workers

ICAIC and Casa de las Américas were created during the first year of the revolution, and ICAIC was seen as providing a fundamental link between government and people.[1] ICAIC, as described in Law 169, was to serve as an ideological chisel that would shape Cubans into revolutionaries or, at least, supporters of the revolution. Accordingly, film production and criticism were defined as political activities that could further, or hinder, the goals of government. This explains the type of review a film like *La Dolce Vita* would receive from *Hoy* and the type of defense that ICAIC had to issue. In framing all culture as political, the new hegemony defined a framework of cultural interpretation and a proper horizon of expectations (Jauss 1982). If cultural works were political, how was politics manifested in specific works? Answers to this question engendered a style of cultural interpretation and became a mental template that reviewers and cultural workers would often, if not always, use. In a very real sense, the idea that "culture is political" occupied the center of cultural workers' horizon of expectations.

The politicization of culture increased the power and social responsibility of the cultural community who, over time, acquired more politico-cultural roles. Georgina Dopico Black (1989) commented on the degree of influence and importance that literature gained during the revolutionary offensive of the late 1960s (115). The novel, in particular, became more political, and new genres that fitted the government's goals began to be sponsored by UNEAC. At the same time, censorship of works that did not support the revolutionary offensive was common, including the work of Padilla (116–18). Similarly, the organization of the Cuban Union of Writers and Artists (Unión de Escritores y Artistas de Cuba, UNEAC), and of other institutions after "Palabras," meant also the creation of a growing cultural bureaucracy that would have the power, at least ideally, to regulate all Cuban culture and to act as gatekeepers of the cultural realm. In their gatekeeping role, cultural institutions promoted and contained the professional careers of most cultural workers (Reed 1991). Though culture that was not politicized was thereafter allowed to exist ("within the Revolution"), revolutionary politicized culture was seen as the only necessary culture.

Cuba's use of culture to aid government is hardly unique. Influenced by the likes of Friedrich Schiller and Matthew Arnold, art institutions, such as museums, incorporated into their functioning the principle of crafting individuals into better citizens and, therefore, became essential to the modernist project of governing the "souls of their citizens" (Schiller 1982; Arnold 1993). The field of culture provided the state with hegemonic ways of structuring taste, objects, and institutions (Bourdieu 1993, 29–73; Bourdieu 1987, 201–5). Paralleling this was the multiplication of governing disciplines, which altered ideas about citizenship and fostered a reliance on art and mass culture to produce in citizens the desire to be governed. Toby Miller (1993) states: "Citizenship is an open technology, a means of transformation ready for the definition and disposal in dispersed ways at dispersed sites. . . . It produces a 'disposition' on [the citizens'] part not to accept the imposition of a particular form of government passively, but to embrace it actively as a collective expression of themselves" (12). It is in the context of the production of "dispositions" that art and culture became, in modernity, an answer to the question of how to govern. It is culture and art that engender the desire for self-formation, cultivation, and the *Bildung* that Hans-Georg Gadamer (1989, 9) sees as the most important idea of the eighteenth century and that served to anchor most political revolutions.

However, most culture and most art existed within capitalist societies and responded to questions of governance foreign to Cuba's changing needs. They were produced by what Antonio Gramsci would call "traditional intellectuals," or intellectuals who defined themselves as independent from political structures. As Bourdieu (1988) commented on relation to art and art institutions in France, intellectuals in these institutions relied on Kantian ideas of disinterestedness to produce distinctions among classes (41). The artistic gaze, which implied the disinterested contemplation of the work of art, was a marker of distinction and thus an activity of self-interest. The reproduction of social classes and distinctions fulfilled the roles of government because it reproduced a habitus that naturalizes the existing social order and legitimizes class distinctions (170).

In Cuba, the coming to power of a new government and a new economic, social, and political system required the creation of cultural institutions significantly different from those before the revolution (institutions not based on capitalism). Soviet realism did not provide all the answers and many Cubans involved in culture, including most of ICAIC, did not embrace it. According to Milena Recio, Michael Chanan, Antonio Martínez Heredia, and others, the work of Antonio Gramsci, popularized during the early 1960s, provided some of the answers as to how to form a cultural field capable of both responding to the needs of Marxism and the needs of the people (Martínez-Heredia 2001, 375; Recio et al. 1998; Chanan 2001). As I show below, in addition, the new regime required an aesthetics that could produce new markers of distinction regarding taste. This aesthetics was politicized, and most of it rejected Kantian ideas about art. One of the reasons why it is so interesting to research Cuba's cultural development during the first decades after the revolution is precisely because Cuba's community of cultural workers had to produce the conditions of production, distribution, and consumption of cultural texts that could create new classes of citizens. The new politicized culture would have to inspire *Bildung*, revolutionary citizenship, and support of the government; similarly to, for instance, Soviet, Chinese Maoist, and Israeli goals of seeking a new citizen, Cuba had to produce a new habitus, new sets of dispositions, and new principles that could be applied as universals in order to judge cultural works (Levy 2007, 129). Aside from the administrative decisions that this setup required, it was also necessary to produce new sets of knowledge that would facilitate and guide the decision-making processes of those involved in administration and that could serve as theoretical grounds for universal principles.

Culture as Transformation

The revolution made culture political because the leadership believed that culture could transform Cuba into a developed, socialist, and law-abiding nation. This idealist project required a new type of Cuban, a new type of citizen, one who would make it his/her personal goal to construct, defend, and protect the nation, and one who would embody a new set of dispositions. As Richard R. Fagen (1969) has observed, individual transformation required a new "political culture" that included "patterns of action as well as states of mind" and nontraditional "domains of action." He notes that Cuban political culture used the ideas of struggle and utopia as cornerstones of ideological framework that would help Cubans become exemplars of "the New Man." Echoing Fagen, Tzvi Medin (1990) argues that the Cuban leaders addressed the issue of forming a revolutionary consciousness by creating institutions of change and transformative practices. The leadership organized the Literacy Campaign of 1960–61, which helped shape educational goals and gave an opportunity to inculcate revolutionary principles. They structured the army and people's militias with training that included a significant amount of ideological elements. They controlled the media and the way it represented current affairs, including cinema, with the documentary, the newsreel, and the fictional film each providing distinctive elements of indoctrination (Medin 1990, 8). Medin is correct in highlighting the importance of creating a new political culture, but wrong in viewing cultural institutions as "controlled." Most of the time, political leaderships had no control over cultural institutions, which were left to the purview of the cultural vanguard (which I discuss below). Cultural institutions, for the most part, functioned (or tried to function) as part of civil society, using Gramsci's term. Cultural institutions, with the blessing of the political leaders, became social locations where Cubans could exercise their agency. For instance, the government, particularly in the early stages of the revolution, supported intellectuals by organizing cultural life and events such as dance, song festivals, literature contests, and, of course, cinema screenings all over the nation. The strategy at once secured the role of the government as the provider of culture while allowing the government to regulate culture (Johnson 1993, 142).

As Martínez Heredia (2001, 380) has noted, reading Gramsci helped Cuban intellectuals understand that the overall strategy to produce a new citizen was a subtle process and required the work of the citizens themselves. The strategy was to incite Cubans to interiorize the principles of the revolution by arousing in each individual a desire to become a new citizen, a new woman or man, a new subject to the law, and a new agent of freedom. Two distinct but related processes came together: governance and self-formation, or rather governance through self-formation. To ignite new desires, to use the language of romance, the Cuban political leaders worked with old objects of desire like freedom, justice, courage, and virility, repositioning these idea-objects within the discourse of the revolution with the goal of producing, at least, a refracted interpellation. One instance of such political and discursive tactics is found in the speech that Castro used after the bomb raids of April 16, 1961, to denounce the American and "gusano" (a "traitor" characterized by those who migrated to Miami in 1959) aggression and where he declared (for the first time) the revolution as socialist. Almost all of his speech was dedicated to denouncing the Bay of Pigs attack. Only in passing, almost as a side commentary, did he announce that the revolution was (and at that moment the revolution became) a "socialist revolution" (Medin 1990, 13). By emphasizing the aggression, Castro framed the historical transition in terms of rebellion, of freedom and survival; socialism was embraced as the reaction of reason against American moral corruption. The resulting discursive formations, a testament to Castro's political savvy, bound together and made interchangeable the terms socialism, rebellion, and freedom.

Medin identifies the three following discursive patterns that served as the cognitive, conceptual, emotional, terminological, and axiological platforms of the revolution and that served to legitimize it (13). The first discourse he calls "existence as confrontation," where "the military" and the ideal epic values of militancy were inscribed in everyday actions (31). A second discourse was that of "Manichaeanism." Its logic helped shape the Cuban identity in an "us versus them" style, and made use of stereotypes that defined the enemy in hyper-negative terms. Manichaeanism was deeply invested in the discursive constitution of the Cuban national identity by defining boundaries and a community through the imaginary relation of all Cubans as defenders of what is good and what is Cuban (Anderson 2006, 5–7). The third discourse is that of Marxism-Leninism, which was fused with Cuban nationalism. The fusion was achieved through the strategic use of symbols, of which the clearest was Fidel Castro. Castro was what Medin calls an "integrative symbol" used to mark the equivalence of discrete discourses and to legitimize each one of them (Medin 1990, 54). To follow Castro meant to follow the revolution, to follow the nation, anti-imperialism, justice, and Marxism-Leninism. It is important to mention, however, that Castro's symbolic power could not have been possible without what Carollee Bengelsdorf (1994) calls the "verticalization of political power," a political structure that guaranteed the centrality of Castro and his acolytes and that made outsiders of the rest of the people (95). Within this system of power distribution, Cubans had no option but to gaze directly to the towering figure (continuing the vertical metaphor) of Castro and his power.

Though these discourses targeted all of the population, they also became common among cultural workers, who often used the discourses as templates for cultural creation and cultural criticism. Each of the films studied in this book presents examples of a view of existence as confrontation, Manichaeanism, and Marxist-Leninism. *Lucia,* for instance, is composed of three stories narrating the role three different women named Lucia played in three different Cuban revolutions. The story of *Memories of Underdevelopment* is enriched by the protagonist's anguish and/or impotence at having to take sides either with the revolution or with his own bourgeois values. *One Way or Another* and *Portrait of Teresa* present issues of gender through the prisms of Marxism-Leninism and revolutionary doctrine. However, it is important to not confuse political culture with culture that is also political. Medin and Bengelsdorf are theorizing political culture; predictably, they fail to account for the subtlety of cultural work. These films are full of textual complexity and ambivalence and they are much more than vehicles for political uses. They are, like all good culture, thinking pieces that use nuanced views of reality and politics.

Given that the transformation of the Cuban consciousness, or at least the attempts at transforming it, were framed by the discourse of freedom, it is possible to see the formation of a revolutionary consciousness in Cuba not simply as a process of subjection. Although the new leadership crafted programs to shape the Cuban citizenry and used technologies of governance that sought normalization and regulation, freedom and self-control were key parts of these programs. Thus, the revolutionary consciousness, which is partly manifested in Cuban film, was and is embedded and dependent on techniques of self-formation inextricably linked to agency and to the ethical manipulation of the self by the self.

From a governmental point of view, the legitimacy and survival of the Cuban Revolution depended on the transformation of Cuban citizens into revolutionary individuals modeled after Che Guevara's ideal of the New Man. This transformation required two discrete ideological processes. The first one targeted the general population, involving the nurturing of *conciencia*. This process was carried on through discursive tactics, institutional alliances between government and people, the politicization of public spaces, and the politicization of culture. To achieve this first goal of *conciencia*, it was required to undertake a second ideological and foundational process to construct some of the cultural tools that would help cultivate the New Man. These tools would be the result of the activities carried on within cultural institutions like ICAIC, UNEAC, Casa de la Américas, and the education system and that would properly constitute what Bourdieu calls the "field of cultural production." Given the characteristics of Cuba, where for decades the state organized most, if not all, economic and cultural activities, the majority of cultural mediators were involved in official cultural institutions. According to Recio, this is how civil society exists in a socialist nation (Recio et al. 1998, 156). Therefore, Cuba's field of culture played ideological and institutional goals. At the ideological level, the field produced the meaning and value of artistic works, including film, and granted as natural and logical certain interpretations. The field normalized part of the phenomenological world of Cuban citizens. At the institutional level, the field coincided with official cultural institutions, producing a stronger link between the cultural vanguard, cultural policy, and the Cuban people (Miller 1993, 15).

Aiding this project were theories of culture and people, which explained and legitimized institutional and personal practices and actions. To arrive at these explanations, the Cuban field of cultural production greatly relied on the ongoing investigation of three theoretical questions: What is the role of the intellectual in the revolution? What works can be considered revolutionary film, literature, or art? What are the proper objects of filmic and artistic reflection? Underlying these theoretical questions was a fourth issue or set of assumptions about the relationship of people to revolutionary or proper culture. Although in the previous chapter I already mentioned some of the ways in which these issues were resolved at different times, the following is a more detailed elaboration.

The Intellectual in the Revolution

Parallel to the politicization of culture was the idea that the cultural community ought to play a vanguard role in Cuban society. As a vanguard, the intellectual was called to perform specific social and personal tasks. Socially, she/he had to lead the people toward revolutionary change, and personally, she/he had to become an exemplar by embodying the principles of the revolution. In Gramscian terminology, the vanguard is an organic intellectual, but the unusual Cuba case makes even this definition problematic. Gramsci referred to organic intellectuals as those who have grown and developed with the ruling class and were self-aware of their class and political role. In his view, a revolutionary movement needed to develop its own organic intellectuals, that is, cultural workers that came from the popular classes and were aware of their political role. In Cuba, the cultural class after the revolution was neither the product of the ruling class (which was displaced by the revolution) nor came from the masses. Perhaps this is why their position wavered. We need only consider the political paradox from "Palabras" (see previous chapter), which states that a revolutionary government obeys the will of the people, yet the people are, according to Marxist revolutionary theory, alienated from their reality. In a sense, the cultural vanguard became caught between two functions: leading the people and learning from them.

Not surprisingly, the vanguard had to be more advanced ideologically and more willing to sacrifice than the masses (Guevara 1987, 130). This ideological advancement required self-reflection, the monitoring of one's activities, and the recognition that prerevolutionary ways of being and thinking had to be eradicated. As Nicolas Guillén (1987 [1961]) stated in his speech at UNEAC's send-off event (the First Congress of Writers and Artists), the socialist intellectual must negate herself/himself and must focus on serving the people (73). As in Christian doctrine where negation refers to the repressing or suppressing of humanity's out-of-grace state, in Guillén's work negation meant the leaving behind or the suppression of any prerevolutionary, socially shaped ways of being (see also Fornet 1971, 33–39).

Part of the affective elements that sustained the appetite for sacrifice and self-negation were the social rewards of being a vanguard. To be a vanguard meant sharing in the "aura" of perfection constructed through mass media, film, literature, the arts, and political speeches. Popular representations of the vanguard were consistently heroic, but, in addition, intellectual and political public spaces were full with references to the vanguard's enviable heroism, sacrifice, and responsibility. In intellectual congresses (that is, Fornet, Guillén), political speeches, and key texts such as the essay "El Hombre Nuevo" by Che Guevara, the vanguard occupied the highest rank in the new order. According to Che Guevara, participating as a vanguard in the formation of the communist society was a sign that the individual had a complete social self, that he or she was a fully realized human being, and that he or she was without "alienation." In film, the measure of a good revolutionary was sacrifice, or at least a type of ascetics related to discipline and measure. Sergio, from *Memorias,* cannot sacrifice and thus cannot become a revolutionary. All the Lucias (*Lucia*), Teresa (*Portrait of Teresa*), Lina (*Up to a Certain Point*), and Yolanda (*One Way or Another*) show a willingness to sacrifice and pay the price of the revolution (Davies 1997, 345–59). For doing so, they are depicted as vanguard characters, as revolutionaries, and as exemplars.

True to the notion of the organic intellectual, the discourse of the vanguard is also a discourse on epistemology that centers on the notion that only knowledge acquired through the people can be real knowledge. Castro, Che Guevara, Fornet, Guillén, and Osvaldo Dorticós Torrado, former president of Cuba, all mentioned different versions of this idea. These versions included the metaphor of a "new optic" (Fornet 1971), the engagement with those who inspire the vanguard's work (Guillén 1987 [1961]), a commitment to be one of the people (Dorticós Torrado 1987 [1961], 43–49). Although fully embracing this populist epistemology was hardly possible, the discourse of 'knowledge through the people' influenced cultural life. For instance, this discourse affected the film industry, which showed a strong commitment to reflect on the lives of the middle and lower classes and to embrace themes that problematized existing social circumstances, both thematics previously unpopular in Cuban film. Starting with films like *Cuba Baila* (1960, Espinosa), which deals with the celebration of the fifteen birthday of a girl who belonged to the "popular classes" (a term commonly used in Cuba to refer to the working class), to *Up to a Certain Point* (1983), which uses working-class revolutionary ethics to teach moral lessons, Cuba's film community represented, examined, commented on, and criticized the "people." In general, the "people" occupied the center of many, if not most, literary and filmic narratives, vindicating the existence of this epistemology (Chanan 1985, 111–18).

A second way in which these epistemological requests affected Cuban cultural life was by providing theoretical support to artistic educational policies and outreach cultural activities. For instance, the Movement of Aficionados (Movimiento de Aficionados) organized amateur artists, filmmakers, writers, musicians, actors, and so forth. Following a resolution by the Congress of Education and Culture to "massify" culture, political and labor organizations such as the UJC (Organization of Communist Youth—Unión de Jovenes Comunistas) and the CTC (Confederación de Trabajadores Comunistas) began organizing the amateur artists that belonged to their ranks ("Dirigentes de Organismos Hablan Sobre el Movimiento de Aficionados" 1972, 24–32; "Informe Central al I Congreso del Partido Comunista de Cuba" 1982, 59–65). With the participation of the CNC (Consejo Nacional de Cultura), ICAIC, UNEAC, the Academy of Sciences, the School of Literature of the Universidad de La Habana, and the Ballet Nacional de Cuba, among others, these labor and political organizations fostered cultural education, production, and distribution between workers, farmers, and youth ("Dirigentes de Organismos" 27). They did so through training, workshops, festivals, and exhibits that showcased the talents of otherwise disenfranchised segments of the population. What was an epistemological challenge for some (those intellectuals and cultural workers who were not from the popular classes) became an easier task for cultural workers prepared *by* the revolution.

Mistrusting universal or abstract knowledge and relying on knowledge that could be acquired through personal experience were two characteristics that furthered the vanguard's pragmatism and organicism. Understanding the task of the revolutionary intellectual in pragmatic ways was akin to Marxist ideas that placed the intellectual under capitalism squarely within the superstructure. Paul Baran, published in 1961 in the second number of *Casa,* contended that the alienated intellectual worker is the result of capitalism, and because of this, in a divided labor system, manual labor and intellectual labor are separated (14–21). This separation has contributed to the disintegration of the individual, from the point of view of self-development and of social development. In addition, the separation has created an ideological gulf that the intellectual worker tries to maintain by producing myths about the difficulties of intellectual work and by creating alliances with the governing classes. The worker is left with the stigma of undervalued labor and the structural powerlessness that goes with it. The real intellectual, conversely, constantly tries to relate his/her experience and/or labor to other aspects of human existence. His or her life is a constant reminder that so-called autonomous areas of existence (government, art, literature, politics, economics) can only be understood insofar as they are perceived as components of a totality. The real intellectual, moreover, is in her/his essence a social critic interested in fighting for a more rational and human society. She/he is the consciousness of society; as Fornet would later comment, she/he is a heroic figure. In a Cuban voice, Francisco López Cámara (1963) added that abstract consciousness, as exemplified by art and philosophy, serves the interests of the ruling class. Art and philosophy can become constitutive of revolutionary consciousness only when they are reintegrated to praxis and become transformative and autopoetic (29–32). Agreeing with López Cámara, the Cuban Mirta Aguirre (1987 [1980]) argued that cultural workers greatly benefited from learning and using dialectic materialism, and, thus, its study should be undertaken by all creators (108–21). When this is not possible, she adds, cultural workers should abide by the following two recommendations: First, artists must align themselves with the proletariat. Second, artists must reject all metaphysical and/or abstract conception of men and society. These two principles should help the cultural worker produce work aligned with the revolution (113).

The Aesthetics of Revolutionary Art, Literature, and Film

The central task of the cultural vanguard was producing the conditions of existence necessary for a socialist society. Their tools were cultural and included activities sponsored and/or promoted by cultural institutions such as art, literary, and film production, and literary, artistic, and filmic competitions. To function, these institutions relied on cultural policies to legitimate standards of artistic and revolutionary merit. The first of these policies, Law 169, stated that cultural work should transform collective consciousness and deepen the revolutionary spirit. Because this did little to clarify the specific aesthetic principles that cultural workers could use either to carry out their cultural production or at least to defend it against ideological attacks, debates over aesthetics began with the revolution and increased after 1961 (the year of the *P.M.* crisis). Because Marxist aesthetics dominated the debates, it is worth detailing what particular strands of Marxist aesthetics were popular among Cuban cultural workers during the 1960s and 1970s. Though I am not claiming that all cultural workers read, learned, or used these aesthetic principles to determine aesthetic value, many of these principles reached most cultural workers, albeit in a "popular" (versus academic) form.

A quick survey of publications reveals a rich discursive and theoretical space that included key strands of Continental and Latin American aesthetic philosophies. Among them were the Marxism of the Frankfurt School, French-influenced structuralist aesthetics, Soviet-style aesthetics, and Latin American aesthetics, to mention a few. Particularly influential were the works of Bertolt Brecht, Adolfo Sánchez Vázquez, and Aguirre, which I examine below, together with the writings of the film theoreticians and filmmakers Julio García Espinosa and Tomás Gutiérrez Alea.

Brecht, whose work was commonly referenced in *Casa* and *Cine Cubano*, influenced theater, film, and television. Of particular interest to Cuban cultural workers were Brecht's concept of distanciation and his ideas regarding the relationship of audiences to theater ("Del Estilo Épico de Bertolt Brecht" 4, 38–42; Laverde 1963, 77–90; Muguercia 1975, 73; Boudet 1975, 73–75). Distanciation is a staging and acting technique that attempts to break the alienating illusionism of classical theater. Brecht conceived it as a way of foregrounding the sociality and historicity of an actor's gestures and theater's production techniques. While acting, actors should be able to support a duality composed of, on the one hand, the character she/he is representing and, on the other hand, the actor's critique of such character. Identification with the character should only be used to highlight the character's social and historical contradictions. In so doing, the distanciation technique engenders a critical representation of reality, via drama, by making reality knowable and transformable (Laverde 1963, 80). The technique of distanciation was useful to Cuban cultural workers because it emphasized the audience's critical engagement with reality and conceived of the audience as a participant in the solution of social problems (Boudet 1975, 74). Given that the leadership saw political participation as a way of gaining the support of the Cuban people, an aesthetics that produced cultural works that invited participation was coherent with public policy. In addition to support, the leadership believed that participation was key to the transformation of the Cuban people. Dealienation by praxis was a common axiom of political thought in the Cuba of the sixties. Extending the axiom to the field of culture meant conceiving of an active audience as an audience that could be transformed by praxis into a subject closer to the ideal of the New Man.

Though some Cuban cultural workers (Grupo Teatro Escambray, ICAIC) used Brecht's work to conceptualize the pragmatics of producing revolutionary narratives and production techniques, an ongoing attempt to investigate the relationships of Marx and Lenin to culture required the examination of questions that were more abstract. According to the Cuban art critic Gerardo Mosquera (1991), the work of the Mexican philosopher Sánchez Vázquez partly fulfilled this purpose. Sánchez Vázquez was one of the most enduring influences in post-revolutionary Cuba, as he was widely published from the 1960s to the 1980s. Mosquera comments that Sánchez Vázquez deeply shaped the field with his writings, his ideological support of the revolution, and his numerous visits.

In his work, Sánchez Vázquez elaborated on Marx's aesthetics and arrived at several conclusions that Cuban intellectuals would repeat throughout the next couple of decades. The most important of these conclusions was the faith in the transformational power of art (Sánchez Vázquez 1962, 3–24). According to him, Marx's greatest contribution to aesthetics was conceiving of the aesthetic as a peculiar relationship between man and reality. Aesthetics is, for Sánchez Vázquez, a particular way of assimilating reality. In this assimilation, the particular of the object is not lost to general laws, but remains as an immediate experience. Conversely, assimilating the world through a theoretical attitude means placing the subject in the sphere of existence of the object, resulting in the subject's alienation and self-abstraction. Abstracting the self, and the self's relationship to the world, impedes self-knowledge and fosters alienation. In opposition, artistic assimilation via the aesthetic experience allows for the display and generation of human potentials in relation to the self and the community. The object becomes the subject's mean of expression (1962, 6). Sánchez Vázquez argued that the possibility of producing art exists only insofar as men and women have the capacity to concretize, through work, essential forces (13). Given that the senses have become humanized through labor in art production, the senses become means of self-knowledge. Artistic labor, hence, humanizes objects but also objectifies the self. Their link is social and productive, mutually generative.

His theories relied on understanding art as labor and not abstraction and on understanding labor as the humanization of reality. Artistic production and the aesthetic experience are, in his theoretical framework, examples of dealienated labor and self. Sánchez Vázquez, like Brecht, understood the self to be transformable only in situations in which the self could be known or objectified. Self-knowledge was an a priori condition to self-transformation, particularly if self-transformation was conceived in relation to a telos, which in the Cuban case existed. If the telos was the New Man, and if the individual was to participate in her/his own transformation, then she/he required a technique for self-knowledge. Because labor in general was alienated, the individual was left with the aesthetic experience as the only technique of self-knowledge.

The Cuban philosopher Aguirre, who later occupied a high position in the Ministry of Culture, theorized an aesthetics that incorporated the cultural policies and the political requirements of her time. Like Brecht and Sánchez Vázquez, Aguirre (1987 [1980]) elaborated on the transformational, and revolutionary, power of art. In her 1963 contribution to Marxist aesthetics, she argued that revolutionary art had specific characteristics and that these worked to create a powerful and critical link between viewer/audience/reader/listener and reality. In order to produce an argument that could account for the political requirements of 1963, which likely included, at least, an acknowledgment of the work done in the USSR, she argued for "socialist realism." Though this term, "socialist realism," appeared to refer to Soviet aesthetics, particularly aesthetics influenced by Lukács, Aguirre used the term in an unusual fashion and, indeed, refashioned it to fit the Cuban cultural climate, which at the time was heavily influenced by Western aesthetics and art.[2] Her definition of socialist realism is an insightful definition that could be applied today to most political art and that recaptures some of the spirit of Lukács' work.

Aguirre contended, echoing Lukács (1979, 28–59), that socialist realism is the best type of artwork if the goal of art is to transform individuals and society. She wrote: "The world does not satisfy men and he, with art, can contribute to perfect it, deepen it, improve it, re-create it, if he ably reflects in his conscience the objective reality" (Aguirre 1987 [1980], 108). As in the work of Brecht and Lukács, art's meaningful contribution to life is its power to reflect on reality and make reality objective, knowledgeable, and, thus, transformable. However, for her, realism in art is not a type of representation of reality, the sometimes crude aesthetics of Soviet realism. Instead, realism refers to the work's property of successfully conveying reality's more important characteristics. Aguirre's moderation in this regard wisely accommodates a wider array of representational styles and audience competences. In order to convey reality one must, Aguirre argued like Lukács, use artistic tropes. These do not hinder realism or truthfulness because they are shortcuts that reveal the interconnectedness of objects, phenomena, and reality. They are habits, consensual, and communicative. These resources, tropes, suggest the possibility of boundless communication and also the limits of communication. Tropes are communal. Moreover, the contingency of tropes is actualized in the contingency of reception, profiling the historical location and ideological formation of their existence (1987, 111–12).

Using Marxist-Leninist aesthetics, Aguirre argued for an idea of beauty not dependent on the ephemeral satisfaction of the senses but on the ability of things to awaken the desire to appreciate reality affectively and without alienation. Though her ideas were quite permissive, she recognized that not all art was equally able to facilitate the audience's understanding of reality. Abstract art, for instance, was a poor vehicle for revolutionary ideas. For her, this type of art is hopelessly a-ideological and unlikely to foster understanding. Its only revolutionary usefulness can be its use in industrial design and for educating the masses about form. Regardless, Aguirre insisted that no art or aesthetic principle should be censored. Even aesthetic idealism, though not particularly apt to carry on revolutionary goals, is Cuba's aesthetic legacy and is always, of necessity, the frame within which ideological debate about art happens (1987, 117). Echoing Castro in "Palabras," Aguirre insists that as long as socialism is not harmed by an aesthetic practice, and abstract art has this characteristic, these practices should not be censored or coerced.

Contributions to the issue of revolutionary art from filmmakers Espinosa (1993) and Alea (1997) echoed the ideas of Brecht, Sánchez Vázquez, and Aguirre. Espinosa's essay, "For an Imperfect Cinema," printed originally in 1969 and a key text for New Latin American Cinema (NLAC), argued for a new poetics for film. Much in line with Brecht's dissatisfaction with classical theater, Espinosa reacted against the illusionism of Hollywood cinema; he proposed an imperfect cinema that would rely on a dialogic relationship with the viewer. Hollywood cinema, he contended, hides the means of its production and positions the viewer as a consumer who passively reconstitutes its alienation. Imperfect cinema attempts to break with this modality of reception by showing film as labor. The dialogue between text and viewer makes the viewer a participant in the production of meaning and uses the viewer's artistic labor to concretize, echoing Sánchez Vázquez, the viewer's essential force (García Espinosa 1993, 81). Imperfect cinema activates reception and has the potential to transform viewers because this activity is shaping reality, and is thus labor; imperfect cinema humanizes filmic language and the objects represented in the narrative, but it also objectifies the viewer's self. As in Sánchez Vázquez's work, the link between film and viewer becomes social and productive, mutually generative.

In "The Viewer's Dialectic," Alea (Gutiérrez Alea 1997) proposed an aesthetics able, simultaneously, to prepare the individual ideologically and entertain him/her. This dual task can be performed by the use of "show" and "spectacle" and by assuming a real "popular cinema." His definition of realism is close to Aguirre's. Like Aguirre, Alea argues that film must be able to communicate with the people and thus it has to use existing tropes. Though the goal of film can only be reached by a new understanding of reality, this goal cannot be attained without recourse to the senses. Thus, entertainment and emotions (what Aguirre calls beauty) can be used as the vehicle of intellect and reason (120). Given these requirements, the realism of popular cinema cannot be the consequence of a straightforward reflection of reality; instead, popular cinema's realism must be able to produce a *new reality* resulting from the bridging of "genuine reality" and fiction (122–23).

Brecht, Sánchez Vázquez, Aguirre, Espinosa, and Alea were trying, in different ways, to answer the same question: how to use art, film, and/or literature to change the audience. Their proposals have in common the idea that the best art, revolutionary art, should be able to perform the following functions: first, it should transform the viewer/audience. But true transformation cannot result from coercive means or ideological manipulation; it should result from the viewer's actions. Therefore, revolutionary art must engage the viewer's self-knowledge. To do so, it had to communicate with the viewer by using languages and representational styles familiar to the viewer (competence). However, these familiar languages and representational styles have to be used in such a way that they could move the viewer, take the viewer out of his/her ideological inertia. These two functions could be achieved either by denaturalizing tropes, denaturalizing reality, or denaturalizing the self. Denaturalizing tropes involved showing the social and normative nature of languages and representational styles. Brecht, Espinosa, and to a lesser extent Alea, believed in this tactic. Denaturalizing reality implied representing a piece of reality in a different way, a tactic also espoused by Aguirre and Alea. Denaturalizing the self required the participation of the viewer in order to make the object of art a product of the viewer's self. This is more clearly seen in Sánchez Vázquez, though present in all. The three denaturalizing tactics are deeply interrelated because the three are intrinsic elements of experience, and a change of one will bring a change to all. However, the distinction is useful because it replicates the way cultural workers often divided their objects of reflection, discussed in the next section.

Proper Objects of Aesthetic Reflection

To produce art with transformative potential, art and culture had to be political, intentionally transformative, be the proper articulation between vanguard and society, embody a proper aesthetics, and reflect on objects (issues) that had the potential to form proper citizenship. Of all the objects for reflection, Guillén (1987 [1961]) believed that "national culture" and "the Revolution" had the most transformative potential. His views on the topic proved to be quite close to what was going to happen in the future, particularly in the literary, theatrical, and filmic worlds. Cuban cultural workers, for the most part, became concerned with a revision of Cuba's past (for example, use of historical themes) and tried to produce a new political world by questioning the workings of the revolution. In literature, most novels had either a prerevolutionary setting that included an existentialist hero or an existentialist critique of prerevolutionary life, were an actual reflection of the revolution, or were works concerned with *Cubanidad* (Menton 1975). In theater, the new cultural climate fueled the organization of theater groups concerned with examining the revolution and its advances, as well as the challenge of generating revolutionary values in a population still displaying prerevolutionary attitudes (Boudet 1975, 78; Muguercia 1975, 69–72). To do so, they employed vernacular ways of communicating (*decimas*), oral traditions, and peasant folklore.

In theater and literature, proper objects of reflection became common objects of reflection and constituted a finite set of themes and representational styles. Objects of reflection, insofar as they become a "thematics," are evidence of normative ways of representing reality and of hegemonic cultural-production values. In addition, thematics help constitute the viewer's horizon of expectation that triggers specific modes of reception and hermeneutic techniques. As in literature and theater, Cuban films can be organized in terms of themes. Two were often present and require closer examination: historical themes, often centered on revolutionary struggles, and examination of the workings of the revolution, often dealing with contemporary social challenges and/or individual responses to revolutionary needs.

For the Cuban leadership and the cultural vanguard, one of the key areas colonized by Spanish and, later, American rule was the representation of history

(García Mesa 1983, 35). Through academic, political, and artistic arguments, Cubans contended that Cuban history was, up to 1959, a distorted narrative that supported, legitimized, or naturalized Cuba's oppression. Revising this history was therefore a fundamental goal of the revolutionary academy and the field of cultural production (Pérez Jr. 1985, 1–13). The reasons were not purely historiographic, but also political. The leadership commonly argued that historicizing Cuba's struggles, for instance, would inspire the citizenry into revolutionary action. Commander Rigoberto García commented in 1980 on the inspiration his soldiers drew from learning the history of the struggles of the Cuban people (Medin 1990). According to him, history fueled heroic deeds and insulated them from the imperialist propaganda: "Whoever studies the true history of Cuba in depth will never be able to cross the 'bridges' that imperialism builds" (151).

Most approaches to history benefited the new government by representing revolutionary struggles in a benign light and by validating the government's agenda (Pérez Jr. 1985, 2). History, for instance, explained the revolution as the natural result of Cuba's past. History also represented the past as a site of revolutionary struggle that the new Cuba would have to emulate. The first revolutionary generation learned the values of sacrifice, selflessness, reading, and observing history. The following generation learned these values by reference to historical accounts of the first generation, their sacrifices and struggles. The importance of history has been so great that its study has been carried out within and outside the academy. For instance, the Department of Historic Assessment of the Cuban Institute of Radio and Television (Departamento de Asesoramiento Histórico del Instituto Cubano de Radio y Televisión) assists writers and directors on the production of programming about history. Some of the large cane mills, the Revolutionary Armed Forces, the Cuban Communist Party, and most of the cities and municipalities maintain resident historians (1985, 3–7). It is amid this emphasis on history that cultural workers from the fields of literature, theater, and film (and also workers from radio, television, and periodicals) commonly produced narratives that explored historic events (Barnard 1993, 143, 154).

Films dealing with historical themes often represented historical events involving revolutionary or armed struggles. Examples of this include *Lucia. The First Machete Charge* (*La Primera Carga del Machete*, 1969, Manuel Octavio Gómez) dealt with the War of Liberation against Spain in 1868. *The Other Francisco* (*El Otro Francisco*, 1975, d. Sergio Giral) and *The Last Supper* (*La Última Cena*, 1976, d. Alea) explored life in sugar plantations and colonial slavery.

Innovative treatment of historical themes was common. In *A Cuban Struggle Against the Demons* (*Una Pelea Cubana Contra los Demonios,* 1971, d. Alea), the camera is in continuous circular motion. *Girón* (1972, d. Manuel Herrera) is a historical reconstruction through interviews of participants in the Bay of Pigs invasion. The film uses an impressive array of representational techniques: direct narration, interviews, re-creation, voice-over, and archival footage. *The Days of Water* (*Los Dias del Agua,* 1971, d. Manuel Octavio Gómez), which explores religious hysteria in the 1930s, uses a highly expressionistic palette and dreamlike narrative often photographed with a hand-held camera.

If the past was a topic of historic and creative exploration, the present was examined against the backdrop of the revolution. As in the novel, feature films that centered on postrevolutionary themes took years to appear.[3] When they did, they showed a tendency to explore the ways social changes affected individuals and the way individuals responded, or failed to respond, to revolutionary ideals. Addressing the former are films dealing with the difficulties of housing (*House for Swap—Se Permuta,* 1984, d. Juan Carlos Tabío), bureaucracy (*Death of a Bureaucrat—Muerte de un Burócrata,* 1966, d. Alea), governmental administration (*Now It's Up to You—Ustedes Tienen la Palabra,* 1974, d. Manuel Octavio Gómez), and urban renewal (*A Man, A Woman, A City—Una Mujer, Un Hombre, Una Ciudad,* 1977, d. Manuel Octavio Gómez) (*Aufderheide,* March 1984, 28–34). The latter category includes all the films that will be discussed in the next chapter. As a group, these films reflect on the way revolutionary values (such as gender equality and socialized property) challenged individuals whose sense of self depended on non- or prerevolutionary ideologies (like sexism and private property).

Analyzing the most relevant objects of aesthetic reflection shows the ongoing importance of using culture to further the goals of government. The otherwise vague comments made by Castro in "Palabras" regarding the issues that should concern cultural workers (that is, "serving the people" and producing culture that is one with the revolution) were often articulated through an array of representational tactics (Brechtian tactics, expressionism, neorealism, and other types of realisms) and thematics. The latter included depictions of history, the revolution, and the challenges to revolutionary life. Though it would be untrue to state that all Cuban culture used these themes, their commonality suggests a field of cultural production where material and ideological rewards were given to workers willing to put these important political issues at the center of their aesthetic explorations. The resulting cultural works provided the populace with an agenda of public discussion and set ways for interpreting the past (history) and the present (the revolution) and the best way to arrive to a socialist society and to become the New Man.

The (Ideal) Relationship of the People to Culture

Each of the previous discourses rests on assumptions about the Cuban people and the role of culture in shaping Cuban subjectivities. These assumptions reflect formal and informal theories about the subject, disseminated in discourses about politics and culture. Because political and cultural media became relatively centralized, the most popular theories about the subject, at least in the public sphere, were few but key for understanding notions of criticism, citizenship, and ideology. Among the thinkers that were more influential on this matter, three stand out: Gramsci, Louis Althusser, and Che Guevara. Although quite different from each other, the three understood the importance of culture in the formation of the new society.

Gramsci, who first came to Cuba through Argentinean publications, was published in Cuba from 1964 on, and throughout the decade became widely read in philosophy departments (Martínez Heredia 2001, 370). He was particularly helpful to Cubans during the 1960s, a decade when the political and cultural leadership were trying to find innovative ways of thinking about Marxism (Martínez Heredia 2001, 370, 376; Chanan 2001, 393; Berta Álvarez, quoted in Recio et al. 1998, 157). Partly because the Italy of the 1920s seemed more similar to the Cuba of the 1960s than, let us say, the USSR, Gramsci's heterodoxical views on social structures, hegemony, and civil society became attractive ways of thinking about Cuba's present and future. According to Martínez Heredia (2001), Gramsci allowed Cubans to theorize the transition to socialism in terms of cultural transformations, not economics, and to recognize that this transition required a type of hegemonic domination, though one that would weaken over time (380, 381). Culture, therefore, was key, and so was forming cultural institutions that would work as civil society.

Although in Western liberal political cultures the notion of civil society is typically understood as a mediating social structure (relatively) independent from government, Cubans read Gramsci differently. In explaining the role of Gramsci in Cuba, Chanan (2001) establishes that in Gramsci's work, civil society is a set of institutions and spheres that are formally independent from government, but informally related to it. Different configurations of relations between government and civil society would correspond to different historical moments (392–93). At times, government and civil society occupy opposite positions, as in Latin America, where neoliberal forces in government energized the emergence of counterhegemonic NGOs in the 1990s. At other times, government and civil society support each other, as in the case of syndicalism. This argument is important to Chanan, Martínez Heredia, Recio, and others, because it allows them to theorize Cuba's official cultural institutions *as* civil society. In this way of theorizing, cultural institutions mediate between formal political structures and the people, and these institutions become the key to establishing a state of healthy hegemony.

Like Gramsci, Althusser helped Cubans to think of Marxism as much more than economic theory. Both thinkers placed culture at the center of societal stasis and change. The similarities end there. Unlike Gramsci, who understood the process of hegemony as a fluid one, prone to discontinuities, Althusser's views on ideology presuppose a more rigid social structure. As Stuart Hall (1982) notes, in Althusser's ideas it is difficult "to discern how anything but the 'dominant ideology' could ever be reproduced in discourse" (78). Althusser, however, is also great for thinking about the formation of subjects by institutions and for calculating the possibility for real popular change.

According to Louis Althusser, "the category of the subject is constitutive of all ideology . . . *insofar as all ideology has the function (which defines it) of 'constituting' concrete individuals as subjects"* (italics in the original. Althusser 1971, 171). Cubans were concrete individuals formed as subjects not by the revolution, historical materialism, or guerrilla warfare, but by prerevolutionary ideologies. Cubans, by and large, were ready to respond to interpellations coming not from the government's ideology but from the ousted hegemony's ideologies. To constitute a revolutionary ideology that would form, over time, a revolutionary citizen, the Cuban leaders needed to undo a historical trajectory, a way of being a subject. Castro recognized this. He believed that the greatest obstacle facing the revolution was "the force of custom, of the way and habits of thinking and looking at things that prevailed in the vast section of the population." These prejudices and ideas, supported by the dominant classes before the revolution, "constituted one of the most powerful forces with which the revolution had to contend" (Fidel Castro in Medin 1990, 7). The prejudices included *amiguismo* (nepotism), gangsterism, *chapucería* (shoddiness), *el choteo* (a specific Cuban type of humor that trivializes serious subjects), and *blandenguería* (wimpiness) (Fernández 2000, 91). To create a bridge between the ideologies of the Cuban people, the leadership used, as mentioned before, already established discourses and *some* prerevolutionary cultural values such as virility, justice, and sacrifice. These were activated toward the goal of forming a revolutionary consciousness, an interiorized civics (Behar 2000, 137–40). If Gramsci helped Cubans understand the role of cultural institutions in the creation of a benign hegemony, Althusser shed light on the articulation between institutions and subjects.

Che Guevara's work at times resembles Gramsci's and at times Althusser's. His discussions about the New Man and the development of *conciencia,* which anticipated Foucault's later theories on technologies of self, left an important mark in the Cuban intellectual and political worlds. Like Foucault, Che Guevara discussed the process of transforming consciousness in a technological fashion (Guevara 1965[1978]). That is, the process of transformation required of a basic material that would be shaped with specific techniques to take the form of a final product (Foucault 1988, 18). By way of these technologies of personal transformation, individuals address issues of personal identity, community, personal freedom, and historicity. They do so by embracing culturally specific ways of ethically taking care of themselves.

Che Guevara theorized that the masses, because of their alienation, depended on the transformation of their material conditions of existence to become fully human: "I think that the simplest thing to do is recognize [the capitalist individual's] quality of not-done, of un-finished product" (Guevara 1965[1978], 9). To become complete, the individual must engage "in a conscious process of autoeducation." For Che Guevara, the transformation of the individual has to happen at the level of *conciencia* (consciousness or subjectivity). In his writings, *conciencia* is the raw material on which society, state, and self must work (Foucault 1985, 340–72). *Conciencia* must change at the moral level, and this is done with direct education, whereby the state inculcates new habits, and indirect education, whereby social experiences (such as film viewing) teach the individual the necessity to enter the new and just society (Guevara 1965[1978], 11–12). Che Guevara is aware that the ideological separation between vanguard and masses signals the underdevelopment of society's subjectivity. In his model, the vanguards embody the characteristics of the New Man and become the goal or telos of the masses' transformational trajectory (14).

According to Che Guevara, this work of producing *conciencia* is performed with techniques borrowed from Marxism that involve labor and culture. The use of labor as a technique of dealienation is a Marxist idea that works on the assumption that alienation is the product of the capitalist system as expressed by the relationship of worker, profit, and final product. Che Guevara, like other Marxists, believed that alienation could be overcome by breaking this system (Guevara 1960 [1987], 128). To do so, he proposed the institution of moral, instead of material, incentives, an economic strategy popular in Cuba during the 1960s. In this way, he reasoned, the worker would stop seeing her/his own work as a commodity and, in its stead, she/he would begin seeing it as an expression of social duties (131). A second technique involved the use of culture and art to shape the Cuban's subjectivity into the *conciencia* of the New Man (132). Echoing Sánchez Vázquez, Che Guevara saw art as a technique that individuals could use to appropriate the world in its particularity. Reacting against theory and theory's tendency of abstracting object and self, Che Guevara and Sánchez Vázquez proposed art practice as an epistemological tool that allowed the opportunity to acquire self-knowledge (132). Because the benefits of culture depended on individual praxis (art practice as self-expression), a different notion of viewership and audience was required. The viewer could not be thought of as passive observer of the world (film, theater, television). Instead, the viewer had to be thought of as actively engaging the world, actively producing meaning, actively crafting social criticisms, actively expressing herself/himself *through* the world and, thus, humanizing it. Moreover, this activity was a technique necessary for the individual transformation from a subject of capitalism toward the telos of the New Man.

Che Guevara's ideas about subjects shaped the way filmmakers and critics conceived of a film audience. An active film viewer was a necessity for the revolution because the viewer needed to take part in her/his own decolonization. Viewer activity was understood as a political action. Supporting this idea, Alfredo Guevara (ICAIC's director) had stated in 1959, regarding the popular response to the showing of *Esta Tierra Nuestra* (the film received standing ovations), that "each showing of the film had the same significance as a plebiscite" (Chanan 2005, 125). The axiomatic linking of active audience to politicalization went hand in hand with the discourse of politicized culture and Marxist aesthetics. In the emerging Cuban discourse of active viewership, viewers' reflection and critical assessment of film were not only political but expressly revolutionary gestures. Santiago Álvarez, Cuba's leading documentarian, argued this at the Havana Cultural Congress of 1968, where he stated that ICAIC's objectives were "The formation of a new film public — more critical, more complex, more informed, more demanding, more revolutionary" (Álvarez 1971, 48). To produce this type of critical, active viewer, cultural workers used different tactics including, as I mention above, aesthetic and also media literacy. ICAIC's efforts on media literacy included cine-mobiles (mobile screening units), which were organized in 1962 to take film to the provinces and rural Cuba (Vega no. 73-74-75, 85; "En Cuba el Cine Busca al Público" 3, 13-16). The goal was to use film as a modernizing force but also to educate the people on filmic language and set up the competence that Cuban film, Cuban documentary, and Cuban television required from their viewers. In this spirit, a Q&A session followed a typical screening, during which the personnel of the mobile unit would answer questions about the film. These questions included basic ones regarding the making of the film, editing, special effects—things that audiences elsewhere would take for granted. Film was so unfamiliar to some of these audiences that operators of the mobile units witnessed many people talking to the screens, engaging in conversation with the film's characters, and, in general, marveling at the fact that events depicted on the screen were make-believe. The screenings were successful to the point that sometimes audiences from one town would walk miles to the next town, chair in hand, to watch the film again. Another example of media literacy was the weekly television show *24 x seg*. The goal of the show was to teach viewers the mechanisms of filmic narration and their ideological underpinnings (Colina no. 73-74-75, 102). It included clips from films followed by expert commentaries. The titles to their themes are telling of the decolonizing impetus of the show: "Cinema in the Battle of Ideas," "Film and Colonialism," "Cinematographic Language and Ideology," and "Latin American Cinema, a Combat Weapon" (104).

Unlike in Europe and the United States, where active viewership has been discussed mostly in terms of counterhegemony, Cuban discussions on the topic elaborated on active viewership in terms of the Cuban cultural and political leadership's hegemonic goals. These different ways of theorizing active viewership support Gramsci's ideas on culture. Although in Europe and the United States, an active viewership may be a sign of resistance and political opposition, in Cuba, active viewership ideally resists American and European cultural imperialisms, but not the Cuban hegemony.

The Policing Culture

In 1959 the cultural leaders of Cuba, together with the political leadership, passed Law 169, only months into the revolutionary period. This was a strong signal that Cuban culture was going to be regulated by policy. Since then, the production and exercise of a national cultural policy has given shape to the field of culture. Policy has defined what is permitted and forbidden and how culture ought to be administrated, promoted, and controlled. This strong push toward normativity reduced the types of official culture that could exist in Cuba at any given time, but it also gave great vitality to a field that before 1959 was anemic, elitist, and, with some notable exceptions, marginal in the international cultural landscape.

Cultural policy was a type of formalized discourse that attempted to set guidelines regarding which types of culture could exist in revolutionary Cuba (that is, "within the Revolution anything . . ."). Law 169 expressed this need through the organization of the film institute to propagate the message of the revolution. In 1961, "Palabras" expressed the need to protect the revolution from internal attacks, something doubly important in light of the Bay of Pigs. And second, the government needed to further the reach and power of cultural institutions, and it thus organized the First Congress of Writers and Artists and UNEAC. In 1971, amid a wave of international protests regarding the treatment of Padilla, the First National Congress of Education and Culture was organized to draw new policies and defend existing cultural policies. In each instance, organization, congresses, and mobilization followed political, social, or cultural instability.

Cultural policy in Cuba has often been written in vague language. Complex terms like "negation," "decolonization," and "alienation" have been an integral part in official speeches, writings, and declarations about culture. That these concepts and others lent themselves to different interpretations depending on philosophical traditions and rhetorical styles made most of cultural policy subject to interpretation. This has been one of my arguments throughout. What this implies in terms of cultural policing is that given the possibility of different interpretations to the same general legislature or policy, the official interpretation would be the one uttered by the speaker with the highest status and not necessarily the one with the soundest argument. This feature of Cuban cultural policy gave way to institutional communities highly sensitive to the leadership's speech regarding the interpretation of policy. This feature also produced blatant contradictions in the way cultural policy was applied. One such example is when Alfredo Guevara first opposed the film *P.M.* and the newspaper *Lunes*. His reasons included a repudiation of formal experimentation. Yet, only weeks thereafter, Alfredo Guevara declared that ICAIC would espouse formal experimentation and use form to create an authentic Cuban film tradition.

While policing culture through legislation affected Cuban culture and its development, what perhaps had the farthest-reaching consequences regarding the policing of culture was the constitution of the myriad government-sponsored cultural organizations. From aficionado organizations, reading circles, and dance contests to art schools, revolutionary museums, and free education, the field of culture after the revolution multiplied in size, reach, and formal plurality but always under the auspices of revolutionary ideology, revolutionary citizens, and revolutionary resources. Because of the way these cultural institutions and organizations were organized, they attracted those who wanted to participate in their self-formation while artistically manipulating realities approved by revolutionary instructors. In formal education, most aspects of the curriculum were taught using examples that complimented the revolution. For instance, Gramsci may have been common in universities in the 1960s (when cultural workers and politicians were trying to figure out ways of thinking Marxism) but he was absent from curricula in the 1970s, when the Sovietization of institutions would have contradicted Gramsci's insights on civil society.

Conclusion

Investigating discourses about culture that official communities fostered shows a normative system of ideas invested in legitimizing a stylistics of being public, a way of being a citizen. All the discourses were centered on principles that linked culture to governance and that made culture a fundamental aspect of the social and political transformation that Cuba would have to undergo to fit the political ideas of the leadership. Among these leaders, which included the cultural vanguard, it was understood that culture was political. If culture was political, then it had to have a political role, and this was to make the Cuban people proper subjects of government, proper citizens, proper revolutionaries.

Though culture had a political goal promoted by the leadership, the means to achieve such a goal had been a matter of continuous debate since 1959.

Simply put, even if one wanted to use culture to transform people into revolutionary citizens, and if this was perceived as a clear goal (which is at least questionable), one must still find the right type of cultural work, cultural institutions, and cultural workers to achieve this goal. A field of cultural production had to be structured, and though some of the structuring happened because of struggles for hegemony, its development depended in part on the production of knowledge sets that could power the field's existence and performance.

No other knowledge sets are more important to a politicized cultural field than those associated with subject transformation, such as formal and informal education. For this reason, popular culture, the greatest force in informal education, is always under scrutiny and policing by official institutions. Yet, the power of popular culture to produce citizens can only be harnessed if the field of culture is organized coherently and if the cultural artifacts disseminated through media are built on the proper aesthetics. In the previous chapter I showed how the field of culture (film, television, journalism, literature, and theater) became increasingly dominated by official institutions and the vanguard. In this chapter I explored issues of aesthetics, which go a long way toward explaining the theoretical rationales used to support or criticize cultural work. After considering some ideas by Brecht, Sánchez Vázquez, Aguirre, Gramsci, Espinosa, and Alea, I suggest that the proper or revolutionary aesthetics would have to denaturalize tropes (as with imperfect cinema or epic theater), denaturalize reality (new content or new ways of presenting content), and/or denaturalize the self (making the viewer reflect on meaning production). These aesthetic characteristics were present in the ideas informing official cultural production and cultural texts. Imperfect cinema and actual films showed a tendency to question the stylistic nature of film language and to establish reflective conditions of reception. Similarly, the new socialist theater capitalized on Brecht's ideas of estrangement, and some troupes, like Escambray, relied on a dialectic reception style.

In addition to these modernist questionings of form and their critical potential, cultural workers tried to present reality in unusual ways or present unusual aspects of reality to fit revolutionary goals. For instance, some forms of folklore and historical topics, such as Abakua religion and Afro-Cuban culture, though intrinsic to the historic evolution of Cuban society, had been displaced from public culture by the Spanish and, later, U.S. cultural influences. A push to constitute a public culture that would speak to the common

Cuban fostered folkloric and historic nationalistic themes and reinscribed Abakua and Afro-Cuban culture within national culture. If these objects of reflection were seen as fundamental to constituting a new national identity, so were revolutionary themes. These themes multiplied from the sixties onward in film, literature, and theater. The exploration of revolutionary themes evidenced the goal of producing a new type of citizen that Cubans often called the New Man. Therefore, most of the revolutionary topics used narratives in which a revolutionary man or woman served as an exemplar and was pitted against other types of "imperfect" individuals (such as bourgeois, oppressive, or sexist characters).

These aesthetic approaches and elaborations are only useful to the field of power and culture if they can be put into practice; practice was understood as helping the transformation of subjects into proper citizens. These aesthetic approaches are to culture what pedagogic theory is to formal education. That is, they are fundamental, but only a part of the whole process of transformation. In Cuba, this whole process was the development of the New Man, which was a key cultural goal framed in terms of technologies of self. Although a theoretical creation that contradicted pragmatic Cuban attitudes, the New Man was the telos of the process of social transformation that Cubans were subjected to since the early 1960s. Championed by Che Guevara, this "individual" was an archetype of the communist citizen, a social and subjective goal that required the methodic self-work of, ideally, all Cubans. Like all work, this labor would try to transform an object into something else. The object of transformation was, according to Che Guevara, the ethical relationship of the individual to itself and to the world, what Cubans often named *conciencia*. The resulting subject/self would possess the leadership characteristics of the vanguard as well as the vanguard's drive toward self-sacrifice. Instead of being driven by profit and self-interest, this New Man would be led by moral incentives and social rewards. The techniques used to facilitate this process of self-transformation were self-education, reflection, and self-knowledge inspired by the new society and by a new relationship to cultural works and, thus, national history, national folklore, the revolution, and ideologies.

In all of this process, the critic played the role of vanguard; she/he was the only cultural worker whose sole duty was to monitor the way aesthetics were properly used in cultural work. The critic's labor was thus at the conjuncture of politics and culture, policing others' practices while publicly performing the role of citizen. The debates about *La Dolce Vita* were thus necessary and expected in a field of culture that required the ongoing monitoring of one's actions and the constant reflection on whether cultural works used the right aesthetics. The next chapter explores how the performance of citizenship shaped the critics' roles as film viewers and interpreters.

Chapter 3

The U.S. Field
of Culture

A huge historic fluke frames the reception of Cuban film in the United States, a fluke that gives significance to this chapter and this book. The Cuban Revolution coincided with the sixties in America, and just as the revolution shaped the culture of criticism in Cuba, the sixties deeply influenced the U.S. culture of criticism. Though in Cuba the 1960s was the decade in which the revolution showed its brightest promise, the sixties in the United States was an epoch of radical cultural changes that included changes to notions of citizenship and to ideas of freedom. I see these changes affecting cultural criticism in general because they helped redefine the role of politics in culture and the relationship of the cultural field to the field of politics.

The sixties, as a cultural and political continuation of previous radicalisms, is not the only meaningful background to American criticism of Cuban film. The globalization of culture is another one. By this I mean that the sixties were also a global phenomenon fueled by globalized cultural products and transnational cultural labor markets. Although traditionally the globalization of culture is understood as the Americanization of the world, cultural products and cultural workers circulated in all directions, and the American system of media was also shaped by foreign products and people. This book offers some such examples. Cuban film was distributed and exhibited in the United States partly because it spoke to Americans through the lens of the cold war and the fear of communism. But it also relied on the restructuring of American film exhibition during the 1950s and 1960s, which lent growing cultural relevance to foreign film. These sociohistorical spaces frame the culture of criticism and the critical interpretations of the Cuban films under investigation and correspond to a period expanding from the 1960s to the 1980s.

As in the Cuban case, the American culture of criticism is bound to the field of power, and this articulation makes the practice of criticism a way of performing citizenship. The similarities end there, because unlike in Cuba, the American field of culture relies for its definition on a stated independence from the field of power. The critic, much like the artist, performs his/her cultural role assuming independence, even in cases when their cultural products are clearly political (such as reviews of political films). The resulting performances of citizenship are eminently ambivalent (that is, they have contrasting values), unlike the more normative way in which Cuban critics performed their citizenship through official criticism. In my view, American cultural workers embraced an ambivalent hermeneutics that could help them negotiate the discursive contradictions resulting from the field of culture's pressure to define itself independently from political influence even while performing within established political frameworks. This ambivalent hermeneutics applied liberal aesthetic principles to cultural production and evaluation as ways of responding to the, at times, contradictory requirements of the American government and to already existing cultural traditions of dissention. A caveat is required. I am assuming some familiarity with 1960s to 1980s U.S. history. Hence, and in contrast to the Cuban chapters, I concentrate on those elements of history and culture that are less likely to be known by readers, and that are central to understanding the American cultures of criticism and citizenship.

The Sixties and Beyond: Politics as Context to Criticism

There is general agreement between historians and cultural commentators on the political nature of the sixties. Although clearly "the sixties" does not refer only to the decade that begins in 1960, the sixties have served as a historiographical shorthand referring to the epoch that began roughly in the mid-1950s and ended at the beginning of the 1970s. Below, I use "1960s" when I am referring to the actual years composing the decade and "sixties" when I am referring to the historiographical category. What makes this epoch distinctive, what links the sixties to almost twenty years of U.S. history, is the sense that the American field of politics was radically transformed from without (Polletta 1997, 436).[1] Not surprisingly, many place the beginning of the sixties in 1954, the year that the U.S. Supreme Court decided in favor of Oliver Brown et al. and against the Board of Education of Topeka (Kansas), a decision marking the symbolic dismantling of Jim Crow law in America. In these views, the sixties began with the legal system recognizing a basic social right of citizenship for African Americans, a recognition that came about partly because of the legal and activist work of the NAACP, an organization commonly at odds with the field of power and politics. Using 1954 as the beginning of the sixties (the same can be said of those who date the beginning of the sixties to December 1, 1955, and Rosa Parks's arrest in Montgomery, Alabama) means arguing that what binds these decades was citizen activism and the concomitant expansion (or hope of expansion) of the political field. During the sixties more Americans believed that they had the right (and civic duty) to demand the field of power to incorporate new definitions of law and politics and to give citizenship rights to a more diverse set of Americans, from African Americans to homosexuals. More important, many hoped their activities would produce actual social change. Although citizen activism is a constant of American history, the sixties as a historiographical category had as much to do with citizen activism as with the hope that activism would work. This is why the sixties is typically remembered nostalgically. Its end does not mean the end of activism, which continues today, but the end of a particular definition of hope.

Although catchy, the standard of hope is an extremely subjective way of marking history and making it understandable. That is why I side with social historian Peter Clecak (1983), who finds too many continuities in the decade following the 1960s to warrant the standard periodization. Clecak links the sixties to a political culture where dissent became one of the chief ways in which to express politicization and seek self-fulfillment. The same, he argues, can be found in the seventies. "Dissent not only affected people in every part of the spectrum of the American political ideology. It penetrated the regions of culture and personality—of individual consciousness—to such an extent that large numbers of citizens acquired the habit of dissent or at least exercised it with increasing frequency" (21). Clecak is trying to explain deep changes in the way politics was understood and exercised during these decades, but he is also exploring a deeper shift in the way American subjectivities were constituted. With others (Damovsky, Epstein, and Flacks 1995, xiv; Hunter 1995, 332; Klatch 1995, 83; Marcuse, 1964; Klatch 2004, 497), Clecak attempted to give a theoretical form to changes in the way personhood (the self) and self-fulfillment had become a political goal of an increasing (and diverse) number of Americans.

The way politics of dissent were carried on at the beginning of the sixties had changed by its end (Gittlin 1987, 420; Klatch 2004, 499–504). *Brown v. Board of Education* symbolized the broad social goal of ending Jim Crow law, the voting drives of the early 1960s attempted to extend basic political rights to millions of African Americans, and the antiwar movement catalyzed millions of people in America, but by the sixties' end, the movement became a set of fragmentary mini or micro movements. Terry Anderson (1994), in an optimistic note, describes this as follows: "The movement fractured, making social activism more difficult to describe, but it also spread as participants turned to other concerns and confronted the establishment in almost every level and at almost every institution: the university and even high schools, the church, business, military, and all forms of government, from city hall to the White House" (356).

Toward the end of the sixties, and during the seventies, the justice claims and forms of dissention by hippies, the Youth International Party (the yippies), the Black Panthers, the Black Nationalist movement, the Chicano movement, the Symbionese Liberation Army, the Weathermen, the gay rights movement, liberal feminists, radical feminists, and the fragmented Republican and Democratic Parties, were based on different and even contradictory ways of imagining equality (for example, Fox-Genovese 1979–80, 94–97; Martin-Lipset 1978, 445–46). They had to be. By the 1970s, enacting politics through highly specific ways of dissention had given way to a richly textured, fragmentary, and contradictory ideological field of counterpolitics that included claims from the right (owing in part to a religious revival), the left, and everything in between. Dissent multiplied to incorporate a huge variety of perceived or presumed oppressions. From oppressions linked to the body (for example, race, sexuality, gender, ableness, age) to those of culture (for example, cultural citizenship and representation), dissenting practices were found under structures of traditional politics, but often, increasingly, under more small-goal, single-issue, politics of dissention (Clecak 1983, 186; Pescosolido 2000, 63; Wuthnow 1998, 30). If citizenship is understood as the aspect of identity that articulates the individual's relationship to the field of politics, then, dissention became central to the experience of American citizenship.

Insofar as citizenship allows individuals to inhabit, or at least relate, to the field of politics, the popularization and privatization of dissent is a significant historical development in American politics and culture. I am careful here to remind the reader that dissent has always been part of American citizenship and of all citizenship traditions belonging to nations that began under the aegis of revolution. Several decades in U.S. history had been marked by strong popular dissent including, in the twentieth century, the 1910s and 1930s when socialist, feminist, and labor organizations and political activity galvanized large sectors of American society (Denning 1997, viii–xx; Ross 1989, 21). What is different in, and after, the sixties is the effect dissent had on political participation, its popularization, and the way dissent became privatized.

Dissent's popularization was not easy to detect if you were only paying attention to traditional civic and political communities. Not surprisingly, Robert Putnam's (1995) "Bowling Alone," on the decline of civic associations, became extremely popular and was commonly used as evidence of America's decline in political involvement. However, when researchers began to investigate new, nontraditional ways of enacting civics and politics, they came to opposite conclusions. For instance, Everett Ladd (1999) observes that the proportion of Americans that voted in 1992 was actually larger than in 1948. He also argues that overall civic engagement has grown, although often in new organizations (bowling league membership may indeed have decreased, but youth soccer organizations have grown enormously). While there has been a growth in civic engagement, there has also been a growth in more privatized politics. Civic engagements are likely to be related to single-issue politics (for example, antiabortion or anti-WTO) or temporary, individual-centered politics (for example, opposing Wal-Mart in specific neighborhoods, banning *Harry Potter* from the school library) (Frank and Meyer 2002, 90; Thomson 2005, 438). Although I do not assume that this historical turn is negative, and find value in many of these types of political engagements, particularly when they become bridges to larger issues and broader politics (for example, Muncy 2004, 287), the privatization of dissent has changed the culture of citizenship and is now a central part of the public behaviors that are interpreted as civic and political.

Traditionally, liberalism has been understood as based on the citizen's free and consensual association with the state (Schuck 1998, 20; Tienda 2002, 587). Yet, based on the changes discussed, consent is a much more complex process that needs to be renegotiated and is in need of ongoing maintenance. I am not suggesting that the notion of consent is unproblematic. At the very least, consent is an awkward term that wrongly suggests that individuals regularly engage in a calculation regarding whether they ought to be subjected to the government. Consent, which relies on notions of free will and rational choice theories of politics, is a weak concept that leaves out complex psychological and social elements of action and choice and that fails to explain the role of culture in shaping subjectivities. However, in America, the notion of consent has been part of the field of politics and is commonly used to give government legitimacy. This is achieved by discursively constructing some political actions as evidence of consent, including voting and law abidance.

Dissent is the antonym of consent, but their opposition does not mean incompatibility. Just as democracy and liberalism are based (at least discursively or theoretically) on consent, they rely on the possibility of political rebellion, revolution, or, at least, political change. Discursively, consent becomes meaningful because it can be weighed against the specter of dissent. The field of politics relies for its long-term stability on the management, control, and suppression of dissent, but it cannot exist without it. Dissent is, like consent, constitutive of the discourse of American politics. Thus, the popularization and privatization of dissent signals an important change in the way the field of politics secured stability and affected the way the field constructed itself discursively. For it is clear that the popularization of dissent can be managed if dissent is fragmentary and not based on a unitary definition of oppression and justice. Dissent's plurality, multidirectionality (for example, right, left, libertarian, anarchist, local, global, sexual, racial, class-based initiatives), and privatization secure the relative stability of the field of politics while allowing for a rich and textured political culture and civil society.

Cultures of Dissent and Difference

Just like the 1930s, among the things that mark the sixties as an epoch are precisely the types and popularity of cultural expressions that used politics of dissent as their referent. In *The Cultural Front*, Michael Denning (1997) narrates the relationship of 1930s politics of radicalism (the "Popular Front") to cultural production and cultural workers. In this compelling cultural history, which begins with the formation of the Popular Front in 1934, Denning shows how the complex mixture of labor, feminist, and socialist political concerns were energized and given shape by cultural productions such as Paul Robeson's "Ballad for Americans," John Steinbeck's *The Grapes of Wrath*, and Billie Holiday's "Strange Fruit," all from 1939. Although the Popular Front (and its companion cultural front) lost force after World War II, the symbiosis of culture and politics did not. As Denning and others have shown (Helen Langa in *Radical Art: Printmaking and the Left in 1930s New York* and Robert Shulman in *The Power of Political Art: The 1930s Left Reconsidered*), and as I argue about Cuban cultural workers, artists and cultural workers are not ancillary to political quests, but central. Similarly, Arthur Marwick (1998) argues that the sixties can better be understood as a cultural revolution, and one of global magnitude. The sixties happened across the globe and took the center of the political stage in places as dissimilar as France, Mexico, Cameroon, England, Nigeria, Cuba, Chile, and Brazil. It is precisely in the global politicization of dissent in cultural texts, cultural production, and cultural consumption where one may find one of the most lasting legacies of this historical period, and a direct historical context to Cuban film in the United States (Denning 2005, 17–34). A second, more troubling legacy is the way dissent in American culture became commodified and subject to hegemonic appropriation. From *The Wild One* (1953, directed by Hungarian László Benedek) to Jimi Hendrix (whose power of dissention also resulted from globalized economic arrangements and colonialisms), dissent became big business, often global, and its commodification relied on, at best, mildly progressive industrial arrangements (for example, black labels discussed below) and, at worst, on traditional ones. Perhaps because of this, mediated cultures of dissention often manifested a difficult ambivalence toward the field of power (which includes the corporate field) and even the field of politics.

Although the counterculture meant the formation of new political and life-style arrangements, it depended, particularly in a nation as large as the United States, on mediated cultural forms that could give expression to the immensely affective aspects of the social revolution. When mass mediated, these cultural forms played a fundamental role in constituting an imaginary community of people across geographies and social strata, and, as importantly, a veritable new market (Moore 2005, 231). Music of the sixties, for instance, was often inscribed within discourses of dissent that targeted the youth market. As Andrew Ross (1989) observes: "The new ideology of 'people's culture' was most visible in the realm of folk music, which had replaced the proletariat novel as the cultural form most privileged at social gatherings, while it shared honors in the pages of the *Daily Worker* and *New Masses* with 'progressive' literature, theatre, and even Hollywood films like *The Grapes of Wrath* (1940)" (23).

This is not to say that the 1960s music was always political or that the youth market was, in the United States, the same as the political culture market.

For many Americans, the 1960s were a continuation of the (relatively) apolitical 1950s, and this was reflected in much of the music, youth culture, and movies of the time. Beach culture, surfers, twisters, and party animals of the 1950s continued existing during the 1960s, and their explorations of sexual mores, hedonism, and drugs continued until the second half of the 1960s. But aside from the important, relatively apolitical cultural traditions of the time (which were also associated with other variations of the youth market), the sixties gave way to important countercultural music forms that were used as political expression and by individuals interested in constructing political identities. Two examples: The folkniks, a group of mostly white, middle-class urban youth, embraced old-time ballads and new ways of singing folk music and blues. This group of musicians and singers, including Joan Baez, Bob Dylan, and even older artists like Pete Seeger and the Weavers, catered to the intellectual, university-centered youth and constructed imaginary links between Madison and Berkeley, Austin and Chicago, and hippies and leftists (Rodnitsky 1999, 109). Their music and lyrics ranged from traditional forms such as old work songs and blues to contemporary ballads that protested the social conditions of the time (Stern and Stern 1990, 103–23). Certain types of rock 'n' roll and certain musicians were considered political and therefore good cultural material with which to build a political identity.

In sixties folk and rock music, dissent was commodified and packaged in a way amenable to youth consumption. The popularity of youth culture was evidence of youth's economic viability as cultural consumers and, by the end of the 1960s, of the importance of political signifiers to the success of certain youth-marketed cultural products, which were often filtered through discourses of dissent. Volkswagen made a point of linking their products to the peace and the hippie movement, and record labels were created to cater to specialized youth audiences not interested in consuming run-of-the-mill music. This new market meant new business opportunities. Countering hegemonic industrial music arrangements, black labels and recording companies specializing in R&B music and political songs joined the group of existing corporations profiting from rock 'n' roll and other youth music. For instance, Ace Records, specializing in rhythm 'n' blues and rock 'n' roll, was founded in 1955. Challenge Records, which also recorded jazz and country, started in 1957. Del-Fi Records, initiated in the same year, specialized in recording "pachuco" artists from Los Angeles. Etiquette Records released its first single in 1961 and specialized in garage rock 'n' roll. Goldwax Records, also a 1957 enterprise, recorded gospel and soul music. Jerden Records, now associated with "grunge" music from Seattle, released its first single in 1963. Stax Records, a celebrated soul label, began in 1959. The Acta label, with their brand of psychedelic rock, was established in 1967.

On a different cultural front, but obeying similar patterns of commodification, publishing houses in San Francisco, New York, and Chicago served the highly specialized tastes of a growing politically savvy readership. Magazines like *Village Voice, The New Republic, The New York Book Review, Ms., Mother Jones, Socialist Review, In These Times,* and *The Nation* gave a distinctive and politicized view of the world to a largely leftist, liberal, and feminist national readership (Clecak 1983, 49). Local magazines and underground presses did the same for local readers. The sixties, and its complex intermixing of hegemonic culture and discourses of youthful dissention, was published, recorded, reviewed, and exhibited in a growing field of cultural production where politics and dissent had become an everyday conversation topic and great business.

Music and magazines were not the only cultural industries invested in helping (re)constitute communities of dissent and politics for a profit. The sixties also shaped film distribution, exhibition, and reception, and some of these changes directly impacted foreign film and criticism. Under the aegis of global culture and transnationalism, the 1950s and 1960s witnessed the multiplication of foreign film distribution, which brought to American audiences art and revolutionary national cinema previously unavailable. A pause is needed here. Foreign film has been distributed in America from the beginning of U.S. film history. Before the 1950s, the great majority of these films were distributed in foreign-language neighborhood theaters serving ethnic communities (Towmey 1956, 240). The shift we see in the late 1940s, 1950s, and 1960s is the distribution of foreign film in art house theaters and the increasing tendency to equate foreign film to art film and to fit it within a cultural politics of dissention. This tendency did not immediately materialize, but the way it happened brings to relevance political economic factors that since have structured cultures of criticism and have shaped the field of culture's popularization of dissent as identity.

Foreign Film and Cultures of Dissent

How foreign film exhibition came to signify a certain type of politics is a great example of a mode of film reception intimately bound to industrial and political structures. Because the way foreign film distribution came to be since the 1950s and through the 1980s, the actual activity of attending a foreign film screening (and participating in its popularization) became a cultural activity with political undertones because it signaled to self and others a distinct taste structure that separated the viewer from the masses. I am using here the term "masses" in the nastiest possible way, as a way of understanding and qualifying consumers of mainstream culture in America. These were the masses that Adorno and Horkheimer warned us about (*Dialectic of Enlightenment,* 1944); the ones that David Reisman argued lacked leadership abilities (*The Lonely Crowd,* 1950); the masses that Erich Fromm believed were afraid of freedom (*Escape from Freedom,* 1941); the ones that Sloan Wilson feared were lost in the world of management and business (*The Man in the Gray Flannel Suit,* 1955). Massification, and the fear of massification, were common in the 1950s, prompting social strategies of difference. To some, the structure of film exhibition helped them construct identities different from the masses by bringing cosmopolitanism into their lives through the cultural consumption of art and foreign films.

As Barbara Wilinsky (2001) argues, several factors came together to open the American art house market to foreign films. The 1948 Paramount decision and other litigations in the 1950s separated the business of exhibition from production and distribution and forbade block-booking (66–67). No longer able to guarantee the distribution of B-movies, and, as Janet Staiger (1992) notices, no longer able to see profit on cheap films, movie production decreased. After World War II, Hollywood majors reduced the number of films, leaving second-run theaters without (from 263 features produced in 1950, the number of releases went down to only 140 in 1963) (183). Changes in the film industry's structures in the United States because of production shortages benefited the recuperating film industries of France, Italy, and Germany that had been devastated by World War II by opening exhibition opportunities (Mayer 1985, 2–3). In addition to these shortages that threatened exhibitors, television had begun to compete with movie theaters, and studios had begun unloading many of their older B-releases through television. Foreign films, however, were not desirable television products. Second-run exhibitors thus showed outstanding foreign films from Italy (Federico Fellini, Michelangelo Antonioni), Sweden (Ingmar Bergman), Argentina (Torre Nillson), India (Satyajit Ray), and England's Angry Young Men (3). In addition to these second-run exhibitors, the end of the 1950s and beginning of the 1960s saw a huge increase in the number of first-run theaters dedicated to showing art films, the majority of which were foreign. In 1950 there were eighty such theaters; by 1963 the number had jumped to 450 (*Film Daily Year Book* 1950, 1036; *Film Daily Year Book* 1964, 1033). Magnifying the importance of art film and foreign film in America is the fact that during the same time, from 1950 to 1963, the total number of theaters in America went down from 17,000 to 12,500 (drives-ins excluded) (*Film Daily Year Book* 1964, 117). These changes in the structure of exhibition brought competing national industries and film traditions to American audiences, transforming in the process audiences' and critics' aesthetic and narrative expectations. From Italian neorealism to French New Wave to Third Cinema, audiences and critics praised the aesthetic and political quality of these films, often noting the serious and intellectually responsible qualities of art and foreign cinema (Staiger 1992, 182–95; Wilinsky 2001, 18–25).

The popularity of foreign films in the United States was never total nor their acceptance widespread. According to Christine Ogan (1990), the potential audience for these films was never more than 10 percent of the total (58–77). This 10 percent, she continues, tended to exhibit specific demographic characteristics that included a university education and living close to a university campus or in large urban settings (Adler 1959, 7–15; O'Guinn and Hardy 1988, 53). However, the proliferation of foreign films in these types of locations and among specific audiences helped established specific audience expectations regarding the films. These include overall filmic quality (so many of these films received critical acclaim), sexuality (more frank depictions of sexuality were typically found in films from Europe) (Mayer 1985, 63; Wilinsky 2001, 24), "sophistication" (these films were shown among the educated in places like New York and San Francisco), and politics. As Staiger (1992) notes regarding art cinema and its audiences, common expectations included finding a "message" presented in a frank and serious way about a social problem (185–86). This message was often politicized, even when dealing with issues like sexuality, which from the sixties onward became a key way of understanding politics (and an example of the privatization of politics). Though never producing a huge audience, these films and their audiences influenced the definition of what it meant to be a university student, an educated person, and a discerning moviegoer.

The ability of foreign and art film to mark audiences with distinction was particularly important at a time when class distinctions were losing ground as eminent markers of difference, especially among white, middle-class, populations. Partly because of the economic boom of post–World War II America (articulated through the G.I. Bill), and partly because of changing racial understandings, the middle class grew in its traditional urban locations and in new cultural spaces, such as suburbia (Brodkin 1998, 101–6; Kenyon 2004, 2–5). This growth accelerated, or was aided by, the incorporation of populations previously understood as nonwhite, ethnic European, such as Jewish and eastern European immigrant groups, into the general category of white (for example, Brodkin 1998, 107–10). Alongside these economic shifts was the growing importance of mass media as a homogenizing force and as a cultural articulation of desires to belong to the middle class. Amy Kenyon (2004) examines the latter when exploring the role of film and popular literature in creating images of ideal suburbia during the 1950s (40). The former relates to, for instance, the rise of television during the same time, which brought these same ideas about suburbia, middle class, and whiteness to most American middle-class households, constituting a cultural homogenizing force that many felt ambivalent about. Jackson Lears (1989) investigates the latter when examining the growing importance of taste as distinction, amid the massification of culture of the 1950s (38–57). Bourdieu's work shows that taste is not simply a psychological response to cultural products, but it is also a wider process of consumption of spaces and technologies that facilitates specific social relations and discourses. For instance, distinction through film consumption, John Belton (1992) argues, was also at play in the popularization of widescreen theaters among middle-class audiences of the 1950s and 1960s. The same can be said of viewing foreign film in art houses, a cultural practice that created hierarchies and fragmentation between knowledgeable and ignorant, cosmopolitan and provincial, sophisticated and brutish, and urban and rural (Wilinsky 2001, 82–86). As importantly, viewing foreign film also engendered new cultural communities based on taste and on the art house as meeting place and cultural hub. For these communities, viewing foreign film gave them distinction from the masses, who were watching Hollywood films and television and siding with Archie Bunker. Viewing foreign film was (and continues to be) a dissenting practice constructed through the discourses of intellectualism, cosmopolitanism, and taste.

In addition to the increasing number of exhibitors willing to show foreign films, film festivals, which, beginning in the late 1950s, were increasingly popular and also served as venues for foreign and political film. Following the success of the Academy Awards, which began in 1927, international film festivals multiplied around the world during the 1940s and 1950s. In the United States, the San Francisco Film Festival began in 1957 and the New York International Film Festival began in 1963 (Meyer 1967, 74–79). More important, film festivals catering to specific political identities, including leftist and feminist identities, began to be organized around this time. Let me comment on two examples.

Even though the 1960s marked one of the high points of the cold war, some movies from behind the iron curtain had made it to American screens. From Poland, Roman Polanski's *Knife in the Water* was shown at the first New York Film Festival at Lincoln Center in 1963. Other films from the USSR, such as *Ballad of a Soldier* (1959), *My Name is Ivan* (1962), and *Dimka* (1962), were also exhibited at other festivals (Meyer 1967, 60). However, because of the special place that Cuba occupied in the American imagination, no film from Cuba was shown to general audiences during the 1960s. In 1971, American Documentary Films (ADF) joined efforts with the Instituto Cubano de Artes e Industria Cinematográficos (ICAIC) to organize a festival of Cuban films in several U.S. cities, with an opening festival in New York City. The festival was held in 1972 to a highly politicized audience and was opposed by a politicized citizenry. ADF, a leftist, pro-Cuban, grass-roots organization that had distributed and exhibited leftist films throughout the 1960s, trusted that a politicized audience, accustomed to watching international film, would support the festival. They were correct. The films that were exhibited played to big audiences.

Also in 1972, feminist filmmakers from New York hosted the First International Festival of Women's Films, which attempted to continue radical feminist consciousness-raising efforts. Kristina Nordstrom (quoted in Gregg 1995), the film programmer, commented: "We had been in a consciousness-raising group and I was tired of just talking. I wanted to do some kind of action. . . . I had worked for the New York Film Festival . . . and I knew the steps of organizing a film festival. . . . I knew there had been some films made by women but I didn't know how many. And I thought a festival of women's films would really spotlight that for women and be something positive that they could identify with and encourage more women to do it and convince the world at large that women have those kinds of capacities so that they could get more work" (55). In the two instances commented, film festival organizers understood their goals to be political and trusted that a politicized audience would be responsive to their efforts. As importantly, film organizing was considered a political "action," challenging the notion that politics was only traditional activism. Much like Castro understood, immediately after the triumph of the revolution, that he needed to garner the power of media to make the revolution viable, Americans understood that media (music, film, and, increasingly, television) were fundamental at constituting and expanding the field of power. Not surprisingly, culture became essential to the definition and maintenance of political identities and to the creation of difference among all people, and in particular middle-class white populations (although this pattern is evident across races and ethnicities). The magazines and books read, the music heard, the movies seen, and the marches and concerts attended identified the individual and spoke of her/his political convictions. This was particularly true of leftists and feminists because their identities were partly built on a critique of mainstream culture and the way such culture represented the ideology of the powerful and/or patriarchy.

Conclusion

The American sixties normalized political dissent and, over time, allowed for the expression of dissent in increasingly more private ways, through narrower and more personal issues. This effervescent political culture has allowed for the constitution of dynamic (and multiple) political identities, which have relied on cultural consumption to identify themselves and craft discrete identities. Cultural industries happily accommodated, producing the structural and cultural conditions for culture centered on dissent and politics. Music and publishing were key industries, but I also show that film exhibition and consumption played an important role, particularly with the art house exhibition structure and with the screening of foreign films.

The mode of reception that we now associate with foreign film distributed in art houses from the 1950s onward, and film festivals, includes the notions that these are serious, intellectual, and, often, political films. Whether they were, indeed, serious and intellectual becomes irrelevant, because among Americans, watching these films (and their supposed sophistication) was a social action that gave distinction to the viewer, a discursive outcome quite desirable during the 1950s (and the growth of the middle class, mass media, and homogenization) and the politicized sixties. I am not suggesting that watching foreign film was a badge of honor for radical leftists in the sixties, who more often than not relied on underground presses, popular art, and radical film; rather, I propose, with other researchers, that foreign film gave distinction to a large number of educated, left-leaning liberals and feminists. But it would be naïve to think that the films, in and of themselves, achieved this outcome. Distinction was possible because the films were given meaning through their association with specific leftist-liberal institutions (for example, university campuses), cultural geographies (for example, New York, Madison, Berkeley), and media institutions and their critics (for example, the *New York Times, The Nation, Ms., The New Yorker*).

The discursive labor of critics and cultural commentators of the time authorized specific meanings and interpretations of films and viewing practices. In the following chapter I discuss the function of the critic in film interpretation and the types of knowledge sets mobilized to make sense of political and foreign film in general and Cuban film in particular. These knowledge sets, which constituted a specific hermeneutics, came from 1950s and 1960s auteur theory, new cultural knowledge sets from academia, and the broad cultural knowledge sets of communism and cold war ideology. Instead of using history's broad strokes to paint a context, in the next chapter I use history to explore politicized criticism in America and the discursive and epistemic traditions informing film interpretation in general and Cuban film in particular.

Chapter 4

U.S. Criticism, Dissent, and Hermeneutics

The rise of foreign film distribution and art house exhibition during the 1950s onward helped constitute the field of professional film criticism in America. By the 1970s and 1980s, the decades in which the Cuban films were reviewed, criticism had a defined place in the field of culture and in the film world, and so did critics. In 1973, the year that the first postrevolutionary Cuban films were distributed and exhibited in the United States, *Newsweek* magazine published a small piece in which Arthur Cooper commented on the film critic as superstar (Cooper 1973, 96). Cooper was not referring to Jean-Luc Godard or François Truffaut, who had been film critics and were, no doubt, superstars. Instead, Cooper was referring to a group of critics that in the United States were establishing the influential practice of popular film criticism in newspapers and magazines. Critics like Vincent Canby (the *New York Times*), Pauline Kael (*The New Yorker*), Judith Crist (*TV Guide, New York*), Stanley Kauffmann (*The New Republic*), Andrew Sarris (*Village Voice*), and John Simon (*Esquire*) had given the practice an aura of respectability that before 1960 was less impressive (Blades Jr. 1976, 205). To Cooper, these critics were superstars because, at that time, their opinions were respected, influential, and, as importantly, their opinions reflected a great deal of knowledge about cinema. As practitioners of popular film criticism, these critics professionalized the field, making it a field of specialists (Cooper 1973, 218).

Critics, superstars or not, depend on a public willing to believe that the qualities they possess are proper to their social/economic/cultural role. In this, the critic resembles an author and, as such, "functions" within a system of practices and expectations that constitute her/his uniqueness and distinction. The function of the critic as such is complex because it is overdetermined. It is inscribed within a field of cultural production and, simultaneously, it serves as mediator between this field and society, this field and power, this field and similar fields from other nations. Different elements go into constructing the critic's function: economic, cultural, social, artistic, class, and, of course, political. Critics may be guardians of the elite's taste; critics may try to reposition cultural works within the field; critics may inform a community of the works and proper interpretations that the community should "consume." Finally, some critics use the place they occupy in society to highlight their own politics and to bring, through culture, political texts to specific communities.

During the 1970s, superstar critics were not the sole commentators on culture, nor their publications the only sources of film criticism. Specialized magazines like *Variety* and journals like *Film Quarterly* existed to provide different types of reviews and interpretations, and other political journals like *Jump Cut* and *Cineaste* and magazines like *Ms.* were catering to an increasingly politically varied, ideologically fragmented, and knowledgeable readership. Critics, like media and readers, varied in their political and ideological stances and existed in a diverse American field of cultural production. However, variations among critics were not only a matter of individual taste or expression of a distinctive genius, like *Newsweek* seemed to suggest.

Critics performed their jobs in ways that gave expression to social and historical dispositions to view film in specific ways, with specific interpretive and meaning-making frameworks. For instance, Kauffmann, one of the superstars to whom *Newsweek* referred in 1973, participated, as a critic, in the public protest against the American government for stopping the First Cuban Film Festival in New York in 1972. With other notables, including Kael and Sarris, the other superstars, he sent a harsh protest letter to the *New York Times* in 1972. To these critics, this letter was a way of enacting dissention. In 1973, when *Memories of Underdevelopment* (*Memories* from here on) was finally distributed, he reviewed it for *The New Republic*. Placed right after a review, also written by him, of a book that criticized the House Un-American Activities Committee (HUAC) and the cases of censorship and repression sponsored by that organization, *Memories'* review begins with a paragraph in which Kauffmann mentions the censoring and repression of the Cuban Film Festival in New York by the State Department (Kauffmann 1973, 22, 32). In these writings, this professional critic takes direct action to participate in a cultural struggle with clear political meanings.

Kauffmann's review of *Memories* is interested in the film not only for its textual characteristics but also for the place it occupied within the U.S. field of cultural production and the field of power. *Memories* had spilled over whatever boundaries had existed to separate politics from culture and had confirmed, yet again, the way the U.S. government exercised governance through the control and the shaping of the cultural world. That Kauffmann recognized this style of governance as similar to the one used during the McCarthy years is hardly surprising and, simultaneously, deeply significant. Like other intellectuals of the time, Kauffmann understood that the fear of communism underscored the reaction against Cuban film by the U.S. government during the 1970s, and this fear brought with it a threat to the civil liberties of Americans, including political freedom and freedom of expression. Relying on this fear, the State Department impeded ADF's legal rights and censored the first Cuban film festival. Other branches of government acted similarly. Notably, the Federal Bureau of Investigation (FBI) was involved in activities that threatened Americans' civil liberties. COINTELPRO, which spied on communist U.S. citizens, was a program originally organized by J. Edgar Hoover to the end of discrediting and disrupting specific groups and individuals. COINTELPRO was finally exposed in 1971 and the FBI was forced to reform intelligence practices (Gelbspan 1991).

If Kauffman's review is significant because it is inscribed within a political struggle against the U.S. government cold war apparatus, it becomes doubly important to American film reception when such a political act is carried on through the interpretation of, and commentary on, a Cuban film. His actions were hermeneutic and entangled in a web of issues that included professional and political expectations about Cuban films in particular and foreign film in general. Andrew Kopkind, writing for *The Nation* in 1985, corroborates this point with the following commentary:

> There were six showings of *Memories of Underdevelopment,* the classic chronicle of bourgeois alienation in revolutionary Cuba. . . . This was not a rare event, and yet the theatre was packed for all performances. Since it was made . . . Tomas Gutierrez Alea's [sic] film has been staple fare for radical repertory and revolutionary retrospectives from Cambridge to Santa Cruz, and it is hard to imagine that anyone old enough to recognize the face of Che on a poster and honest enough to admit a romantic loyalty to Cuba does not have a functional acquaintance with it. . . . The persistence of *Memories* in the consciousness of a political generation is like the permanence of a sacred text in the cul-

ture of a sect. . . . The crowds that saw the movie that weekend at the Film Forum went to take part in a ritual that told them who they were or what they had been, which is not only a wonderful way to spend an hour in the dark but almost redeems the whole painful, extravagant and self-indulgent process of movie making.

In this brief piece of writing, Kopkind manages to convey many of the reasons for the importance of researching the reception of Cuban film in the United States. Because of their origin (a revolutionary third world nation) and their aesthetics, films like *Memories* became part of the experience of being a radical, a leftist, and a socially conscious American citizen. Their dialogue and scenes became part of the lore of political communities, and attending their screenings became rituals that celebrated the potential meaningfulness of cultural consumption.

As Kopkind implies, *Memories* and other foreign political films occupy unusual positions within the field of cultural production in general and within the film industry in particular. Typically offered in special screenings, festivals, universities, and art houses, the exhibition life of a political foreign film in America usually has been one of relative isolation. But several factors aid their exhibition: given the minuscule budgets for advertising that these movies have (often none), word of mouth becomes essential to their success. For this same reason, critics like Kopkind or Kauffmann can be key to attracting a sizable audience. Kopkind, who published in *The Nation,* a reputable liberal-leftist magazine of some prominence in the field of cultural production, for this very fact, had access to a segment of the public that was likely interested in a film from Cuba. A positive, or at least an intriguing, review from the likes of Kopkind had the potential to generate enough buzz to propel otherwise obscure films like *Memories* and *Up to a Certain Point* (another film reviewed by Kopkind) into relative commercial winners.[1]

The critic's importance to the field of culture, and his/her power within the field, lies in her/his ability to influence the commercial survival of a cultural product. This happens because the critic mediates between the field and the larger habitus where a community, bound by lifestyles, traditions, systems of taste, and political beliefs, awaits to participate in activities of the field. Other cultural workers perform similar mediating roles, and their importance to the field is related to their economic roles. Film magazines and journals, because they reach festival organizers and art house exhibitors, are also important to these films. In the following chapters, I comment on writings published in newspapers, mainstream magazines, cultural magazines, film magazines, nonacademic film journals, and assorted academic journals. Each mediates between the field of cultural production and different audiences and each is partly constituted by the critic as a key mediator between cultural knowledge sets and texts.

This is not to say that these cultural workers are always capable of addressing film and other cultural expressions as ideology (cultural workers are "inside" ideology), as politics, and, in the case of foreign film, as international texts that require specific command of foreign histories and aesthetic traditions. Cultural workers occupy specific subject positions that, though politicized and at times counterhegemonic, are constituted in ideology and thus likely to rely on seemingly natural hermeneutic frameworks at the textual, contextual, and extratextual levels. Some of the cultural repertoire from which cultural workers may draw were sketched in the previous chapter, including romanticized notions, dissent, and the expectation that foreign film would grant distinction to viewers. Below, I add to this repertoire the ideological construction of Cuba's rebellion and the formal cultural knowledge sets that were also available to leftist and feminist cultural workers, with a particular emphasis on feminist criticism and epistemology.

Cuba in the Leftist Imagination

Although Michael Denning (1997) is correct at drawing attention to the 1930s as a decade that prepared America for the sixties, the cold war and revolutionary movements across the world also influenced America's political culture and were instrumental in the popularization of dissent during the sixties. Of all these revolutionary movements (which included struggles in Nicaragua, Vietnam, and Indonesia), Cuba's was arguably the most popular and most positively depicted by U.S. media. During the 1950s, these depictions were not based on cold war ideology; Castro's agenda was strictly nationalist, and only when the United States denied its support did Cuba turn to the Soviets. Instead, aided by new media technologies and under the auspices of transnationalism, U.S. media represented the 1950s Cuban revolt in narratives of rebellion and romanticized violence.

Because of Cuba, revolution was in the minds of many in America. On May 17, 1957, CBS aired a special report by Robert Taber called "Rebels of the Sierra Maestra: The Story of Cuba's Jungle Fighters." In an old journalistic tradition (the journalist-as-explorer), Taber had gone to Cuba to search and find a mysterious rebel fighter, and he had succeeded. Taber told his viewers that he was in the Sierra "not to explore the maze of Cuban politics, but to find a man the government says isn't there, the Rebel Leader Fidel Castro" (Taber quoted in Gosse 1993, 83). The footage of the rebels reveals a group of young men and women, including three young Americans, sharing cigars, food, and otherwise acting as if they were in a scout camp in the middle of the jungle. The documentary follows Taber's crew through the Sierra to finally find the rebel group described as "clerks, technicians, students, townspeople, and simple campesinos." They are led by "Doctor Fidel Castro, thirty-one, holder of four university degrees." The three American boys, who had left Guantanamo Bay to join the rebels, are particularly interesting to Taber, and he asks all of them the reason for their dangerous odyssey. Chuck Ryan, who at twenty-one is the oldest of the three, answers: "Well, we came to do our part for the freedom of the world. We just heard so much about how, uh, about how Batista was so cruel. . . ." Then Taber pleads to the parents of the other two (one of whom is only fifteen): "They should be proud of their sons. . . . I only hope that they can try to realize what their boys are doing. Their boys are fighting for an ideal . . . for their country and the world. This is for world peace" (84). From the jungles of the Sierra Maestra, CBS viewers were witnessing something unusual: the power of a mysterious and charismatic young man, Castro, to capture the imagination of young Americans to the point of securing their greatest support and solidarity.

Though CBS's special report was the first television piece dedicated to the 26th of July Movement in Cuba, the rebel movement had been of interest to media during the previous couple of years and, increasingly, during the previous months (Schwartz 2000, 315). The *New York Times* had published extensive pieces written by Herbert Matthews in February 1957, and the *Chicago Tribune, Time,* and *Life* magazine had followed with written and photo essays in the months that followed (Gosse 1993, 67–69). The appeal of Castro and the way these reports framed the movement created an aura of idealism, manliness, and courage that surrounded the Cuban revolutionaries until the end of the decade. Among the youth, Castro's persona strengthened this aura, an image that was easy to incorporate into personal fantasies of courage, individuality, and sacrifice that were central to much of youth popular culture (53). The rise of rock 'n' roll, the 1955–56 films *Rebel Without a Cause, The Wild One,* and *Blackboard Jungle,* and books like Allen Ginsberg's *Howl* and

Jack Kerouac's *On the Road* provided young men with a catalog of attractive options regarding masculinity that could set them apart from previous generations and that could bring meaning to what some feared was an overly stifling epoch. That Castro was routinely described as a mixture of Robin Hood, George Washington, and Gregory Peck and that Carleton Beals, writing for *The Nation,* tried to discredit Castro by writing a piece titled "Rebels Without a Cause" helped consolidate the link between some American youth and the revolutionaries (55).

Not surprisingly, much in the same way that idealist young Americans had joined the Spanish Revolution two decades before, restless members of a new generation of Americans tried to join the Cuban revolution, and some succeeded. Of those who did not, many joined the effort symbolically by organizing prorevolutionary activities meant to support the revolution financially and politically. Some accounts of the sixties place its beginning in these organizations. One of these, the Fair Play for Cuba Committee (FPCC), gave an opportunity to create alliances across races, across campuses like Berkeley, California, and Madison, Wisconsin, and gave the opportunity to a new group of student and political leaders from different ideological credos to taste political battle against the establishment (147–54, 162).

The sex appeal of the Cuban Revolution dwindled after 1960, and what was left of its popular force was lost during the Missile Crisis, at least for a few years. Although most of the New Left ceased publicly supporting the revolution, radical groups, including the Weathermen, at the end of the 1960s retook Cuban imagery in the forging of their own mythologies. In culture, several plays dealing with Cuba appeared at the end of the 1960s. *Cuba, Sí* (1968), written by Terence McNally, was about a New York woman named Cuba who supported the revolution and gave pro-Castro speeches in Central Park (Schwartz 2000, 330). That same year, Jack Gelber (who does a cameo in *Memories of Underdevelopment*) staged *The Cuban Thing,* which presented the gains that the Cuban revolution had brought to a middle-class family. The Cuban American press and the Cuban American community opposed the play so fiercely that the theater was bombed the day of the preview. The play closed after one day (330).

Because of the strong presence of the Cuban exile community in American culture and politics, the fact that Cuba is communist (rather than a government of any other politics), and that the United States had always desired to influence Cuban affairs, the island has been a catalyst for political emotion. On the one hand, for good or for bad, Castro and Ernesto "Che" Guevara became symbols of third world revolutionary struggles. On the other hand, the nation of Cuba, the whole ten million of its people, its culture, and its history has been presented to Americans since 1960 through the eyes of the cold war. Cuba's "imagined" politics have eclipsed almost any other reality that may have been used to understand the island. Because of this politics, Cuba has been a heroic nation to many on the Left, or a rogue state to most Americans. As such, Cuba was systematically lumped with the Soviet nations and defined as a military communist dictatorship.

By the beginning of the 1970s, the animosity between the two nations had become a strange tradition, particularly in light of what the U.S. government was doing regarding other socialist and communist nations. For instance, in 1971, Richard Nixon ended the twenty-one-year trade embargo with China. This was part of Nixon's and his advisor Henry Kissinger's strategy of pressuring the Soviets to forget about Hanoi. The following year, 1972, Nixon made the historic trip to visit Mao Tse-tung at Peking to tighten a relationship that could make the world a better place. The same day of the momentous gala evening presided over by Chairman Mao acting as host to the U.S. president and his wife, the U.S. State Department denied visas to the, by then internationally acclaimed, Cuban directors who were to participate in the First Cuban Film Festival in New York. Senate Foreign Relations Committee Chairman J. William Fulbright questioned why the "U.S. government should consider four filmmakers a security threat and not Mao Tse-tung and the People's Republic of China" (Myerson 1973, 30). Other senators also protested, including Edward Kennedy and George McGovern. The *New York Post* and the *Los Angeles Times* also questioned this act.

The festival's organizer, Michael Myerson, was a leader of the New Left since its inception. A Berkeley student, Myerson organized SLATE, a radical leftist political party within the university, and went on to construct an ongoing link with the Cuban revolution. He argued that the U.S. government's treatment of the Cuban directors was unlawful, and that the eventual halt of the film festival was linked to a group of Cuban exiles, all of whom had participated in the CIA-organized Bay of Pigs invasion and were "serving" the Nixon administration (1–3). Myerson's strong evidence was the presence of other anti-Castro associations in the Nixon administration: four of the five men arrested on June 17, 1972, at the Watergate Hotel were Cuban Americans who had been linked to the CIA and to the Bay of Pigs affair.

Besides their potential relation to Nixon's government, conservative Cuban Americans played another important role in making the First Cuban Film Festival a politically laden event. Similar to the violence directed toward Gelber's play in 1968, radical Cuban Americans organized protests in front of the Olympia theater (which was to host the event), stoned the theater, and threatened to bomb it (32). Though the festival opened March 24, 1972, the pressures to impede its continuation were too great, and the U.S. State and Treasury Departments stopped the festival March 25, seized the prize-winning film *Days of Water* (1971), and committed an old-fashioned act of cultural repression.

The critics protested. Vincent Canby of the *New York Times* and Jay Cocks of *Time* wrote to complain about the government's halting of the festival, and, as I mentioned, a group of film critics published a letter "To the Editors" in *The New York Review of Books,* also protesting. This letter poignantly stated: "We think it either sinister or absurd when access to foreign art can be turned off and on like a tap to suit the government's current policy, when Americans are not allowed to see Cuban films only weeks after the President has been televised worldwide cheerfully applauding the Peking Ballet. . . . The blockade of Cuba by the United States has been a foolish and destructive mistake" (Vogel et al. 1972). The signers were Amos Vogel, Sarris, Annette Michelson, Dwight MacDonald, Gelber, Cocks, Jonas Mekas, Nat Hentoff, Richard Gilman, Ricki Franklin, Kauffmann, Stephen Koch, and William Wolf. Several of the signers would be reviewers of Cuban films.

Racialization

Politics regarding Cuba and Cuba's media construction have also been determined by the way Cuba has been constructed in the minds of Americans as a third world nation, a Latin American nation, and a nonwhite nation not only by news but also by mass culture, chiefly film. If Castro could so readily occupy a place in the pantheon of rebels without a cause, be the youth hero of the 1950s, and later become a "classical" dictator, it was partly because of a tradition of seeing Latin Americans since Pancho Villa—and, closer in time to Castro, Augusto César Sandino in Nicaragua—as violent leaders. The myth-making machine of Hollywood absorbed these historical figures and created a set of expectations and prejudices based on race, country of origin, and class.

Racial preconceptions about Latin Americans had been common in American popular culture since the nineteenth century's expansion of Anglo culture into Texas. The expansionist drive had needed an ideological system to legitimize violence, injustice, and land theft (Montejano 1987, 311–12). Racism against Mexicans played this role. By the twentieth century, this racism had translated into popular stereotypes such as El Bandido and attempted to convey a sense of racial, moral, and intellectual superiority to naturalize the acute social, political, and economic disparities between Anglos and Latinos and between the United States and Latin America (Noriega 2000, 3–6). Throughout the first half of the century, American popular culture provided a consistent flurry of representations of Latin Americans as violent and macho and their societies as chaotic, dirty, corrupt, and often in revolution.

That American popular culture has continued serving as a propaganda machine for the U.S. government's economic, military, and cultural expansionism into Latin America is, perhaps, obvious. The only glimmers of fairness regarding representation of Latin Americans came about when the United States needed a stronger alliance with the region because of World War II. Two films shaped by diplomacy were produced during this epoch: one, *Juarez* (1939), starring Paul Muni, depicted the war of Mexico against France. The second, *Viva Zapata!* (1952), starring Marlon Brando, narrated the revolutionary war of the 1910s. As is clear from the selection of themes that these Good Neighbor films dealt with, even with diplomacy as a factor, Latin America was considered a vehicle for narratives of war, revolution, violence, and civic chaos. In the same tradition, John Huston directed *We Were Strangers* in 1949. In this film, John Garfield plays Tonny Fenner, a professional soldier who goes to Cuba to help fight the repressive regime of Machado. With other Cubans, Fenner organizes an assassination attempt that is discovered, and he dies, machine gun in hand, just as the people of Havana go to the streets to overthrow Machado.

The news treatment of the Cuban revolutionaries and the popular images of Latin Americans produced the disposition to see Castro, at least momentarily, as a hero, though clearly one that commanded violence. He was the embodiment of dissent and could be romanticized as such. Racialized assumptions about the nature of Latin American people and their societies served to reconfigure Castro's image during the 1960s and to make him, and the revolution, one of violence (the Missile Crisis) and repression, and Cuba as the perfect land for "communism" or at least the perfect site for the transfer of American preconceptions about communism. The enduring link between the Cuban Revolution and cultures of dissent in America is manifested in the ongoing and growing commodification of Che Guevara, whose image as a radical revolutionary is emblematic of dissent and revolution around the world.

Formalized Culture:
The Academy and "Subjugated Knowledges"

Popular representations of Cuba, cold war ideologies, and racialized ideas about Latin Americans were discursive contexts generally available to most Americans. Typically, anyone wishing to write or speak about Cuba had to engage these discursive contexts and used them or opposed them. In addition to these contexts, liberal-leftist and feminist cultural workers and critics had access to more specialized knowledge sets about culture and politics that they would typically activate to interpret Cuban political film. Most of these knowledge sets were circulated through the expanding post–World War II university system and progressive social movements, and existed in close proximity to the sixties' way of understanding politics.

One of the most significant changes in the epistemology of justice in the last fifty years is the centrality of culture to understanding issues of politics and economics. If at one point it was possible to lay down a theory of social justice based on relations of production (for example, Karl Marx and Booker T. Washington), this became increasingly difficult after the Frankfurt School, the Birmingham School of Cultural Studies, and French structuralism. What began with Ferdinand de Saussure and Roman Jakobson as the linguistic turn in academia became, by the end of World War II, the cultural turn, an epistemological shift of huge magnitude that placed culture and cultural problems at the center of the issue of distributive justice (Denning 2005, 80). During the century prior, the term "culture" itself had transformed from one denoting either the beaux arts, morals, customs, or "folk" culture to a term encompassing the economic and political realms. In a classic example, Theodor Adorno and Max Horkheimer's arguments about the culture industries figure culture (mass communication and philosophical idealism) at the center of (in)justice. In a world of signs, they presciently state, where equivalencies of incommensurable quality constitute all the possibilities, language and discourse become the vehicle of totalitarian identity (1944 [1979], 16). In attempting to theorize Germany's fascism and America's turn to advanced capitalism, Adorno and Horkheimer made it impossible to separate material reality (for example, relations of production) from the world of discourse, language, and entertainment (see also Ross 1989, 50). Although prior to the 1940s writers like György Lukács (1920 [1979]) and W. E. B. Du Bois (1903) recognized that (in)justice could not be theorized without reference to culture, the cultural shift marks the beginning of the transformation of the social sciences and humanities canon to incorporate cultural concerns in the exploration of justice.

The cultural turn coincided with the biggest-ever expansion of the American university system. In 1945, universities hosted 1.5 million students. By the year 1970, the number of students had multiplied to 8 million (Marchese 1997). Partly because of U.S. economic expansion post–World War II, and partly owing to the G.I Bill, which financed the education of millions who otherwise would not have attended college, the university system expanded, with the biggest growth during the 1960s, allowing the rank and file to accommodate lower-class students, a growing number of women, and, slowly, racial minorities. As Linda Eisenmann (2006) comments regarding the years 1945–65, the university system's transformation provided "a generational bridge from the energetic women of World War II to the activists of the late 1960s" (233). The expansion of the university system, the cultural turn, and the incorporation of new types of students to the academic field were transformational forces that changed university institutions since the 1960s and that revolutionized the social sciences and the humanities (Gitlin 1987, 420–38; Duberman 1999, 197, 216; Clecak 1983, 232). In this veritable educational and academic revolution, racial minorities, women, and leftist students pushed for a radical revision of canonic disciplines and for the formation of other disciplines that could account for the experiences of counterhegemonic and marginalized groups. African American Studies, Women and Gender, Latino Studies, Queer Studies, and Cultural Studies, as well as recently developed disciplines like communications and film studies, became proof of a shift of expectations regarding postsecondary education (Aranowitz 1990, 214). Although there has been a backlash against leftist college faculty that began in the 1980s (and evidence that the biggest political change among faculty is toward the right), the social sciences and the humanities continue being dominated by left- and liberal-leaning faculty (Hamilton and Hargens 1993, 608).

Climbing the ivory tower, and occupying a traditional position in hegemony, was no longer the only reason for acquiring a university education: since the politico-cultural prominence of Berkeley in 1960, being at university meant also the possibility of constructing a social location from where to be counterhegemonic. To many, the university became a location of and for dissent. Within these new departments and old departments of literature, philosophy, history, and anthropology, these post-1960 scholars created new knowledge sets that attempted to explain the force, direction, and defeat of radicalism across the world and the upsurge of women, racial and ethnic minorities, and the colonized toward the center of the public sphere. Culture became a key way of discussing these areas of inquiry, for through the study of culture one could understand central issues of philosophy, politics, and historiography. For instance, what is the impact of the past on the present (inquiries into the way that ideologies, histories, social structures, and also the past, the general, and the universal constitute the present or presents)? How are social subjects constituted? What new ways of seeing reality must be considered, given marginal standpoints? How do we conceive of utopian ideas that could manufacture a more egalitarian future (for example, the revolutionary potential of counterhegemonic culture as manifested in, for instance, women's writing, racial and ethnic art, and disenfranchised cultural practices)?

The centrality of culture to these academic endeavors made hermeneutics central to the production of knowledge about society and the theorizing of liberating practices. Indeed, the ideological import of culture has never been more essential to the social sciences and humanities than within the last fifty years. With this, I am not trying to suggest that the importance of ideology and the social are recent theoretical insights, but rather that the interest in culture because of the huge influence of cultural studies, the Frankfurt School, the civil rights movement, the New Left, and feminism in the American academy brought to centrality issues typically explored only in regard to art, literature, politics, the nation, and civilization. The necessity to account for ideology's maddening subtleties and treacherous effects on the social drove academic discourse and produced a community of cultural workers, including myself, committed to finding better tools to interpret cultural works and practices and their relationships to the individual and to the social.

The quest for a theory that fits all realities and cultural practices is, however, no longer popular. Though I see my community invested in hermeneutic tasks, I do not see a drive to find *a* hermeneutics. That said, within the social sciences and humanities, Marxism, feminism, and critical race theories are common approaches, and there has been a tendency to use some of these theories' principles as general hermeneutic principles for the interpretation of culture. So, in presenting in this chapter and the previous one some of the ways in which the New Left and feminists saw the world, I have already introduced the principles of the hermeneutics that, I argue, are at play within the leftist, liberal, and feminist communities that reviewed the Cuban films that I am interested in investigating.

The "insurrection of subjugated knowledges," as Foucault calls them, were not simply the result of the 1960s social movements (Foucault 1980, 82). As Aranowitz has commented, these "knowledges" were a continuation of a critique of positivism that had taken root in American and European social sciences from the mid-nineteenth century (positivism continues today in disciplines such as economics and political science) (Aranowitz 1990, 212). Because of the mostly Marxist critiques of positivism in the last century, and more contemporary critiques of reason coming from feminist and critical race theory, the investigation of culture has been carried on for the last few decades through methodologies that share some of the positivist goals to scienticism and others that reject them. Though different professional fields have been influenced by their particular relation to the positivist battle, criticism, a professional branch of literary studies, film studies, media studies, and art history are typically undertaken with antipositivist methodologies and theories. Below, I briefly explore these.

The role subjugated knowledges have played in shaping academic standards of criticism is something that has been researched within the fields of film, literary, feminist, and critical race studies (Gunn 1987). Not much has been written on nonacademic criticism, such as criticism carried on in newspapers, magazines, and other nonacademic institutions; however, postsecondary educational and academic disciplines such as literature and film are common backgrounds among those writing film criticism in magazines, newspapers, and other media. Because of this, most critics have been exposed to similar theoretical and methodological considerations regarding film, aesthetics, and criticism, and they either embrace some of the ideas representative of subjugated knowledges or at least have to acknowledge their existence and importance to criticism and their readership.

But what is included in these hermeneutic frameworks that were in use during the 1970s and 1980s by academic and nonacademic critics? First, one must consider that heavily influencing these hermeneutic styles were Marxisms (particularly Marxist aesthetics as it is found in French poststructuralism and cultural studies), feminisms, and critical race theories that provided fundamental templates for cultural criticism. Because the majority of the films I analyze deal with gender, and because I am particularly interested in feminist and leftist critical reception, I concentrate on those factors that helped form a feminist and leftist hermeneutics and their theoretical outcomes.

Feminism as Preamble to Feminist Hermeneutics

Although, in a broad sense, feminist film hermeneutics and criticism are linked to other subjugated knowledges, feminist criticism's specificity can be explained better by reference to the epistemological challenges and social practices of feminist activisms of the 1960s (Thornham 1997, 5; Polletta 1997, 432). Given the richness of the subject matter and its philosophical and historiographical intricacies, this brief study cannot do justice to the topic. However, even this description is useful to contextualize the interpretive approaches of critics in the 1970s. Finally, given that the reviews and cultural commentaries by U.S. critics of Cuban films span from 1970 to 1985, in this section I am only concerned with the state of feminist film criticism until 1985.

Roughly speaking, feminist film criticism came from general feminisms of the era. Feminist activism since the 1960s can be divided into two key strands of social and political practices. The first, espoused by mostly white professional women and carried on in policy circles, was a quest for equal rights in the tradition of liberalism. Policy organizations like the National Organization for Women (NOW) formed this strand of feminism, often called liberal feminism, which reached national presence and influence in the 1970s. The second, espoused by white and black women and carried out at the grassroots level, was a quest for a revision of the systems of sex and gender in the tradition of Marxian and post-Freudian philosophies, in particular theoretical claims about the formation of gendered, sexual, and capitalist subjects. This strand is often referred to as radical feminism. Each version of feminism engendered a specific style of being political. A strong historiography of feminism gives me the luxury of not having to recount or retell the histories of these two strands. To learn on the topic, I recommend Winifred D. Wandersee's *On the Move: American Women in the 1970s* (1988, 239–48). There, she organizes the literature on feminist histories in relation to focus areas. A more specific historiography that centers on feminist film criticism is found in Maggie Humm's *Feminism and Film* (1997, 6).

NOW was formed in 1966 when the Equal Employment Opportunity Commission (EEOC) refused to enforce the provision for sexual equality in Title VII of the Civil Rights Act. Headed by Betty Friedan, Pauli Murray, Mary Eastwood, and Kathryn Clarenbach, NOW began as a lobbying organization working within the structure of government and attempting to effect change in the status of women in the public realm. Although proposals from NOW included issues regarding the private lives of women such as abortion and birth control, the bulk of the demands related to public policy such as alimony, divorce law, child custody, and job discrimination (Wandersee 1988, 18–19).

The women that participated in NOW at the beginning were white professionals interested in changing women's consciousness so that they could participate in mainstream society (Wandersee 1988, 39; Evans 1980, 17). NOW's commitment to speak their issues in terms of policy and liberal theories of rights made it easy to label NOW a conservative organization, particularly in the activist landscape of the 1960s. Though over the years NOW embraced progressive agendas like abortion, lesbian rights, and racial and gender equality, other leftist, lesbian, and radical feminist organizations considered NOW's identity as an organization interested in societal and political reform to be inadequately aggressive. That said, to the conservative mainstream, NOW seemed radical. Within the overall schema, then, NOW and similar groups advocating women's rights through equitable policies are liberal feminisms.

Other women were interested in transforming a wider gamut of gendered and sexed structures that included the private realm, a culture of sexism, and the way women (and men) were constituted as subjects to gender and sex. Though the development of radical feminism is too complex a phenomenon to be fully explored here, examining some of its connections to the 1960s civil rights movement illustrates how culture, hermeneutics, and self-construction became common concerns in this socioepistemological practice.

Radical feminisms (including "cultural feminisms") (Humm 1982 [1993]), 4), Sara Evans argues, "first developed from within the ranks, and revolt, of young southern blacks" (Evans 1980, 25). A core of women activists involved with the Student Nonviolent Coordinating Committee (SNCC) and who participated first in sit-ins and sit-in-related activities (such as boycotts of Woolworth's and other corporations) and later in the voter registration drives in southern states (in particular Mississippi) made important contributions to the development of early radical feminism (25–59). In general, women's participation in the struggles offered opportunities for self-assertion (through breaking with familiar constraints and conservatism that would typically forbid them from joining an activist organization working for and with blacks), self-discovery (through doing things they never thought they could do, and doing them well), self-construction (through experiencing fear and violence as old selves were shed like old skins), and self-recognition (through knowing and following other courageous black and white women) (65–75; Polletta 1997, 437).

Beside these benefits, women's participation in Students for a Democratic Society (SDS) was important in establishing useful principles for later radical feminist organizing. Beginning in 1963, but with more emphasis in 1965, SDS began organizing impoverished communities in urban settings. The Economic Research and Action Project (ERAP) applied grass-roots techniques to organize neighborhoods around social issues. These consciousness-raising efforts consisted of bringing together communities to talk about problems affecting their members that could be solved by collective action (134). These and other tactics of ERAP were later used in feminist organizing: "The anti-leadership bias and emphasis on internal process in ERAP found counterparts in the women's movement's experiments with rotating chairs, intensely personal meetings, and distrust of public spokeswomen; the theory of radicalization through discussions that revealed the social origins of personal problems took shape in the feminist practice of consciousness-raising" (137).

Radical feminism has relied on ideas and theories that understand gender and sexuality as constitutive of the modern capitalist subject. The implications of such ideas and theories are far reaching and have troubled activists and academics since. For instance, liberal feminists can apply theories of emancipation to women and thus hypothesize that granting and protecting the rights of women will result in their liberation. Not so for radical feminists who, in lieu of the constitutive role of sex and gender in our lives and subjectivities, cannot conceive of emancipation as the acquisition of equality with men because masculinity and men, as well as our ideas of equality and rights, have been formed by oppressive social and ideological structures. Unlike in liberal feminism, the categories of gender and sexuality for radical feminists occupy a paradoxical position because they are both oppressive and oppressed; that is, these categories constitute the platform on which a non-oppressive subjectivity can be built; and at the same time, these structures have been produced by oppression and thus are embedded and constitutive of patriarchy and capitalism.

At the center of radical feminism has been an impetus to learn to interpret the world in a new way. As a set of theories and activities, radical feminism was a call for a feminist hermeneutics that would see the world through the looking glass of women's experiences and their oppressions. This hermeneutics would make evident the connections between personal feelings and experiences, social events, and disparate lives, and would rekindle a passion for the community of women while unearthing the patriarchal foundations of nonfeminist perspectives and of commonsense, everyday life. Given this focus on a feminist hermeneutics, radical feminists gave a great deal of importance to women's cultural production and to feminist criticism, and in doing so, these people and organizations produced lasting contributions to academic discussions of culture, one of which is feminist film criticism. This is not to say that liberal feminism has not given importance to cultural production and criticism, but to emphasize that culture and criticism have played a different role in radical feminist circles. Although for liberal feminism women's culture is an expression of their equality, for radical feminism, women's culture is a way of exploring the categories of gender and sexuality and a way of reconstituting communities of women.

Feminist Film Criticism

From 1970 to the early 1980s, feminist film criticism analyzed the role film and other cultural forms play in the constitution, reproduction, and/or challenge of gender and sexual systems of oppression and, increasingly, incorporated racial and class concerns. As a critical tradition, feminist film criticism was quite varied in terms of methodologies, theories, and even political concerns. To organize this otherwise too complex subject, I center on four areas—similar to those I examined in relation to Cuba (chapter 2)—that correspond to challenges issued by feminist film criticism against traditional film cultural practices and texts. These areas are: the politicization of film and culture; hermeneutics and critical approaches; feminist aesthetics; and feminist epistemology. It is important to remark that this section is more succinct than my examination of similar issues regarding Cuba. The reason is that although all of the Cuban reviews and writings investigated in the following chapters had a very close relation to the hermeneutics explored in chapter 2, feminist film criticism informs only some of the reviews and writings to follow. Finally, paralleling the dates of the evidence found in the next chapter, in this section I review writings on feminist film criticism up to 1985.

The Politicization of Film and Culture in Feminist Film Criticism

As discussed above, feminist activisms of the 1960s, in particular radical feminism, understood the importance of culture for the constitution of systems of oppression. Because of this, feminist circles saw cultural criticism as a fundamental political activity (Thornham 1985, 4–5). But how exactly cultural systems oppressed was a matter that required the development of ways of seeing gender, sex, women, and men in terms of their cultural constitution. Feminist film criticism owes early insights into this matter to the work of Simone de Beauvoir, who had discussed the marginalization of women arising from the woman's cultural construction as "Other" (3). Influenced by Jean-Paul Sartre's existentialism, de Beauvoir argued that the woman was a "creature" necessary to man as an Other, for the notion of "woman as other" confirmed man as Self. As such, woman was a changing category filled with male fantasies and fears as well as ideas of eternal beauty and sacrifice (4).

A couple of decades later in 1969, Kate Millet (*Sexual Politics*) reapplies some of de Beauvoir's concerns when she explores how canonical literary works rely on misogynist representations of women and are thus invested in the reproduction of patriarchy. Millet investigated sexual images in the works of Norman Mailer, Henry Miller, and D. H. Lawrence (among others) and analyzed them in terms of the authors' and implied readers' expectations regarding female sexuality and power dynamics of gender. Her second chapter is an exploration of patriarchy where she uses anthropology, sociology, and psychology to construct a systemic theory of patriarchy-as-society. Millet observes how female characters in the classic works of Mailer, Miller, and Lawrence are cultural constructs where male fantasies of the woman as sexual object are repeatedly played. In 1972, only two years after Millet's book, the first feminist film criticism journal, *Women and Film,* appeared. Its critical agenda, Sue Thornham (1999) observes, was political and born out of an awareness of women's oppression at the "psychological, social and economic" levels (9). The woman as object and as Other were also central issues that this journal wanted to address. Sharon Smith, for instance, was concerned with the objectification of women in film (Smith 1972 [1999], 14–20). For her, film's distorted ideas reflect male fantasies. Thus, in film women are possessions (for example, *The Cheat*) and sexual objects (for example, Mae West). One of her main propositions was to have a more varied and realistic set of female characters in film (15–18). Other feminist film criticism echoed Millet's concerns and questioned the way women were represented in film and the way particular genres have been devalued because of their relationship to women (Haskell 1987, 153–88; Johnston 1973, 24–31).

Shortly after, in 1973, Marjorie Rosen and Molly Haskell (who also happens to be Andrew Sarris's spouse) published two key monographs where they explored how women were represented in mainstream film. Rosen and Haskell are also two of the critics commenting on the Cuban films upon their release in the United States. Their approaches, sometimes called "sociological," understand the politics of film in relation to film's distorted representations of women's reality (Thornham 1997, 16). The function of these representations is political because "the woman as myth" functions not only to mirror reality but also as an ideology that naturalizes gender and sexual discrimination (14). Smith, Rosen, and Haskell fall somewhere between a liberal and radical feminist position. They analyzed the constructed nature of sex and gender but often tended to assume that merely producing more realistic representations of women would solve problems of women's oppression.

Shortly later, Claire Johnston and Pam Cook explored a more precise way in which the ideological import of film texts and practices functions as a politics of oppression. Johnston, writing in 1973, associated film texts and practices with ideology, but her ideas of ideology went beyond deception (which was implied in previous feminist work). For her, ideology is more subtle in that it is embedded in all aspects of the filmic text (for example, codes of realism, the camera lens, and narrative techniques); therefore, the political goals of feminist film criticism could not be achieved simply by addressing the truth-value of filmic representations but required the examination of film's "depiction of reality; . . . the language of cinema/the depiction of reality must also be interrogated, so that a break between ideology and text is effected" (Johnston 1973 [2000], 30). With Cook, Johnston continued problematizing ideology in 1974 and foregrounding the subtle ways in which patriarchy functions in filmic texts (Cook and Johnston 1983, 379–87). Using psychoanalysis (see below), Cook and Johnston explored the textual depths at which the Law of the Father is at work in the films by Raoul Walsh, films some feminist scholars considered progressive. Pointing out how women are reduced to signs that male characters exchange, Cook's and Johnston's work further problematized the political task of feminist film criticism by rendering oppressive textual elements previously unseen as that by critical eyes (Thornham 1997, 27–32).

Given film's perceptual characteristics and its reliance on the visible, the political character of feminist film criticism continued emphasizing new "ways of seeing" film and other culture work as a prelude to political action. During the 1970s and 1980s, a continuous push to see deeper textual structures as factors involved in women's and men's gendered oppression gave way to more nuanced ideological and psychological analyses of film texts and practices, including Screen theory approaches that sometimes utilized Marxist/ideological methods such as semiotics. In summary, being a feminist film critic was simultaneously being political—intervening in gender politics.

Hermeneutics and Critical Approaches

Early feminist film criticism relied on sociological approaches to analyze film. Centered on female stereotypes and straightforward notions of representation (as true or false), researchers investigated the realm of the visible in relation to issues of referents. Film images and representations were thus criticized for indexing nonrepresentative elements of women's realities or for indexing cultural myths and male fantasies rather than women's everyday experiences. But as the 1970s progressed, the visible was going to become a more complex matter.

Christian Metz extends the hermeneutic impulse of film criticism with his investigations of psychoanalysis and cinema. He links the spectator's ocular structures to cinema's visible and perceptual apparatus. Furnishing this link is a primary system of desire ("the desire to see") whereby the film spectator experiences voyeuristic pleasures that reinforce the ego's sense of epistemological mastery. Laura Mulvey (1974 [1992]) further elaborates on Johnston's and Metz's ideas by theorizing the visual pleasures of male viewership (22–34). Like Johnston, Mulvey uses the insight of psychoanalysis that "Woman then stands in patriarchal culture as signifier for the male other." The woman is "bearer of meaning, not the maker of meaning" (23). For her, and echoing Metz's ideas, Hollywood narratives were constructed for a voyeuristic male viewer who can easily identify with the typically male central characters and who can fetishize or punish through visual investigation the female characters. Visual pleasure, then, was an expression of the desire to see the woman as a sign that stands for men's erotic fantasies and also as a sign of men's "more powerful ideal ego" (Thornham 1997, 41).

Mary Ann Doane (1982 [1992]) expands on Mulvey to argue that the male viewer relies on the distance existent between him and the screen to experience desire. This distance makes the film-viewing process one that locks the male viewer into a sexual identity of oppression but that leaves open female viewership to other possibilities (234). Female spectatorship is for Mulvey and Doane a problematic thing that Mulvey explains as passive and thus masochistic and Doane, given that the preferred viewer subject position is masculine, as an instance of masochism, cross-dressing (taking up the male's position), or masquerading (taking up the female's position but from a distance). For Doane, this psychic step that women have to take to see mainstream narrative cinema in any sort of positive way renders female spectatorship as potentially subversive, for it relies on the masquerade; in the end, this proposition denotes the social construction of gender and lays down the possibility of placing constraints on it (240). In an optimistic note, Doane reminds her reader that as Michel Foucault has observed (and as I have discussed earlier), repression (such as female repression) should not only be theorized as a lack of power but as a position from which potential power also exists (241).

Though psychoanalysis played an important role in setting up a theoretical agenda for 1970s and 1980s feminist film criticism, feminism also includes ideological approaches. Marxism informs feminist ideological approaches that understand gender and sexuality as social, cultural, and ideological phenomena manifested in film texts and practices (Kuhn 1993, 4). Although to a certain degree, all the approaches above assume Marxist aesthetics, theorists like Annette Kuhn have placed materialism at the center of their projects, with ideology as one of the points of entry into cultural analysis (Humm 1997, 26–28; Thornham 1997, 27). For Kuhn, both "sex/gender systems" and "the cultural" are subsumed under ideology, which means that it is possible to intervene in culture and have an effect on sex/gender systems (Kuhn 1993, 5). She takes this insight to argue for cultural practices (for example, challenges to the television and film industries) that can affect the systems of sex/gender. Because Kuhn also identifies feminism with oppositional practices, and because she recognizes that cultural texts do not have inherent meanings, her ideas about feminist practices relate more to the political nature of the practice than to its aesthetic qualities. Favoring the social aspects of cultural consumption is a way of addressing the conditions of existence of filmic texts and viewers. Indeed, for Kuhn, the moment of reception of the filmic work is the moment at which meaning is constructed, and because a plethora of social, historical, and economic factors influence reception, sense making ceases to be purely a psychic process (16).

Kuhn's emphasis on viewers and the potential of reception as a site of political rebellion marks a shift in feminist film criticism. Over the course of the late 1980s, audiences and viewers would share, with the text, the central spot in feminist criticism. The shift happened slowly. Several factors influenced it, including the recognition that meaning was not embedded in the text (for example, Kuhn), the necessity to theorize the female spectator (for example, Doane), and ideas of narrative excess (for example, melodrama and other woman's genres).

Though Mulvey's early work had left little room for a female spectator, Doane's work provided a space for thinking of a more political-progressive female spectatorship. As she observes, if Mulvey is correct, and mainstream films construct filmic systems optimally for the heterosexual male viewer, female viewers, in their quest for identification with the protagonist, might masquerade as women in order to view dominant cinema (Thornham 1997, 52). Though Doane finishes with an optimistic note and states that power is possible within oppression, one must not be overly hopeful. As Doane points out, the process of spectatorship becomes unstable in particular when women are viewing "woman's film." Because these films seek out female identification, and the identifying process is masculine, female viewers are placed in the position of having to enact masochistic scenarios to deal with the instability of the female viewing process (54). This is not a healthy option.

It is also prudent to mention here Elizabeth Cowie's contribution to the matter of what might count as progressive identifications (1979 [1988], 104–40). In her analysis of the detective film *Coma,* Cowie challenges the idea that a single look exists in cinematic texts. Instead, in her analysis she shows how the relationship of spectator to filmic text is better understood as a "continual construction of looks, with a constant production of spectator-position and thus subject" (137). Based on the process of knowledge acquisition in this film and for its female protagonist who struggles to make her questions believable within the narrative and to the audience, Cowie argues that the narrative offers the viewers only intermittent identifications (120–35).

Though cultural studies' influence in feminist film criticism can be traced back to the end of the 1970s, by 1985 this influence was very clearly felt. According to Mary C. Kearney, cultural studies was mentioned as a viable research approach in feminist film circles as far back as 1973 (Julia Lesage). However, Kearney continues, it is by the end of the decade when Christine Gledhill and Maureen Turim firmly placed cultural studies as a desirable alternative to psychoanalytic approaches. At this time, the dominance of Screen theory was such that those who used cultural studies were marginalized in the field. Throughout the 1980s things changed and cultural studies became more central to feminist film criticism.

In 1985, Ien Ang (1989) gave an account of television viewing that used film theory in unusual ways. Her study of the reception of *Dallas* in Holland characterized that televisual text as a melodrama that, like film melodrama, is full of intensity, excess, and contradictions. Moreover, this endless narrative and its multiple characters produce ambiguous identifications (75). Though Ang sees women's identification with the melodramatic imagination (its fatalism and powerlessness) as masochistic, she contends that this is experienced in the realm of "fantasy" and thus bracketed off from reality (135). While Ang recognizes that women's pleasures watching *Dallas* are hardly the pleasures of feminism, she sees them as necessary to women's engagement with a reality that is otherwise precarious.

From 1972 to 1985, feminist film criticism included sociological (for example, stereotypes and representation), psychoanalytic, Marxist, and cultural studies approaches. In general, and as elaborated in the introduction, these criticisms began giving more importance to the complexities of the filmic texts and only later opened up to questions of the multiplicity and complexities of audiences.

Feminist Aesthetics

In 1978 several feminist film critics (Michelle Citron, Julia Lesage, Judith Mayne, B. Ruby Rich, and Anna Marie Taylor) briefly discussed feminist aesthetics (Citron 1978 [1999], 115–21). At issue was not simply what types of films feminists had produced, but rather, how likely it was that mainstream filmic texts would offer radical potential to women. These critics were not very confident. Addressing the issue under the spell of Metz and Mulvey, they saw little promise in popular film. Except for Marlene Dietrich's persona (which offers a possible lesbian identification) and Brecht's Marxist aesthetic, an actual filmic text having liberatory potential had not happened.

Yet, feminist film practices existed and tended to have certain aesthetic characteristics that several scholars, including B. Ruby Rich and Kuhn, documented. Trying to come to terms with the growing and factitious field of film criticism, Rich proposed a set of unusual categories of films to unify the language of feminist criticism and the aesthetics identified with women or feminism (Rich 1994, 27). Among the categories are the following: films of validation are works that in a realistic fashion explore women's lives and cultures; films of correspondence are those works that use personal styles of writing; reconstructive films are ones that use a genre and fashion it for feminism; medusan films are those that use laughter and camp as subversion; films of corrective realism use realism to care for women and centered on women; and projectile films are those films made by patriarchy, aimed at women (37–41).

These unusual categories reveal a complex subfield of film production that could be considered feminist or for women's consumption. Not surprisingly, Kuhn later recognized that imposing a film aesthetics on feminist practices was, indeed, counterintuitive. Instead, she provided a set of feminist uses of film aesthetics (Kuhn 1993, 129); in so doing, she highlighted the reception of aesthetics as the central issue to feminist film practices (176–96). As an example, realism, she observed, though broadly used in Hollywood cinema, was a good medium for the presentation of political issues. Thus, 1970s Hollywood films organized around a woman's self-discovery (for example, *Alice Doesn't Live Here Anymore,* d. Martin Scorsese, 1975; *Starting Over,* d. Alan Pakula, 1979), for instance, lent themselves to feminist uses by female audiences because they allowed for identification with winning, female protagonists (135).

Other realist genres such as socialist realism, direct cinema, and documentary also offer opportunities for feminist film reception. Socialist realism often provides representations of heroism and processes of self-construction (*Salt of the Earth,* d. Herbert Biberman, 1935). Feminists have used direct cinema and documentary to represent the lives of women, often using autobiography and, thus, self-construction as a political and epistemological tool. Women's experiences are foregrounded, and viewers are invited to identify with the lives of women (144–49).

The second general tactic used by feminist film practitioners is counter-cinema. This filmmaking approach attempts to break with dominant filmic codes. As Kuhn observes, the tradition often borrows from Brecht and proposes an active engagement between viewer and text based on the deconstruction and questioning of filmic codes (161). As an example of counter-cinema, she uses Sara Gómez's *One Way or Another* (1977), a film that draws on documentary techniques such as interviews with real people and that addresses social issues (see next chapter and chapter 7).

What Kuhn and Rich show in their discussions of feminist aesthetics is the foregrounding of works that can be used by women (and men) to further the varied political goals of feminisms. Moreover, in foregrounding some works, they helped construct a new film canon, one that accounts for the social and aesthetic needs of women and that uses political value as a valid standard of quality. Millet had already shown that the literary canon was implicated in the reproduction of patriarchal structures, which meant that it needed to be criticized, revised, or, simply, dumped. Since the early 1970s, therefore, the substitution of misogynist cultural canons became one of the tasks for feminist critics. During the 1970s and 1980s, feminists challenged canons in literature, film, television, and art. They were ready to consider revolutionary cinematic practices as political expression (Showalter 1977; Chadwick 1990; Kuhn 1993; Staiger 1994).

Each of the previous issues has provided feminism with fertile ground from which to build critiques of epistemology. This has turned feminist film criticism into a complex philosophical enterprise that challenges all elements of the production of knowledge and the interpretation of the world. As a long-lasting critique of knowledge, feminism is a social practice that has underlined the ethical and the aesthetics of epistemology, their interrelations, and their codependences. And, at the point where ethics, aesthetics, and epistemology converge, feminism has discovered tyranny and freedom. The insight is that our knowledge has been built on an ethos of oppression. From this kernel, the body, emotion, the feminine, women, the nonwhite, the non-Western, the particular, experience, biography, autobiography, black culture, women's pictures, *écriture féminine, Latinidad,* sexuality, pleasure, and love become philosophy. As seen above, they also become the guidelines for a critical hermeneutics.

Conclusion

In 1973 critics may have been superstars, but, as all superstars, they depended on a public willing to believe that the qualities they possessed were special and outstanding. Because the critic is a type of author, her/his function in society is characterized by the roles she/he performs to fit within the grids of culture and power. The critic's function is overdetermined and multiple. In this chapter I commented on contexts that had the potential to politicize the critic's social function from 1970 to 1985.

The modus operandi of the critic, her/his mode of reception, is not con-stituted through sheer will. It is historic and historicizable. Critics' modus operandi relate to the constitution over time of specific political identities available to them. It is within such historical identities and ways of being that a political critic finds dispositions to view culture as political and thus to view cultural criticism as an activity that forms part of the process of be-coming a political individual. In addition, it is within the historicity of these identities that a political critic encounters specific hermeneutic styles proper to interpreting the world.

Returning to the reception of Cuban films by critics in the United States, as I argue here and as I show in the following pages, some of their hermeneutic styles originated on broad historical factors affecting most members of society. Among these were the U.S.-Cuba political relations and the politicization of culture occurring during the 1960s. Others were more specific to the critic's cultural positions, such as the aura of foreign films, the way these were dis-tributed (for example, film festivals, universities), and the normalization of the study of culture's politics.

Because most of the films I am concerned with have female protagonists and deal with issues of gender and sex, I discussed feminism and feminist film criticism as two social and epistemological practices that cut across the factors previously mentioned. A feminist hermeneutics has been elaborated everywhere in society by committed feminists interested in debunking patri-archal culture; however, this elaboration has happened more intensely within the academy. As part of the academic revolution that occurred because of the critique of positivism that began in the nineteenth century and the rise of subjugated knowledges and peoples within academic communities since the 1960s, feminist hermeneutics is itself a critique of epistemology, ethics, and aesthetics. Moreover, the personal as political, one key aspect of radi-cal feminism (and critical race theory) since the 1960s, is the center of this challenge to epistemology and the center of feminist hermeneutics. Thus, the body, emotions, experience, and autobiography become common and valuable ways of fashioning interpretations of film. At the opposite end, critiques of epistemology have become critiques of universality and the recognition that mainstream culture and classical epistemology are invested in the reproduc-tion of subjection. Thus, a second aspect of a feminist hermeneutics is the investigation of universalizing structures that may constitute oppression.

In the following chapters, I analyze the reviews that feminist and leftist/

liberal critics performed for the four Cuban films in which I am interested, and I compare them with those by Cuban reviewers. I will treat the reviews not solely as evidence of the subject position of the reviewer or solely as the exercise of historically determined modalities of reception that the reviewer has learned to use as proper cultural communication. As I have argued, when the critic's function is political, his or her modes of reception and hermeneutic processes can and must be seen as social actions geared toward the performance of the critic's political identity. Using a proper interpretive apparatus is part of this performance, and for feminist and leftist critics this will mean using feminist and leftist criticism. The personal as a political statement, the body, emotion, and patriarchy are some of the hermeneutic features likely to be encountered in feminist reviews. Social and class oppression, subjection, and deep structures such as ideology or semiosis are features likely to be present in leftist reviews. But what is more important than simply recognizing that feminist critics use feminism, my insight is recognizing that this use is a social practice of freedom, as Foucault describes technologies of selfhood. That is, these reviewers perform normative hermeneutics as political actions and thus within an awareness of the need for social change. The reviewer, in using a political framework, defines herself/himself as an agent of this change, one acting in freedom.

PART II

Performing Film Criticism

Sergio, always a critic, overlooks the city and re-creates the distance that so defines him. Screen grab from *Memories of Underdevelopment* (Alea, 1968).

Chapter 5

Memories of Underdevelopment

Memorias del Subdesarrollo (*Memories of Underdevelopment*, 1968), directed by Tomás Gutiérrez Alea, develops in Havana in 1961, at a time when the nation was undergoing profound changes and just before the Missile Crisis. Sergio, an educated, middle-class, thirty-something white man has seen his family and friends leave Cuba. Left behind, almost alone (except for his friend Pablo, who continuously criticizes the social changes the revolution is bringing), Sergio walks through the city observing with melancholic interest and, at times, with disdain the altering force of the new order. Through inner monologues, the viewer learns of Sergio's feelings of superiority. Rooted in a strong sense of class, racial, and gender privilege, he observes ordinary Cubans who are, to him, vulgar, underdeveloped, unattractive, irrational beings. These opinions affect his subjectivity and engender a strong sense of alienation. As the observer, he is in a position of negatively defining a Cuba that he cannot yet leave.

Sergio becomes involved with a very young woman, Elena, whose social extraction he finds unappealing, but who is otherwise attractive. He seduces her and seems committed to "develop" her intellect. He takes her to Ernest Hemingway's house, to museums, to bookstores, to bed. All of this, he feels, is to no avail. When things go sour, Elena's family confronts Sergio and reports her rape to the authorities. Though the ruling is in Sergio's favor, his feelings of alienation increase. In the final scene, he is alone in his luxury condominium, looking at Havana getting ready for a possible U.S. invasion during the Missile Crisis.

As a counterpoint to the fictional narration, the narrative weaves in nonfictional footage of historical and/or symbolic importance, creating a dialectic between objective reality and Sergio's subjectivity. The film shows Marilyn Monroe, U.S. soldiers at Guantanamo Bay, blacks beaten by soldiers, Fidel Castro's speeches, and the trial of individuals who had participated in the Bay of Pigs invasion, all of these interspersed with the morose observations of the fictional character.

Memories in Cuba

Memories was Alea's fourth feature film. As one of the founders of ICAIC, Alea occupied a privileged position in the field of cultural production and in the world of film. He was part of the editorial team of *Cine Cubano,* and took part in the direction of ICAIC and in the training of new generations of film-makers, including Sara Gómez, Sergio Giral, and Juan Carlos Tabío (Paranagua 1996, 77–89). He directed the first feature fictional film of the revolution in 1960 (*Histories of the Revolution* [*Historias de la Revolución*]) and consistently produced some of the best films in Cuba well into the 1990s (Downing 1987, 279–301). Alea's institutional identity within ICAIC provided a strong context for the reception of *Memories.*

Though *Memories* is today considered one of the most important Cuban films, the film went relatively unnoticed upon its release. One must remember that its release came only months after Che Guevara's death in October 1967 in the jungles of Bolivia. This tragic event brought a grim, overzealous mood to the Cuban political landscape that infused most public culture with new revolutionary vigor. Most journals and magazines, including *Casa, Bohemia,* and *Cine Cubano,* published special issues about Guevara, exulting his actions, words, ideas, and influences on Cuban politics and culture. 1968 was named the "Year of the Guerrilla Fighter" ("Año del Guerrillero Heróico"). In this cultural and political environment, the image of Guevara was transformed from influential figure to exemplar, and in many of these articles and biographies Guevara was defined not only as the ideologue that championed the idea of the New Man but as its embodiment.

Given this patriotic mood, it is hardly surprising to find that critics received a film about a timid, self-centered individual with calculated apathy. *Memories* opened in Havana on August 17, 1968, in six theaters dedicated to new releases. Despite Alea's standing in ICAIC, and despite having received several international prizes, *Granma* did not review it. The journal *Unión,* the official cultural organ of UNEAC, also distanced itself from the film when it published, the same year, a short piece paying tribute to revolutionary cultural production, which praised *Lucia* and other feature films but not *Memories* ("Ellos Habrían Sido Como Nosotros" 1968, 236–37).

The film revolves around some of the themes that had come to be expected from revolutionary culture. It dealt with politics and the political attitudes of Sergio; it represented postrevolutionary Cuban life as formed through confrontation; through its protagonist, it explored the difficulties some had in adapting to the new social expectations, including decolonization; it used some distanciation techniques and attempted to denaturalize the filmic structure by mixing fictional with nonfictional footage; it explored revolutionary reality and the process of undoing prerevolutionary behavior. The journal *Cine Cubano*, edited by Alea, published several written and photographic essays about the film. The first appeared in August 1967 and consisted of the director's "work notes." Other articles appeared after the film's release, and, because of its substantial international success, the film continued being mentioned in practically every article dealing with Cuban film thereafter in *Cine Cubano* and other journals.

Alea's "work notes" came a few months before the death of Guevara, and thus, his comments inhabited a cultural landscape quite different from the one in which the film would be released a year later. In spite of this difference, Alea's privileged position within the cultural field gave his ideas unusual weight. Future references to the film would repeat the themes that he developed and would even quote his words (Díaz 1970, 79–84; Cossio 1968, 74–75). Alea proposed that the film was a lesson about how difficult it was to decolonize the self: "Why *Memories of Underdevelopment?* I remember that during the beginning, immediately after the triumph of the revolution, we all (all) believed that this island . . . could be transformed overnight in a type of Caribbean Switzerland" (Gutiérrez Alea 1967, 20). Yet, this transformation did not happen. The reason, Alea argues, is that underdevelopment is also mental, and that Cubans would have to assume their condition of subjective underdevelopment if they wanted to transform themselves (21–22).

Memories invites Cuban viewers to recognize their own underdevelopment in Sergio, who is presented to the viewer as wavering between a colonized definition of civilization and revolutionary ideologies. This colonized identity favored liberal ideas of the individual and freedom over communal revolutionary ideas. As Alea points out, Sergio always chooses self-involvement, individuality, European civilization, his house (property), as well as his memories

(23). Contrary to Sergio, Alea favors public and communal values. For instance, self-involvement, a private activity, is valued less than self-formation, a public activity. Self-formation, thus conceived, required a continuous engagement with the outside world, what Alea and most members of the intelligentsia would likely call "reality."

The film investigated the procedural nature of *conciencia* and suggested that becoming a revolutionary was a process that some, not all, could bring to completion. *Memories* also allowed the viewer to identify the elements of the technology of self they would have to undertake to reach the state (the status) of a New Man. The first step in the process of transformation was recognizing the underdevelopment within. The second step was recognizing that to become a revolutionary, one would have to get rid of the old self and build a new one. Sergio's inability to do so was a cautionary tale about the risks of underdevelopment in a developing society. Finally, a third element of the technology of self was forwarded by *Memories* in the suggestion that the process of change involved a change of ideology. Sergio's bourgeois and individualistic ideology existed in contrast and tension with the ideology of a transforming society. A new ideology, the film also suggested, is manifested in a new hermeneutic. Sergio's suspicious subjectivity was shown to the viewer through his "odd" hermeneutic tactics; Sergio saw and interpreted the world in ways that separated him from it and that devalued common life and common Cubans.

Though the aesthetic strategies of the film were common in the Cuban cultural field, it is clear that having Sergio as the main object of reflection could be considered problematic in Cuba even before the death of Guevara. This is evident where, despite the fact that Sergio can provide such useful services to the viewer (such as helping develop a critical stance to underdevelopment), Alea harshly criticized the character, almost to excess. As if Alea was trying to erase the possibility of being criticized for having created a character that glorified the bourgeoisie, he vehemently dubs Sergio's character as immoral ("He is incapable of loving"), deluded, cowardly ("he is not capable of assuming the risks the Revolution brought"), and irrational (as he is ill-equipped to describe reality).

Alea's efforts to distance himself from Sergio signal nervousness, a tension within the cultural community and its relationship to the field of power (similar distancing efforts are evident in a photo essay published by *Cine Cubano* upon the film's release) ("*Memorias del Subdesarrollo:* Film Cubano/ con Sergio Corrieri y Daisy Granados" 1968, 152–55). Though conceived as a critique to Cuba's naiveté regarding development and its subjects, the film, as the book had before, could be criticized for glorifying nonrevolutionary values and for too ably interpellating its audience with capitalist ideologies. This tension is evident in the reviews published later.

Nicolas Cossio (1968), a regular film reviewer for the magazine *Bohemia*, wrote about the film in 1968, roughly a year after its release. Like Alea, Cossio criticized Sergio's inability to engage reality (he is "deluded") by juxtaposing the character's subjective persona with what Cossio, echoing Alea, calls "objective reality." The review is quite critical of the film, though it criticized it without openly questioning its politics. Rather, what calls the attention of Cossio is the "roughness" of the film, its imperfect aesthetics, and Alea's inability to narrativize psychological problems. Ultimately, Cossio calculates, the film will be memorable because of its international success, not because of its quality (75).

What is most interesting about Cossio's article is expressed in the following words: "No, I don't share the criteria of criticism benevolent to national cinema, even less that of paternalistic or interested criticism. . . . I believe that the honest thing to do is dive into the truth." Given that this declaration is a type of truism ("criticism should be honest"), including it begs the question of why.

Cossio suggested that some criticism in Cuba was carried on in a dishonest fashion, with an interested attitude, in a self-serving manner, unlike his own. These critics, one suspects, attempted to benefit national cinema without regard for what would benefit the nation. Good criticism, honest criticism, was a revolutionary task, like Espinosa stated, required to influence, create, and reproduce the revolutionary field of cultural production. Cossio also created a clear standard of behavior that separated him from the rest. By doing so, he acknowledged a community-based standard to separate the self from the "other": The self, constituted by those vanguards responsible to the revolution, "dives into the truth," and others do not.

All interpretation is hermeneutic, but not all interpreters feel compelled to state that theirs is an honest and truthful interpretation. Putting such emphasis gives a clue to the role truthfulness should occupy in the specific practice of reviewing national cinema. For instance, Cossio wrote regularly the cultural criticism section of *Bohemia*, but of the dozen pieces I read, the review of *Memories* is the only one that mentions honesty. This intimates that the standards of work may be different depending on the type of cultural artifact that is being criticized. It is easier to be critical of North American films and to use the full arsenal of a revolutionary hermeneutics on capitalist narratives than it is to be critical of national cinema. Other reviewers, Cossio implied, were not doing it. One may speculate about the reasons for this. Among them is the size and cultural influence of ICAIC. As commented in chapter 1, ICAIC had, during the sixties, waged some cultural wars against other institutions and had triumphed. This meant that ICAIC sat strongly in the middle of Cuba's field of cultural production. Another point is the recognition that Cuba needed a national cinema and that this had to be nurtured, not harmed or squelched.

Finally, Cossio's declaration is a brief definition of the writer's ethical makeup (honesty), civic qualities (he feels his honesty is required for the good of Cuba), and individualism. This last aspect is particularly relevant for it suggests the ongoing importance of acting independently from the community. Moreover, this independence is deemed important for the fulfillment of the writer's civic duties. Cossio's declaration is, therefore, one that fits liberal definitions of selfhood for they suggest that autonomy, a key characteristic of the liberal self and citizen, benefits society.

Elena Díaz (1970) published in *Cine Cubano* a review of the film roughly one year and a half after the release of *Memories* (79–84). By 1970 the film had benefited from a successful run at theaters, had collected a number of prizes, and the revolutionary fervor brought about by Guevara's death had dwindled. All of these factors gave Díaz the opportunity to engage the film-text in a different way, putting together a series of positive arguments regarding the film's aesthetic and political qualities.

For her, the film was an example of a complete artistic work that enriched the cultural national heritage. Asserting the film's national character, Díaz suggests that *Cubanidad* is felt in the totality of *Memories* and in each of its parts: the music, the dialogues, and the photography. This ability to express the identity of the nation corresponds to the rightful application of a Cuban aesthetics. Form and narrative, Díaz implies, express something essentially Cuban that is reinforced by the realism of the characters and by the situations depicted by the narrative (80). Given that Sergio's fictionalized subject position cannot be defended or suggested as exemplary or desirable, and, yet, that Sergio is the character through which the viewer enters into the *Memories* world, the problem of identification is one that has to be discussed and solved. Díaz proposes that the viewer recognizes situations but does not identify with them. In this way, the relationship of viewer to text is not one of ideological compliance to Sergio's interpellations but one of objectification of the subject position Sergio represents. Once objectified, this subject position can be understood and, perhaps, avoided or eliminated. What Díaz hypothesizes is a viewer that can construct a critical distance in relation to the text and be able to reflect, laugh, and, in general, make an "other" out of Sergio. Accordingly, the viewer is invited to identify with the situations Sergio is encountering and morally value his inability to join the revolution.

Perhaps surprisingly, all of these spectatorship maneuvers do not stop the viewer from enjoying the film and from being sutured to the narrative. Díaz assumes that the audience is made active by "coherence of action." This quality maintains the attention of the audience and makes them participate in the action developed onscreen. Díaz's ideas about active audiences are different from what we find today in the U.S. academy. For her, to be active is to have a range of experiences through watching film and replicating its radical point of view (POV). Contrary to the American way of understanding an active audience as one that rejects or negotiates the reading of the text, Díaz believes the film to be a revolutionary statement about the world, and for this reason audience activity can be theorized as a replication of the film's POV.

Although most cultural institutions ignored *Memories* at its release, the few that commented on it give me important clues to the way criticism was used to present the self publicly. Alea, the director, presented a piece where he linked his cultural practice to the pedagogic principles of revolutionary culture. In doing so, he reconstituted a notion of cultural work as civic and political work. Moreover, Alea also used this writing to distance himself from Sergio (*Memories* protagonist) and did so by vehemently declaring Sergio unfit to live in a revolutionary society. If Alea enacted his selfhood in alignment with revolutionary ideas of the time, Cossio's style of selfhood evinces the ongoing influence of liberal notions of autonomy and self, albeit within revolutionary frames of social responsibility. Finally, Díaz presents a writing, published in *Cine Cubano,* that seems exemplary of the type of criticism revolutionary ideologies required. Her piece carefully walks the film's ideological minefield, and in her journey she manages to support Alea, criticize Sergio, and qualify the film as flawed but good revolutionary work. Her criticism as practice shows the type of careful interpretive work that "responsible" critics had to perform to continue existing in cultural institutions while fulfilling a vanguard role.

Memories in the United States

The economic and cultural embargo placed on Cuba at the beginning of the 1960s erased most Cuban culture from the American cultural field. These embargos were part of government policies aimed at containing the spread of communism. Often fitted within the discourse of viral infections, communism was a political disease that threatened the healthy American political body (Ross 1989, 47). Not surprisingly, most Americans' perceptions of Cuba were rooted in fear of communism, of nuclear destruction, and also on existing popular notions about Latin America and the third world. Except for the efforts of organizations such as American Documentary Films (ADF), Cuban films were simply not available to most American audiences or critics. Ironically, by the time this happened, revolutionary Cuban film had little chance to affect the identities of American radicals, but was still capable of energizing fantasies of dissention. The sixties were ending, but private dissention continued. By 1973, when *Memories* was first shown, political radicalism was retreating, except for feminism. Todd Gitlin writes: "A Harris poll reported the first drop since 1965 in the percentage of students calling themselves 'radical' or far Left—from 11 percent in the spring of 1970 to 7 percent in the fall. From spring to fall, the middle-of-the-road category leaped from 26 to 34 percent, and the 'conservative' and 'far right' groups, which had been sliding steadily since 1968, from 15 to 19 percent" (Gitlin 1987, 419). These changes in the articulated constitution of politicized groups and identities of the late 1960s marked the end of the era. In April 1971, the antiwar movement organized a march attended by one-half million people, but by then, organized dissention had lost force. From 1970 to 1972, what was left of the movement dwindled because of military deescalation in Vietnam. Nixon was succeeding at containing discontent.

The U.S. government finally allowed the film's distribution by Tricontinental Film Center in May 1973. *Memories* was first exhibited at the First Avenue Screening Room and the Rugoff Theater in New York (Lofredo 1972–73, 56–57). A flurry of reviews followed these first showings and, predictably, they were published in some of the most traditionally liberal-leftist media and specialized journals, including the *New York Times, The New Republic, The Nation, Village Voice, Jump Cut,* and *Cineaste.*

Stanley Kauffmann (1973), one of the most prestigious literary and film critics of the time, reviewed the film for *The New Republic* (22, 32). He had been a critic for reputable cultural magazines since 1958, and was part of the group of critics (for example, Pauline Kael, Andrew Sarris) that emerged during the time that American film was considered subpar to European film (Scott 1998; Kim 2001). Kauffmann's opinions of the French New Wave and the great Italian, Scandinavian, and Japanese directors of the 1960s and 1970s shaped his career and reputation (Scott 1998). Unlike Sarris, who early embraced auteur theory, and Kael, who admired film as popular culture, Kauffman's work was that of an aesthete, knowledgeable and elitist, though clearly liberal, just like *The New Republic*.[1] Kauffmann's review was relevant to the reception of *Memories* and of Cuban film in general in several ways. It was the first review of a Cuban film in a popular magazine and thus set a standard interpretation. Given Kauffmann's prestige and that of his magazine, future reviewers would be beholden to read it and acknowledge it.[2] Second, his review was politicized in several ways. Printed right after a review of a book that criticized the House Un-American Activities Committee (HUAC) and the cases of censorship and repression sponsored by that government entity, Kauffmann's review begins with a paragraph about the State Department's censoring and repression of the Cuban Film Festival in New York.

His criticism of the field of power is performed through the vindication of *Memories* as a text that embodies some of the best qualities of cinema. Kauffmann states (1973): "This is an extraordinarily sensible piece of work—exactly the opposite of the gung-ho stuff one might expect from a newly organized government" (32). Such praise discredits those who, like people in the State Department, probably assumed that film from a communist nation is de facto propaganda. He continues describing the film as "tactful" and directed with skill and links its thematic and aesthetic propositions to European art cinema: "[What] the film gives us is an Antonioni character in the middle of a political revolution." He finishes his review with his strongest argument in favor of the film: "Out of a revolution bred on slogans comes a film without answers: thus lending some credibility to the revolution."

Kauffmann uses cultural criticism to oppose the censoring activities of the State Department, demarcating, in the process, his position in relation to the power structure. Because cultural rights (including cultural freedoms) are central to the American cultural habitus (much in the same way that civic responsibility plays a key role in the Cuban habitus), Kauffmann's defense and praise of *Memories* has a dual register: on the one hand, it is an institutional activity that (re)asserts the cultural field's independence from the field of power. That is, *The New Republic* relies on the idea that cultural freedom is a right and that without it the magazine may not survive. Opposing the State Department's censoring hawks and praising a film like *Memories* become necessities. On the other hand, and as Bourdieu comments, cultural fields exist within the field of power and cannot fully oppose it. Kauffmann's language is evidence of this register. He ends the review commenting on how remarkable it was that a "revolution bred on slogans" produced such subtle film. Though likely Kauffmann did not intend to argue Cuban culture was only propaganda, the two commentaries together reproduce stereotypical language regarding communist nations, which are equated to totalitarian states.

Vincent Canby, writing for the *New York Times* the day after the film's opening on May 18, 1973, also set a standard for interpreting its unusual aesthetics. Like Kauffmann, he praised the film by using European standards of quality: "*Memories of Underdevelopment* is a fascinating achievement. Here is a film about alienation that is wise, sad, and often funny, and that never slips into the bored and boring attitudes that wreck Antonioni's later films." Comparing Alea's style to European art cinema, Canby suggests that Alea "is clearly a man, like Sergio, whose sensibilities are European." Assuming their similarities, however, does not lead Canby to believe that Alea's film is antirevolutionary. On the contrary, he states that this is an "essentially pro-revolutionary film in which Castro's revolution is observed through eyes dim with bafflement." His political opinions are further evinced in the last paragraph of his review, where, like Kauffmann, he links the film to the U.S. State Department's censorship.

Though Kauffmann and Canby are not reviewers that would set the standard for a Marxist critique of *Memories,* their prestige and timing, and the fact that they used already established frames for understanding things Cuban (communism, politics, Europeanized culture), made their reviews standard, particularly Kauffmann's. Practically every reviewer took his approach, placing the film within a political backdrop of censorship, and the U.S. government versus communism. What the reviewers brought to the reception was, however, quite diverse, though some patterns were discernable. One had to do with the reviewers' understanding of what Cuban film was or was supposed to be. A second pattern related to positive evaluations of the film based on its critical stance against the revolution. And the third was an acknowledgment of *Memories* as a text in the Marxist aesthetics tradition.

If Kauffmann, a rather knowledgeable viewer, expressed surprise at the quality of *Memories* (given that, apparently, the film belonged to the category of "films made by newly organized governments"), it is normal to find that other reviewers found *Memories* an unexpectedly pleasant surprise that challenged stereotypical notions of communist culture—that is, culture as propaganda. Peter Schjeldahl (1973), of the *New York Times,* somehow naïvely states: "It is a miracle. It is also something of a shock. I'm not sure what I expected of my first exposure to postrevolutionary Cuban cinema; something raw and hortatory, probably." Colin Westerback (1973) gives a clearer picture of the set of expectations when he writes: "Since history tells me that most revolutionaries are straight-laced and literal minded, it seemed surprising that this film . . . is not only ironical, but ribald. Nor can it be said . . . that the film suffers from the humorlessness typical of revolutionary art" (405). These comments show that in 1973, American film critics, like most Americans, lacked exposure to Cuban culture and that this knowledge gap had been defined ideologically. Without being openly anticommunist (though Westerback comes just short of stating his anticommunism), Schjedahl and Westerback managed nonetheless to praise while criticizing. Like Kauffmann, their comments hit a double register that defines an institutional location in which their selves are manifested as independent, but also subject to power. Both reviewers can state, writing in the first person, that they have not seen other Cuban films; yet, they also confess that they went to the theater with strong expectations and that these, luckily, were not met. One senses an aesthetic and political parochialism in these two reviewers, particularly if we compare them with Kauffmann, who, expertly, reminds the reader that other films from communist nations were comparable to *Memories* in their narrative subtlety and aesthetic propositions. Schjedahl and Westerback also use extratextual political information to interpret the film, in particular ideas about Cuba and about communist culture. In a way similar to the Cuban reviewers who used their own relation to the Cuban field of power to interpret the film, these American reviewers privileged the extratextual over the textual and the political over the aesthetic. This is not to say that the aesthetic was dismissed, but that the aesthetic was understood as containing political ideas and as having political implications. Schjedahl (1973) expressed these implications as follows: "Perhaps the jerrybuilt Cold War barriers between the United States and Cuba have now decayed to the point where a puff or two of fresh, humanizing air like that of *Memories* may help blow them down. Let's hope." The aesthetic quality of the film is the humanizing air of hope.

Memories was seen first through the eyes of power and politics and second as a text to be interpreted and aesthetically valued. Because of its contextual framework, and given the specific expectations regarding communist film in general and Cuban film in particular, these and other popular reviewers of *Memories* praised it. The exception was Robert Hatch (1973) who, in reviewing the film for *The Nation,* commented that exaggerating the praise for *Memories,* based partly on the size of the Cuban nation and possibly on the fact that the United States bullied Cuba for the last decade, was patronizing to Alea. From that position, Hatch constructed a negative critique of *Memories* where he explored his antipathy for European art film, which Hatch uses as a framework to see *Memories.* This antipathy is evident in the sarcastic tone of his writing: "As is custom in pictures that explore the spiritual doubts of modern youth, Sergio is much given to solitary walking and prone sprawling on unmade beds."

Hatch's words reconstitute the potential duality found in previous reviews. For instance, Hatch writes at the beginning of the review that "Castro's government seized control" of Cuba, and he uses language that connotes coercion or illegality. In the next sentence, Hatch changes the tone and writes: "Cuba is a small state going through a critical period of renewal." Paradoxically, Cuba's renewal owes to Castro's forceful empowerment. The redeeming qualities of Cuba, however, may not only relate to what the revolution had accomplished socially. This ambivalence also stems from the political identity of the writer, as it is constituted in relation to the U.S. field of power. Empathizing with Cuba and critical of the United States, Hatch points out that Cuba is "being bullied by its huge neighbor." Like Kauffmann, Hatch's engagement with Cuba is colored by his critical relationship with the field of power. Moreover, in performing his work as a critic, he separates himself and the cultural location he inhabits from power, thus enabling me to talk about it as a practice of freedom.

Kauffmann, Schjedahl, and Westerback praised *Memories* but did so in ways that served themselves. These and other reviewers gave praise to those film elements that they interpreted as critiques of Castro's communist, revolutionary, police, and/or underdeveloped regime. Steve Hogner (1975), writing for the *Austin American Statesman,* commented that the film "underscores much of the bitterness and resentment of a nation." Taking at face value Sergio's comments on Cuba and Cubans, Hogner invests his interpretation of the narrative with his desire to see a counterhegemonic text and, sure enough, he found it. For instance, Alea's representation of the Bay of Pigs was, according to Hogner, "a warning and the beginnings of an international chess match where Cuba is the loser." From this interpretive framework, Hogner can turn around and voice his own ethnocentric and racist prejudices and claim that it was Alea or Sergio who uttered them. For instance, his view was that Sergio was a symbol that Alea employed to say to the world and to Cuba that "this particular nation [Cuba] continues to go on its own incessant stupidity." Similarly, Sarris, the renowned film critic and chairman of the National Society of Film Critics (NSFC), commented that the reason the NSFC had awarded $2000 to Alea was because of the film's ability to present the "very personal and very courageous confrontation of the artist's doubts and ambivalences regarding the Cuban Revolution" (Hartl 1978). Similarly, David Elliott (1978) wrote for the *Sun-Times* (Chicago) that "the film is *too* good for a society that still muscles its people with prisons, propaganda and mini-Vietnams in Africa."

The U.S. field of culture is, however, complex and allows for the existence of a diverse array of critical positions. The reviewers previously mentioned occupied a distinctive space from where they wrote for liberal-left and moderate publics. In this space, the idea of Cuba and the meaning of things Cuban could better circulate if they were mixed with liberal values. That a Cuban film was praised for its courage to oppose its centralized, socialist, and even coercive government evidences that Cuba's radicalization has been presented in an unpalatable way to most Americans. That *Memories* was critical was also proof that it was "free" in a liberal sense, free to express and to experiment with aesthetics, free to communicate what maybe was silenced.

Other cultural workers, occupying different critical positions, understood that most reviewers' willingness to accept the film depended on the reviewer's perception of it as anti-Castroist. Julianne Burton (1977), an academic film critic who specializes in Cuba and Latin American film, was disappointed with the "sophisticated circles in this country," which likely included the reviewers and readers of the *New York Times, The New Republic,* and *The Nation.* She criticized their willingness to embrace the "familiar motifs of political and cultural alienation. . . . The film," she continued, "is viewed as openly critical of the current Cuban regime, but its impassioned denunciation of pre-revolutionary Cuba goes either unperceived or uncommented in this country" (16). In a similar vein, Enrique Fernández (1985), an academically trained Cuban American writer who publishes about Cuban film, writes that "Naively, [liberal Americans] had interpreted the cynicism of the narrator/ protagonist as Alea's, forgetting that while this character amuses himself with an anatomy of the Cuban scene, the film is busily dissecting him" (45). This inability of liberal Americans to "see" the narrational point of view of *Memories* was rooted, according to both Burton and Fernández, in the liberal critics' hermeneutic frameworks labeled as either naïve or ignorant of basic Marxist aesthetic principles, chiefly, dialectics.[3]

The rift between these two sets of critics is one formed by the convergence of aesthetic understanding, political beliefs and ideologies, and hermeneutic tactics. Yet, they disputed not simply a proper interpretation but also the rhetorical tactics used to make this interpretation persuasive and "tasteful" to readers. As David Bordwell (1989) comments, the social character of film criticism makes it a ritual where critics and audiences enact ideological dispositions (34). The communicative and rhetorical links of critic and reader can be established in different ways. In seeing *Memories* as a courageous political text, the first set of reviewers used ethical and emotional arguments to produce a rhetorical link to liberal audiences (liberal even when leftist). This "communion" between reader and critic, a self-defining activity, is also a public declaration of faith in the power of film to overcome ideology. Kauffmann (1978) wrote to this effect and stated that the film's artistic merit rested on its ability to conceal the director's opinions, which in the case of *Memories* meant hiding its candid questioning of the changes in Cuban society. Burton and Fernández similarly used rhetorical strategies to evaluate interpretations. Both suggested the application of stricter hermeneutic techniques, more specifically, Marxist aesthetics.

Burton and Fernández specialized in Latin American film and constructed positions within the field from which they could exercise a leftist optic and perform their jobs from a cultural location different from liberal critics. Both were trained as critics within the changing university world where subjugated knowledges, including political and aesthetic approaches, were ways of countering at least some of the power of hegemony in the United States. From that vantage point, they perceived the field differently from liberal critics and thus criticized the critics' shortcomings. The application of Marxist aesthetics as a hermeneutic technique to interpret *Memories* resulted in an emphasis on those narrative elements that could be seen as dialectical. Instead of centering on Sergio's opinions about Cuba and his optic of disillusionment, a U.S. Marxist interpretation highlighted formal and narrative contrasts and the use of contradictory levels of reality. For Burton (1977), *Memories* is "perhaps the most masterful elaboration to date of film's capacity to convey the dialectical interaction between historical circumstance and individual consciousness" (1977). Also centering on dialectics, Fernández (1985) pointed out that intrinsic to the film's rich textuality is the interplay of "identification and alienation, the legacy of two great theorists of materialist aesthetics: Eisenstein and Brecht" (45).

William Alexander (1985) also used Marxist aesthetic theory to talk about the film, but instead of relating it to Westernized narrative techniques, he used the vocabulary of Third Cinema as a theoretical and hermeneutic framework. Third Cinema refers to film initiatives (including aesthetic, institutional, and political proposals) from third world nations that were inspired by the likes of postcolonialists like Frantz Fanon and that appeared at the end of the 1960s. Alexander places *Memories* in the Third Cinema tradition chiefly by arguing that the film has decolonizing power. Evidence of this is Sergio, a most apathetic hero, who is a character that needs decolonizing. According to Alexander (1985), *Memories* decolonizes the viewer by inviting him/her into a narrative that uses Second Cinema aesthetics (European art cinema) and a Second Cinema typical character (Sergio's morose introspection is all too familiar in European art films) and then shows how this aesthetics and the subject position can only produce isolation from revolutionary processes (45).

Alexander's comments partly explain why critics commonly compared *Memories* to European art film and literature. Kauffmann had already written on Alea's training at the Centro Sperimentale di Roma. Schjeldahl, Fernández, and Lillian Gerard found the film reminiscent of Jean-Luc Godard's work. Described by reviewers not familiar with Cuban film as "artsy," "fancy," and "art film," some reviewers interpreted *Memories* through the code of "foreign European art film," and thus understood it as a subjective attack on social and political mores. That *Memories* was coming from Cuba, a nation in the process of revolution, could only mean, to this group of writers, that the film was indeed attacking social and political mores in Cuba. Such an interpretation has the advantage of belatedly negating aesthetic traditions rooted in socialist and communist nations and thus supporting the liberal notion that art can only be an expression of the artist's autonomy and of the autonomy of the cultural field, a view central to the American cultural field.

The distance that many reviewers recognized between Sergio and Cuban society, a distance nurtured by Europeanized ideas and that some reviewers linked to Alea's construction of space (for example, Amsterdam, Queens, and disintegrating Havana) is, Alexander believes, a Second Cinema tactic of alienation. Sergio *is* a critic of society presented through an art cinema aesthetic. However, he also argues that recognizing Sergio's critical stance (and thus Second Cinema) is only one step in the application of the proper hermeneutic technique. A second step, which Alexander thinks is essential for learning the director's aesthetic and ethical intentions, involves recognizing that identifying with Sergio's stance is identifying with a "rapist" (who applied a type of cultural coercion to abuse Elena), a "racist" (this is evidenced in the way Sergio talks about Afro-Cuban women and in Sergio's libidinal obsession with blonds), and a "murderer" (this because Sergio stands still while a counterrevolutionary assassination takes place). Alexander goes a bit too far in assuming that identifying with Sergio means identifying with a murderer. The film does not give enough information to confirm that Sergio was involved in the presumed assassination. The previous two points of identification, however, are warranted, and viewers engaged in a hermeneutics of decolonization must recognize the trappings of uncritically identifying with Sergio. Alexander, agreeing with Burton and Fernández, observes that U.S. reviewers rarely took that second step; thus, they remained identified with Sergio's rapist, racist, and (arguably) murdering position.

Those reviewers who found European analogies for *Memories* and those who saw it as critical of the revolution (at least of its coercive aspects) enacted a disposition to perceive filmic value by applying ethnocentric standards. Those leftist reviewers who saw it as an example of Third Cinema or Marxist aesthetics enacted a disposition to perceive filmic value by reference to an anti-Western political stance. That these two positions were the most common in the United States explains why *Memories* became a critical favorite. Not surprisingly, "*Take One* magazine conducted a poll of prominent film critics that ended with the nearly unanimous choice of *Memories* as the best Third World movie of the past decade" (Alexander 1985, 45).

Comparing the Critical Reception of *Memories*

Although most Cuban cultural institutions ignored *Memories* at its release, the few that commented on it are great examples of the way criticism was used as political identity. Alea linked his film to the pedagogic principles of revolutionary culture. In doing so, he reconstituted a notion of cultural work as civic and political work. Moreover, in declaring Sergio unfit to live in a revolutionary society, Alea performed his selfhood in alignment with revolutionary ideas of the time. Cossio's style of selfhood evinces the ongoing influence of liberal notions of autonomy and self, albeit within revolutionary frames of social responsibility. Finally, Díaz's writing is an exemplar of the type of criticism that revolutionary ideologies required. Her piece carefully walks the film's ideological minefield, and in her journey she manages to support Alea and criticize the film. Her criticism exemplifies the hermeneutic tasks expected from the cultural vanguard.

By contrast, the U.S. field of culture seems rather complex and friendly to a diverse array of critical positions. The reviewers occupied different spaces that intersected with liberal-left and moderate publics. In most of these spaces, the meaning of things Cuban could better circulate if coded in recognizable liberal parlance. Praising *Memories'* supposed antitotalitarian messages was also performing liberalism and socialism. That *Memories* was read as critical was also proof that it was "free" in a liberal sense, free to express and to experiment with aesthetics, free to communicate what maybe was silenced. This interpretation of *Memories* was not across the board, and academic writers criticized popular writers' naïve interpretations, reconstructing the barrier that continues separating the more left-leaning cultural circles of academia from the compromised leftisms and liberalisms of popular critics.

What is clear from both sets of interpretations (Cuban and American) is that *Memories* could easily accommodate ambiguous readings and that this textual feature determined its status in these two national cultural fields. In Cuba, ambiguity gave way to caution, regardless of Alea's standing in the field of culture and the field of power. In the United States, ambiguity often meant the film was welcomed for its courage to stand up to unjust power. Although Americans were the ones shocked by the film's intelligent way of depicting life and politics, the Cubans' reactions suggested they were also shocked and perhaps expected Cuban film to have more of that "gung-ho" communism Kauffmann mentioned: the simple aesthetics of celebratory political films, perhaps something a la Leni Riefenstahl (*Triumph of the Will,* Germany, 1935).

Memories' relative ambiguity and the reviews it elicited in Cuba and the United States shed light on the way critics perceived their relationships to the field of power and to politics. In Cuba, the critics' proper political behavior included ignoring a film they feared they could misread (and Alea's standing in the cultural and political field made this a delicate issue). In the United States, critics consistently performed their political identities in terms of the discourses of dissention, liberalism, and freedom. The Cubans' public political identities were circumscribed (and perhaps even limited) by narrow definitions of what it meant to be a proper revolutionary. These definitions meant, among other things, that critics use their cultural craft in the betterment and solidification of the revolution. The Americans' public political identities depended on their ability to identify dissenting practices and celebrate them. Because of this, popular critics who believed the film criticized Castro's Cuba, celebrating dissent, admired *Memories*. Similarly, academic critics who believed popular critics were wrong identified their own practice with dissent by theorizing that popular critics' mistaken interpretations were the product of hegemonic anticommunist ideologies. In each case, the cultural worker's position is politically legitimized through recourse to dissent, reconstituting liberal ideas of human worth that value independence above anything else and that define freedom as the separation of individual from the state and society.

With *Memories,* Alea challenged stereotypes and exceeded expectations, and the film can be credited with opening the gate of auteur-land to Alea: the art house circuit. No other Cuban director had more consistent distribution in the United States than Alea. His relative popularity (most Americans cannot name a single Cuban director, but, almost as a rule, if they can, this director is Alea) and perceived quality was eventually honored in 1995 with the nomination of *Strawberry and Chocolate* (codirected with Juan Carlos Tabío, 1994) for the Academy Awards in the category of Best Foreign Film. The winner of the award was, ironically, the postsocialist Russian film, *Burnt by the Sun* (Nikita Mikhalkov, Russia, 1994).

Chapter 6

Lucia

Lucia (*Lucía*, 1968, d. Humberto Solás) is composed of three stories of three women named Lucia. "Lucia 1895" narrates the story of a wealthy, single, white, sexually conservative Cuban woman in 1895, at a time when Cubans were engaged in a war for independence from Spain. Lucía wants to marry and she is happy when a Spanish man, Rafael, begins to court her. Though Lucía's allegiances are with the independence fighters, who include her brother, she pursues her relationship with Rafael who, lying about his romantic intentions, tricks her into giving him the location of revolutionary forces. Promptly, the Spanish attack the hideout, killing Lucía's brother and many others. Lucía goes mad and kills Rafael with a knife. "Lucia 1932" is the story of an upper-middle-class, white, conservative young Cuban woman in 1932, at time in Cuban history when insurgent forces were attempting to put an end to the ruling of President Machado. Lucía becomes involved with Aldo, a radical member of the insurgency. Abandoning her class roots, she takes off with Aldo, sharing danger, poverty, and idealism. They marry just before the insurgency forces triumph. Aldo becomes part of the new government but, confronted with the slowness of change, he becomes radicalized, only to be killed. Lucía, then pregnant, is left isolated from her class and alone. "Lucia 196 . . ." narrates the story of a poor, mulatto, uneducated woman from rural Cuba during the early revolutionary years. A newlywed to Tomás, she soon discovers her new husband's jealousy and its consequences. Tomás is intent on isolating her, forbidding her to work, interact with others outside the home, and from benefiting from the now-famous revolutionary government's alphabetization campaign of 1962. Her struggles against Tomás's narrow-mindedness are helped by Tomás's coworkers, who try to pressure him into stopping his brutish behavior. Unable to succeed, Lucía leaves him, which causes Tomás to go into emotional despair. Eventually, he recognizes that losing Lucía is more catastrophic to his life than holding on to atavistic ideas regarding gender and sexuality. In the final scene, Lucía and Tomás struggle for a compromise, but the film ends before one can be reached.

Lucia in Cuba

The film was released on October 12, 1968, less than two months after *Memories*. It showed in four Havana theaters and competed for audiences with other Cuban films that included *Memories* (Alea) and *The Adventures of Juan Quin Quin* (*Las Aventuras de Juan Quin Quin*, 1967, Espinosa) (*Cartelera*, Oct. 12 1968). Like *Memories, Lucia* was a film that was textually invested in the revolutionary hermeneutics. It was political, represented existence as confrontation, and narrated Cuba's history as a series of revolutions while exploring the lives of common women. The film was not the first Solás project exploring female characters in revolutionary settings. In 1966, he released *Manuela,* a film about a woman guerrilla fighter who gave her life for the struggle against Batista (Chanan 2004, 255).

Representing women's participation in the armed struggle was common during the 1960s. In 1968, while almost every magazine dedicated issues to Che Guevara's life, to commemorate his death, the popular magazine *Mujeres* published a number of articles about women guerrilla fighters. In 1960 *Mujeres* started offering an interesting mixture of feminist politics, current events, fashion, and cultural news. Women's participation was the emphasis in each of these areas, and this participation was always framed as revolutionary. In this tradition, the 1968 issues of the magazine included articles on Guevara, women's emancipation, hygiene, parenting, animated children's film, and cooking. The magazine's third number that year celebrated Tania La Guerrillera, a fighter who had become a popular icon and who was linked, in the mind of most Cubans, to Guevara (according to *Mujeres,* 1968). Tania and Che had fought together and, with Camilo Cienfuegos and Fidel and Raul Castro, were recurring figures in narratives of revolution.

Lucia began screening about the same time that *Mujeres* released the Tania La Guerrillera issue. Though the three Lucías are not, like Tania, guerrillas (women guerrilla fighters), they nonetheless are involved in revolutionary activities, linking them to Tania and to Che and making them proper objects of aesthetic reflection. To mark the historical appropriateness of the film, *Granma,* the newspaper that failed to review *Memories,* dedicated not one but two weeks to reviewing the film. In addition, during the second week after its release, *Granma* published an interview with Solás. In writing about the film, cultural workers applied the revolutionary hermeneutics that, since "Palabras," had worked under the principles of freedom in form and regulated content.

All the reviewers commented on Lucia's Cuban character, in being a national form of expression. They evaluated *Lucia* in relation to the revolutionary life it represented; they all highlighted how opposing oppressive forces (the domination of Spain, the government of Machado, and prerevolutionary sexist attitudes, respectively) and joining the battle was necessary ethical work for good citizens; they all saw the characters in relation to how close or how far these characters were from the ideal of the New Man. That the film gained international praise allowed reviewers to talk about the success the revolution had in fostering the institutional and cultural environment for the creation of works of international artistic merit. The film was "The Consecration of Cuban Cinema," according to *Cine Cubano,* and a landmark for the cinema of third world countries, according to Alfredo Guevara (Meyer 1970, 156; "Al Pie de la Letra" 1969, 142). There were also important differences in the reviews. One that stands out is the role the reviewer's sex played in determining the focus of the review. Men concentrated on the film's aesthetic elements and evaluated its quality in terms of Solás's success or failure at using highly innovative formal techniques to narrate the stories. Women concentrated on issues of gender and sex, investigating the fidelity with which the social world of the Lucías was represented.

For instance, the reviews by Daniel Díaz and Roberto Meyer characterized *Lucia* as art. For Meyer, *Lucia* was auterist cinema, while for Díaz, *Lucia* was a "work of art." Meyer compared it to the auteur works of Visconti, Kurosawa, Bergman, and Welles, while Díaz compared it to Bergman and Kawarerowicz. The directors' names hailed the cognoscenti and legitimized the reviews. But the readers of *Granma* and *Cine Cubano* inhabit a social world in which Cuban film has the responsibility to be truly Cuban, truly national. As a result, Meyer and Díaz linked *Lucia* to these directors but returned to the island and to the nation, claiming the film as a true expression of Cuba. For Meyer the film is "Cubanisimo," which is an expression that hyperbolizes its Cuban character. For Díaz, the film "has indicated the beginning of Our Cinema, with our character, where fiction has grafted its roots within the most profound of our idiosyncrasies" (Díaz 1968).

Díaz's long review addressed aesthetic and formal qualities, downplaying the ideological and historiographical elements of the film. "Lucía 1895," a story developed in more than an hour, was, according to Díaz, the best of the three stories. Of particular interest to Díaz were three powerful scenes, all of which included visual characteristics that denaturalize them and confer them with a great emotional content. These scenes are the most flawed ones in this section; yet they are, according to Díaz, the ones that show the directorial potential of Solás. For instance, Díaz asserts, a scene depicting a party involving a group of women sewing uniforms for the guerrilla army, which ends in a dance where the camera is circling the room, becomes a vertiginous scene that needed extra cutting. Yet, even though long, this scene, like the others, showed the explosive force of Díaz's formal treatments of national narratives. "Lucia 1932," Díaz comments, shows Solás's unusual sensibility for poetic language. Regardless, according to Díaz, this segment lacks the force of the first and third parts. Given that the historic reality that it narrated was uncomfortably close to 1968, Solás shied away from having a strong historical eye and making historical propositions. Instead, he produced a narrative with an ambiguous ending that foreclosed the possibility of organic wholeness. "Lucía 196 . . .", the last part, is hailed as having a stronger ideological transcendence because it dealt with current social problems: machismo and discrimination against women. Given that this episode was shot in a less affected way, in a neorealist style, without formal frivolities, Díaz's aesthetic evaluation is significantly briefer.

Meyer also interpreted *Lucia* as auteurist work and centered his evaluation and interpretation on the film's aesthetic elements. His position, however, is more political than Díaz's and exceeds Díaz's formalist analysis by questioning the film's successes and failures at using aesthetic elements to engage political issues. For instance, in the final scene of "Lucia 1895," in which Lucía stabs her lover to death for his betrayal, Meyer comments: "The lunacy and madness almost acquire the meaning of an acceptance of *conciencia*." (Meyer 1970). Hinting that a more desirable outcome to the story could have been a complete conscientization signals that those narrative conclusions were common and politically attractive. Meyer's review provides another example of revolutionary hermeneutics applied to film criticism. In his opinion, this segment concentrates too much on the exploration of private emotions to be able to represent history. In his interpretive framework, Meyer imagines history, particularly revolutionary history, a narrative better described by public actions and by multitudes. In contrast, "Lucia 196 . . .", Meyer's favorite segment, is didactic, light, and without complex formal arrangements to distract from the telling of the story (compare this to D'Lugo 1993). The apparent realism of the segment, which includes a less affected style of acting, is able to posit the ideological problems in its clearest light. This segment narrates the story of a truck driver who has joined the revolution yet forbids his wife Lucía from working and learning to read and write. "[I]t presents the inevitable frictions between the great social task and private lives not fully integrated into it, between the change of system and the most difficult change of mentality." Meyer's aestheticism reduces the film to a system of meanings, narrative strategies, and filmic devices able or unable to reflect or advance the political and ideological goals of the revolution.

The reviews by women, several of which were printed by *Cine Cubano* in 1969, are significantly different. The three I will comment on each covered one of the three segments of the film and did not center on aesthetic characteristics, but, rather, each reflected on the content of the narratives as it related to historical realities. This approach is evident from Camila Henríquez Ureña's first paragraph, where she states that *Lucia* deals with the lives of women and the social conditions in which these developed. "Lucía, the protagonist, is at the same time the Cuban woman interpreted in three epochs representative of her development . . ." (Henríquez Ureña 1969, 6). Compare this to Meyer, who had written that the film consisted of "complex analyses of feminine psychologies" (Meyer 1970, 156). Meyer's wording highlights the subjective and implies that there is something dark and perhaps even pathological about women's psyches. In contrast, Henríquez sees the piece as an examination of how Cuban women existed in specific social situations. For her, *Lucia* is an exploration of the relationship of women to society. Henríquez's review centers on the development of women and society and the social definition of love. Each vignette marks a historically specific stage of this development, and Solás parallels a diverse set of oppressions that function to determine the private destinies of women, the well-being of society, and the set of available gendered subjectivities. *Lucia* shows how women moved from being prisoners of suffocating public expectations of their private lives in 1895 to a more evolved being in the 1960s. This is a movement parallel to the rest of Cuban society, which develops from being a Spanish colony in

1895 to becoming a place where freedom and equality can exist. "Similarly to women, the society to which she belongs, fights to discover, define, and affirm the essence of its being" (Henríquez Ureña 1969, 6). Finally, love is transformed from a relationship in which women are subjected, to an equitable relationship. This transformation changes the subjective makeup of women and men by calling for a transformation in the meaning of masculinity and femininity. For Henríquez, following the ideas of Guevara, the revolution is a social structure that allows the existence of social equity and the development of women's true selves. *Lucia* then becomes a narrative that both shows the ideal relationship between people and society and that explains Cuba's present as the natural evolution of the country's historic trajectory.

Henríquez's style of reflecting on the film depends on an understanding of politics and oppression that is different from Meyer. Consider that when talking about "Lucia 1895," she does not blame Lucía for the killing of her brother, as Meyer suggests when he writes: "Restless spinster, asphyxiated by the family and bourgeois environment of fin de siècle, she gives herself to her boyfriend knowing that he is a snitch for the Spanish . . ." (Meyer 1970, 157). For Henríquez, Lucía's lack of political formation and the social pressures she experienced to secure a husband determine the tragic outcome. The type of *conciencia* that could have prevented this from happening was not available to Lucía and the women that surrounded her.

Renee Méndez Capote (1969) is an unusual commentator for the second vignette because she lived during the "Machadato," which is the historical context to "Lucia 1932," and she used her experiences to evaluate the historical accuracy of the segment. The Machadato refers to the period between 1925 and 1933 when Gerardo Machado was president of Cuba. Machado, a member of the ruling class, governed Cuba in a pro-American way and was supported by the United States even though he used blatant repression and violence against dissenting political forces (Pérez-Stable 1993, 39–40).

Méndez's use of autobiographical material to review (understand, interpret, comment on) or contextualize the film is a necessary occurrence because all epistemological, phenomenological, and hermeneutical frameworks are constituted through experiences. What sets her interpretations apart is that aside from the unconscious ways in which her past informed her present interpretation of the world (the film), she had to consciously put together some of her memories in a narrative form to use as evidence. This meant selecting among her memories those that better illustrated both the social reality that "Lucia

1932" addressed or represented and those memories that better illustrated her feelings and ideas regarding the movie. In either case, experiences would have to be narrativized in a coherent and rhetorically efficient way. Though her recalling and retelling cannot be assumed to be a truthful account of history, they evidence her understanding of the way her life had to be narrativized to fulfill the institutional requirements of ICAIC and *Cine Cubano*, the social requirements regarding her subject position as a woman vanguard, and her own personal ideas about how her self should be publicized (Giddens 1991, 53). In so doing, she shows herself a proper spokesperson for *Cine Cubano* and a proper reviewer of a film dealing with the revolution. This was accomplished by demonstrating her past and current political identities.

Méndez writes about a historical transition occurring in the 1930s in Cuba. Before and during the Machadato, she recalls, social, sexual, and gender conservatism were the norm, and most women had a limited range of options for their private and public lives. Marriage was the rule and working outside the home was considered improper. Méndez recalls what people use to say about women in the workforce: "No nurse enters my home; I cannot allow such whores into my home" (Méndez 1969, 9). The dictatorship of Machado and the ensuing social unrest changed some of the social structures around women, and some of these changes allowed for a more political identity and, even, freedom. "Some," Méndez comments, "like Lucía, arrived to [their own liberation] through love," while others arrived "to [their] liberation through the awakening of that conciencia." The economic collapse of Cuba during the 1930s, Méndez argued, resulted in more women joining the labor force, and this continued changing social expectations for women. Echoing Engels, Méndez states that the main cause for women's oppression and subsequent liberation was economic (12). Lucía is the product of this changing landscape and, given her personal and historical limitations, she is a proper revolutionary example.

Though linking women's oppression to economic factors was a way of properly performing a revolutionary identity, Méndez's own biography was more complex. In 1933, she was the director of the Beaux Arts, a public position of significant cultural and political influence that evidences wealth and privileged education. To balance this questionable datum, Méndez recalls that during the same year of 1933, she and her sister would economically help the wife of Juan Marinello every time he was arrested. Marinello is one of the key figures from the 1930s that the revolution has canonized as part of Cuba's leftist history. By mentioning Marinello's anecdote, Méndez conjures up a social affinity with the 1930s social and leftist causes and links her past to official history. Méndez's use of Marinello exemplifies the deep politicization that members of the vanguard had to show in public. It also suggests that politicizing one's biography could help gain social and cultural credibility. Knowledge, in particular historical knowledge, could be made proper by identifying the subject position from which it had been acquired.

Graziella Pogolotti (1969) reviewed "Lucia 196 . . ." using a contextual approach to the segment similar to Henríquez's, and highlighted the social and economic processes behind women's liberation. In her article, she created a narrative that places the revolution in the role of "savior of women." According to her, the revolution destroyed the economic and cultural inequalities that survived the Machadato. In spite of this, conventions and prejudices, such as machismo, which the bourgeoisie had spread to all social classes, survived. The revolution, therefore, had to strive to change both the public realities that were the foundation of gender inequalities and the private behaviors through which inequality survived. According to Pogolotti (and to most cultural workers affiliated with institutions), the revolution was the fuel of *Bildung;* the revolution was a pangenetic structure that transformed the material reality and the mental makeup of inequality.

Like Henríquez, Pogolotti used narrative techniques that in the United States have been associated with feminist writing. In addition to historicizing oppression, Pogolotti uses the personal experiences of women to match or contrast reality, as well as to explain or frame reality. In particular, she uses the life of Adela Legrá, the actress who plays Lucía in "Lucia 196 . . .", to give historical validity to the fictional narrative. It is the biography of Legrá, and its comparison to Lucía, that constitutes the core of Pogolotti's hermeneutics. In doing this, Pogolotti is investing on Legrá a star persona, making her a very peculiar source of ideological meaning making. According to Richard Dyer (1998, 8), film stars bring their personas (constructed through complex blends of biography and public discourses about the actor) to add rhetorical power to their roles. Because of this, Dyer believes that stars are particularly useful for understanding changing definitions of selfhood and, thus, changing historical contexts (30).

Pogolotti uses Legrá's biography to explain the rhetorical power of her role in *Lucia.* To do so, Pogolotti parallels Legrá's biography to the role she plays, arguing in the process for an authenticity in acting and on representation. That is, Legrá is the thing she represents, and "Lucia 196 . . ." becomes realistic through mimesis. She writes:

"Now you know how to read" they told Adela and at that time that was enough. At 14, she faced a decision "to either fall in the void or to marry." They offered her the opportunity of a better life. In Caimanera, with the nearby military base, a lot of women took that road. Adela continued studying, more or less on her own. At the beginning, her man does not place obstacles to her. Only to a limit, because "the woman mustn't know more than the man." She pushes him to continue improving himself. They collaborate in the clandestine fight. The man has the initiative and the woman cooperates. They hide people, give indications for taking the command center. The man loses his job at the base and they must leave town, and they began to work in the fields. The woman also works. It is necessary for the survival of all in harsh times and does not imply that she is emancipated (16).

Legrá eventually becomes involved with the revolution through the Literacy Campaign. Later, she helps harvest sugarcane and becomes an activist for the Federación de Mujeres (FMC). While Legrá is working for the FMC, Solás invites her to be the protagonist of his film *Manuela* and, later, one of the protagonists in *Lucia*. In Pogolotti's narrative of Legra's life and review of Solás's film, the relevance of these two discrete forms of reality, and what makes them proper objects for her reflection, is that a woman is at the center of both the fictional and real narrative and that these narratives share similar symbolic/social constraints. "How the woman-object becomes the protagonist of her own destiny" (17). Pogolloti, like Solás, narrativizes the transformation of women in concrete relation to the revolution, and like Solás's filmmaking, her writing is highly emotional, inspirational, and liberating, a style that implicates the reader's rational and emotional structures. Pogolotti finds in Legrá's life a process of concientization similar to the awakening Lucía experiences in the film. From subject to actor, this trajectory follows similar steps: 1) Legrá and Lucia experience the impact of the 1961 Literacy Campaign. 2) Voluntary labor. In the case of Legrá, this happens when she joins the FMC. Lucía experiences it by rejecting the prohibition against work. Lucía joins the revolution, participating with her back-breaking work at a salt mine. 3) Both women participate in the defense of the germinal society. And finally, 4) the transformation of these women is not presented as isolated, for they both transform the institutions that defined them.

Returning to Dyer, Pogolotti's use of Legrá is indicative of a change in representations of selfhood and a change in the way Cuban women could become part of the public sphere. Just like Marilyn Monroe's stardom speaks to a kind of condensation of concerns about 1950s sexuality in the United States, Legrá's is ideal for speaking about the new social expectations placed on women, including their new roles in changing labor markets, the new educational expectations, and their growing ability to represent ideal citizens.

Lucia in the United States

Like *Memories,* the political interference of the State Department in the First New York Cuban Film Festival in March 1972 affected the critical reception of *Lucia.* It was during the screening of *Lucia,* the only film shown during the festival, when anti-Castro activists released white mice to disrupt the event. The next day's press commented on the unusual conditions of exhibition and failed to review the film. Because the State Department shut down the festival that evening, audiences never saw *Lucia* in a full and uninterrupted fashion until March 1974 (Rist 1985). The film's interpretation began when Michael Myerson released the book *Memories of Underdevelopment: The Revolutionary Films of Cuba* (1973), in which he wrote an extensive interpretation of *Lucia,* and continued in several liberal newspapers, magazines, and specialized film media.

Despite playing such prominent roles in political struggles, and unlike *Memories,* the discourses of censorship and communism were not strong frameworks for the interpretation of *Lucia.* Because *Memories* had set a precedent for Cuban film, because *Lucia* was reviewed mostly in specialized magazines and journals, and because the film dealt with the theme of gender relations, a theme that in 1974 was common in U.S. public culture, the film was interpreted mostly in relation to its textual characteristics, such as aesthetics, representation of women, and genre. This is not to say that communism (or Marxism) and ethnocentrism were not important themes in the reviews; like in *Memories,* these two themes helped framed the expectations regarding aesthetic, gender representation, and genre. However, while in *Memories* these notions were used to criticize Cuba's political system, in *Lucia,* similar concepts and their uses hinted of sympathies toward Cuba and its political ideatic systems. Instead of being surprised at the quality and courageousness of the film, the reviewers employed Marxist terminology to understand and to praise its textual characteristics.

Marxism provided the language to describe characters and situations, including the ideas of social struggle and class conflict. Myerson (1973) sees each Lucía as the representative of a class: Lucía in 1895 belonged to the "landowning class whose national interests gave rise to the independence movement against Spain" (115). Lucía in 1932 represented the petit bourgeoisie of the business class in Cuba. Lucía in the 1960s was the working class. Nora Sayre (1974), Molly Haskell (1974), Peter Biskind (1974), and Meg Matthews (1974), and Marjorie Rosen (1980) and Rist (1985) in the 1980s, also analyze the characters based on the class of each Lucía. When seen through the eyes of class, *Lucia* becomes a statement about the development of historically situated subjectivities as they are determined by class. Biskind (1974) describes Lucía in 1895 as a victim of the class and gender conventions of the time. Fearful of remaining a spinster, "She abandons herself to a grand passion, to a myth of romantic self-fulfillment . . . which is derivative in its way of a bygone Byronism, as the finery of her class is imitative of Paris fashions" (7).

Sayre, Haskell, Myerson, Biskind, Rose, and Rist use class in two ways. First, class provided a unifying logic that brought together the three parts of *Lucia*, giving characters a common rationale for behavior and relationships. The clearest examples were behaviors exhibited by the Lucías and their male partners. In 1895, Myerson (1973) writes, Lucía belonged to the class that promoted the revolution against Spain, and she behaved accordingly. For instance, with her friends, Lucía helped produce uniforms for the revolutionary army, to which her brother belonged. In 1932, Biskind (1974) suggests, Lucía's reaction against her comfortable yet banal bourgeois status was the background for her adventures with Aldo, her revolutionary lover. In the 1960s, Lucía's peasant background explained both her illiteracy and her desire to be a hard worker for the revolution. In each of these cases, class determines the way the Lucías relate to social structures. This is not to say that the characters are perceived to be one-dimensional and facile. Except for Matthews, in these leftist reviews *Lucia*'s representation of subjectivities is explained as fragmented and thus likely to occupy conflicting and even contradictory social spaces. As Myerson points out, "Lucia 1895" belonged to the class that promoted the Spanish revolution, yet Lucía inhabited class and gender systems that made her prone to, as Biskind suggests, romantic passions and catastrophic decisions. Biskind (1974) also comments on "Lucia 1932" as a paradoxical character on the one hand, motivated to action by a desire for liberation; on the other hand, she consistently allowed Aldo, her male partner, to do the talking, the fighting, and the dying (8). In Tomás, the husband of Lucía in the 1960s, Biskind also finds contradictions, for this character was incapable of addressing the impossibility of simultaneously being a revolutionary and a chauvinist male.

In the majority of these reviews, economic and gender-based class categories underscored the reviewer's leftist tendency to believe that a film out of Cuba would present historical change as the result of collective or class action engendered within oppressive economic and ideological structures. Such tendency is in opposition to the liberal and conservative custom of narrativizing and interpreting history in terms of the moral and heroic deeds of individuals. Reviewers found in *Lucia* the opposite of a liberal hero: the deeds of individuals, however heroic, were presented as the products of the types of consciousness available to them in that particular historic time. According to Colin Westerback, the film shows how "history raises the level of consciousness and makes revolution inevitable" (1974, 110). Commenting also on the relationship between self and history, Biskind (1974) writes: "Each Lucía is the locus of intersection between large social changes and sharply perceived personal needs. Each makes choices whose sources are at once public and private" (8). The viewer was thus taught a lesson in Marxist historiography by showing the futility of trying to evade history and take refuge in the self. Besides historiography, John Mraz (1978) suggests that the viewer of *Lucia* is also given a lesson in Marxist aesthetics. This was so because *Lucia* explored the interconnection of perception and history. In an attempt to represent the different ways in which different characters perceived reality in different periods, Mraz argues that Solás strategically used "conflicting visual styles." For Cuban filmmakers, perception was, Mraz comments, "an expression of an individual's historical context" (21). Because *Lucia* used class and collective action as unifying narrative forces, some writers hailed the film as a clearly Marxist text (for example, Biskind 1974, 8). Critics like Hatch (1974) commented (using what sounds like a liberal critique of Marxism) that the film showed an awareness of its didactic goal, and this threatened its overall depiction of human nature (110).

Marxist interpretations were possible because several of these reviews were published in leftist and academic media like *Jump Cut* and *Cineaste*. These journals typically issue cultural critiques of the field of power and the entertainment industry. Even more common than strictly Marxist reviews were feminist interpretive tactics. Because *Lucia* had female central characters in each of the three segments, it was easy for American reviewers to associate the narratives with women's lives, the system of gender, patriarchy, and women's participation in history. As commented in the previous chapter, these elements had been part of feminist criticism since Kate Millet's *Sexual Politics*

(1969). However, simply using some of these elements has never amounted to feminist criticism. In fact, the reviewers of *Lucia* used a significant degree of latitude in the application of these ideas. Three main styles of gendered reviewing are evident: The first interprets women's lives and gender oppression through the framework of Marxism. The second is noncommittal in that it uses gender to criticize Cuba's communism but fails to bring complexity to its analysis of gender oppression. The third style is women-centered and, in at least one of the reviews, embodies a significant amount of the hermeneutic principles of radical feminism.

Myerson and Biskind offer examples of Marxist feminist interpretation. Both are sympathetic to women's struggles but assume that the revolution and Marxism would provide solutions to the problem of gender. Myerson (1973), given his familiarity with the Cuban Revolution, was able to present a brief history of women in Cuba where he emphasizes the economic changes the revolution brought to women (111–14). Myerson uses several Marxist codes to interpret the film and explain the type of gender subjectivities in terms of class oppression. He does not elaborate at all on the constitution of gender as a discrete system of oppression; instead, he comments on the social and economic oppression of women and on masculinity. Ultimately, Myerson suggests that *Lucia*'s lessons are that gender mores are more ingrained than social mores, that both are intertwined, and that the solutions to gender inequalities depend on the transformations facilitated by the revolution. In interpreting the narrative in this way, Myerson is not very different from the Cubans' interpretations of the film and the Cubans' reliance on Engel's theories of gender.

Biskind (1974), echoing Myerson, interprets the film by blending Marxist and feminist concerns. In describing the film, he argues that each segment "chronicles a stage in a . . . struggle: for the personal liberation of the individuals from restrictive roles imposed by class and sex, for the decolonization and transformation of Cuba" (7). According to Biskind, each of the segments shows that the root of each character's problems is gender and sexual characteristics and that these must be subsumed to public progressive structures, in particular, the revolutionary impulse. "Each makes choices whose sources are at once public and private, but it is a testimony to the honesty of this film that political changes . . . are often more easily made than transformations of deeply ingrained cultural and social attitudes which directly oppress individuals, especially women" (8). Contrary to radical feminisms of the time, Biskind removes sexuality and gender from the political, defining them as private, cultural oppressions. By rejecting the radical notion that the "personal is political," Biskind shows that his feminism is one infused with old-style Marxism (not the New Left but the old Left) and thus at odds with 1970s feminisms.

Given that Biskind and Myerson are quite complimentary of the film, we can assume that they approve of the way *Lucia,* according to them, privileges class over gender. Hence, their reviews rely on ambivalent interpretive tactics. These cultural workers seem to be drafting a space within the cultural field from where they can utter declarations of independence from the field of power. Yet, from this same space they issue critiques of feminists who believe that gender and sex may be materially based but are uniquely constructed through history. For these feminists, among whom I include myself, privileging class over gender and sex is a dangerous political strategy because it can nullify the specificity of feminist claims.

Other ambivalences are found in reviewers who believed the film reduced the revolution to sexual liberation. Westerback (1974) observed this in the last segment of the film: "In effect this *is* the revolution. It is to give this girl the courage and the right to defy her husband that the other Lucías suffer violence, betrayal and bereavement" (109). Matthews (1975), who did not share Westerback's neutral reaction to this aspect of the film, complained that in the film, "Marxism working through history seems reduced to the struggle of a woman against the privileges of men" (310). The ambivalence here is constituted again by the use of a Marxist framework that places these reviewers as critics of the field of power, but does so at the expense of levying criticisms toward feminism. These ambivalences construct political transformation as the result of either challenging class structures, which are public, or challenging gender structures, which are private. By constructing this either/or, these writers imagine a world where we ought to choose between a socialist and a feminist revolution. Thus, either feminism is the revolution, or the class revolution should precede gender change.

Sayre's, Haskell's, and Rosen's reviews have a more clearly feminist approach to interpretation. For Sayre (1974), the "extraordinary" *Lucia* "focuses on three generations of women whose lives reflect the society around them." For Rosen (1980), the film is a "woman's picture" that "attempts a virtually impossible task—to artistically integrate its heroines' emotional lives with the political fabric in which they live." For Haskell (1974), the film is the first "goshamamy feminist film in 1974." These writers are not interested in simplistically celebrating the film; in fact, they are quite critical of the way the Lucías were represented. Rosen (1980) observes, cynically, how, for instance, Lucía in 1895 is fooled by her suitor when "she agrees to rendezvous at a coffee plantation which is—whoops—the guerrilla hideout; his deception and everyone's tragedy follow" (29). She is also dissatisfied with the second segment, a story that portrayed Lucía always physically and ideologically following her partner, Aldo. For Haskell (1974), "Lucía 1895" is "apparently rendered even more useless (Marxism or Sexism?) by the absence of men who are off fighting Spain." Sayre (1974) comments of the same segment that "The women have been directed to flutter and squeal until they appear like a parody of winsome maidenhood."

What makes Rosen's, Haskell's, and Sayre's reviews a different brand of feminism from that previously commented on is their political radicalism and their awareness that feminism, as a theoretical and social practice, ought to be able to construct multilayered politics of dissention. The film is measured against a complex set of political structures, including socially gendered constraints, economic dependencies, and sexual repressions. These structures are external *and* internal to the subject. Instead of criticizing *Lucia* for its inability to tell a cogent story, a valuation that Hatch (1974) used, these reviewers criticize it for the inability of the female characters to be freethinkers and for their tendencies to follow the men. They also clearly expect that the characters would be more reluctant to abandon themselves to the system of gender, and they even wish the Lucías challenged prejudicial aspects of femininity. Rosen (1980) writes of "Lucia 1895" in a way that betrays her desire: "Lucia . . . makes blankets and shirts for her brother and other revolutionaries, but drops everything, even her discretion, when a suitor comes calling." Femininity blocks Lucía's political commitment and, Rosen interprets, the system of gender has so weakened Lucía that she is incapable of having consistency of character; she drops everything to respond to the call of love. Rosen (1980) expresses a similar desire to see representations of women as agents when she comments of "Lucia 1932" : "Only with her husband's needless death does she, now pregnant, stumble into an awareness of her powerlessness" (29). Rosen uses the verb "stumble" to signal how little agency the film provides Lucia and how much historical events and social conventions direct the characters.

These female reviewers' expectations, their desire to see characters that show the type of individualism that they embrace, do not stop them from clearly voicing their support for the film. Like other feminist critics, Sayre,

Haskell, and Rosen appreciate the fact that *Lucia* dealt with women's lives. But the reason they so complimentarily label the film as "extraordinary," "goshamamy feminist film of 1974," or a "woman's picture" has more to do with the manner in which Solás represented the Lucía's subjection to the systems of gender and sex than with the fact that the film was composed of stories of women. "What Solás does display," Rosen (1980) reflects, "is compassion for their anguish, whether this anguish be in the (too-melodramatic) hysteria of Lucia I, . . . [sic] or in the pain working Lucia II's anxious, lovely face like a plow." Rosen also comments that Solás may have represented passive women, but at least their passivity "may be history's fault, not (just) his" (30). Haskell (1974), though highly critical of the film, redeems Solás when she states that "he has a feeling for his heroines." Also, she comments, he restrained himself from filming voyeuristically the rape scene in "Lucia 1895," a feat, I presume, not normally achieved by male directors. Of "Lucia 196 . . .," Sayre (1974) writes that "it's the best discussion of equality (and inequality) I've seen on screen." Though the three writers do not agree on the same points, the director's treatment of the characters and his willingness to represent them with compassion vindicate him.

A final interpretive axe was genres associated with women, in particular the melodrama and the love story. Hatch (1974), who issued an almost sexist review, criticized the film for the highly dramatic tone of "Lucia 1895." According to him, "The emotional highjinks that embellish this tale are so counterproductive that the audience guffaws during moments of the most graphically portrayed spiritual torment." His criticism was for Solás, for not being able to imagine high drama during the late 1800s. However, Hatch's own commentaries seemed to originate from an Anglocentric perspective that imagines all nineteenth- and twentieth-century romanticism to be British and not the Latin American or Spanish romanticism, and that imagines the use of melodrama to be always retrograde. Benito Pérez Galdos, the Spanish author, and Alejo Carpentier, the Cuban novelist, are clear examples of the type of baroque romantic style that could be proper to Spanish-ruled Cuba. Moreover, as Ana López (1985) has argued, New Latin American Cinema has embraced melodrama as a way of facilitating the critical apprehension of narratives by the general public (4). Stark (1975) reduced *Lucia* to three love stories. In clear opposition to Hatch, who disliked the first Lucía for its overdramatic tone, Stark preferred that segment for the same reasons that Hatch disliked it. The director's take on drama was, she claimed, "impressive," as was the acting.

Moreover, Stark complimentarily declared that Racquel Revuelta, who played Lucia in 1895, was a "stunning figure of a woman." Though defining *Lucia* as a triptych composed of three love stories hardly does justice to the film, compared to Stark's gendered taste, Hatch's taste borders on the chauvinist. However, that Revuelta is described first in relation to her physical appearance suggests that Stark was using a sexual system of interpretation where women's bodies, and not their ethical or intellectual characteristics, were at the center. Gilliatt (1974), writing in *The New Yorker,* also interprets the film in terms that highlight its romantic aspects, describing it in a manner that resembles a sarcastic fairy tale. "Lucia 1895" is, for instance, overwhelmed by a "handsome stranger" who can "obviously [feel] he can deal with her suffocating girlish confidences." "Lucia 1932" is also sarcastically described. The end of the review exemplifies this tone when she writes: "Love is betrayed because Aldo, Lucía, and unmet others are on their own in refusing to comply with the comfortable." In each of these instances, gender and genre collide, providing basic schemas that reduce the film to melodrama or love story.

Comparing the Critical Reception of *Lucia*

Examining *Lucia*'s Cuban critical reception lends some quick and important insights. There was a clear distinction between men's and women's reviews. The men emphasized the aesthetic aspects of *Lucia,* judging it mostly in terms of artistic merit and linking it to European art film. For them, *Lucia* was revolutionary because it dealt with Cuba's revolutionary past *and* because it established a distinctive revolutionary, national aesthetic. Because of this emphasis, Meyer, Cossio, and Díaz performed their public selves in reference to ideas of professionalism that defined film criticism as a type of reflection on form, aesthetic traditions, and general social themes. Very differently, the female critics were interested in *Lucia* for its historical representations of Cuba's gendered past, and as testimony of women's sacrifices during revolutionary periods. If Henríquez, Méndez, and Pogolotti deemed the film revolutionary, they did so because the film educated viewers about women's lives and participation in Cuban history, and because the film illustrated a more complex, because more gendered, notion of social and economic oppression. The importance the female reviewers attached to a reality behind the fictionalized narratives is underscored by their attention to the historical accuracy of the three Lucías and to the way social theories of gender were woven into each review. These writers fulfilled their professional tasks by performing their (revolutionary) gender, highlighting those things that concerned them as gendered and sexed individuals. Thus, issues of accuracy were more important than whether the film resembled Godard's work, and the stories narrated were more relevant than arguing that the film was truly Cuban. Moreover, the methods used to carry out their writings did not rely on a "mastery" of cinema, but relied on personal experiences, autobiography, and feminist Marxist theory.

In the United States, *Lucia* received different treatments than *Memories*. Though the reviews of *Memories* were often used to criticize Cuba, *Lucia* was reviewed by critics more sympathetic to the revolution and who knew the film was clearly revolutionary. These sympathies were evident by their use of Marxist hermeneutic to describe and interpret the film. These reviewers highlighted class and oppression as heuristic tropes and emphasized *Lucia* as a filmic text that presented specific Marxist ideas about history: to these reviewers, historical change was represented as the result of collective action. Similar to Cuban female reviewers, other American critics used gender and feminism to access the film's narrative, sometimes employing Marxist tools. To the Marxists, the problem of gender was one that could be solved with a class revolution and the application of general principles of material egalitarianism. Not everyone embraced this Engels-influenced Marxist feminism. Other critics used radical and liberal feminisms to describe the characters and their motivations and to evaluate general plot developments in relation to feminist standards. The Lucías, for instance, were thus praised or criticized depending on whether they showed women having characteristics such as intelligence, independence, and awareness of oppression. Often, these reviewers praised Solás for at least allowing the female characters to be presented as the product of history.

There are other significant points of contact between Cuban and U.S. critics, when considered by sex. Male critics in both nations tended to use aesthetic and formal characteristics to compliment or denigrate the film. In Cuba, *Lucia* exemplified a national aesthetics; in the United States, the worst of melodrama. Aesthetics here serves as a framing tactic that allows male critics to establish properly gendered filmic expertise while constructing a socially acceptable distance from the film's subject. By focusing on the abstract notion of a national aesthetics, a critic can mask his unwillingness (or inability) to understand the film from the point of view of the subjects represented. By using the cliché of castigating films for belonging to genres deemed unworthy (genres associated with women and Latin Americans), the critic asserts his taste and sophistication while keeping his distance from the social and historical elements of the plots.

That the male Cuban critics favored the film and that some of the Americans so harshly criticized it speaks to national differences. For the Cubans, the film was self-representation. To some of the Americans, the film was evidence of cultural and racial otherness, a poorly staged melodrama. Similar national differences are also at play in the way feminism was used in Cuba and the United States. The Cubans, publishing in *Cine Cubano,* were always on the side of Lucía's prorevolutionary stance. For Solás (as evidenced in the triptych's progression), the revolution was also a struggle against sexism. The critics corroborated this stance and performed their roles as vanguard by declaring the existence of past sexual injustices and by placing hope in a revolutionary future. Feminist American critics, by contrast, praised the film but understood it as evidence of an ongoing struggle over sexual structures and their intersections with power structures. For instance, because a man directed this women's film, some reviewers noticed a relative lack of sexual reflexivity, as in Solás's decision to portray women who were only partially independent. In these comments, the issue was not only the film text (and its treatment of sexuality and gender) but the Cuban film world: a power organization stratified sexually that made it reasonable to produce pro-women projects without women in power.

Chapter 7

One Way or Another

De Cierta Manera (*One Way or Another*, 1977), directed by Sara Gómez, extensively mixes a fictional narrative with documentary footage and the lives of real Cubans. The narrative, which develops at the beginning of the revolution, tells the story of Mario and Yolanda as they become romantically involved. Mario, a mulatto from Havana's poor shantytown, faces challenges at work because of his relationship to Humberto (Mario Limonta), who has asked Mario to lie on his behalf so that he can justify a lengthy work absence. Humberto is having an affair with a woman who lives in another city. Mario is divided between his responsibilities as a friend and his civic duties. Yolanda, a middle-class schoolteacher, is also in a process of learning. She works at a school attended by poor and at times undisciplined children, and she must learn to deal with her students' difficult lives if she is to become a good teacher, and she must also learn to take criticism if she is to become a good revolutionary teacher. Yolanda and Mario struggle with their values. Mario, supported by Yolanda, decides to act ethically and accuses Humberto of taking advantage of the system. Yolanda struggles more to change her values. The ending shows the couple conversing in the middle of a newly constructed housing project. The fictional narrative is mixed with documentary footage about Abakuá religion, an Afro-Cuban spiritual tradition exclusive for men; footage depicting the demolition of a shantytown in Havana; and interviews with a Cuban fighter who became a songwriter.

One Way in Cuba

One Way has the distinction of being the only feature fictional film directed by a woman in Cuba. This fact provides strong context to the film's reception, and its importance is illustrated by the actions the Cuban cultural workers took to highlight it. Most of the issue 52–53 of *Cine Cubano,* the main film journal in Cuba, was dedicated to *One Way,* and it featured reviews by three women critics: Elena Díaz, Camila Henríquez Ureña, and Gabriela Pogolotti. Echoing the struggles for transformation represented and narrativized by *Lucia, Cine Cubano* (and ICAIC) appears here as an institution in search of *conciencia,* struggling to move away from preconceived gender notions. Before I continue, it is necessary to draw a couple of points that illustrate ICAIC's relationships to women as cultural workers. This will help contextualize how women, sex, and gender were affected by institutional practices, including the use of women, sex, and gender as objects of aesthetic reflection.

Women have been involved in ICAIC since its creation in 1959, but their involvement has been stratified by gender expectations. This has meant that women occupied positions related to stereotypical gender roles or, when women held nontypical jobs, that their presence was seen as extraordinary. Carmelina García, for instance, in ICAIC since 1959, was in charge of the costume department, and, not surprisingly, her department employed mostly women ("El Cine las Decidió," 1974). That this type of work was where many women could be found is not surprising. It fits neatly with social expectations of women and their labor. But even the conditions for this occupation were seen as too harsh for women. García herself defined the work in sexed and gendered terms. In an interview with *Mujeres* in 1974, she commented: "[The work] has a schedule difficult for women. The production work in costumes sometimes requires living outside the home for up to three months, and living in tents and in the outdoors. Besides tailoring, the woman has to enjoy cinema" (47). The first part of her comments is a statement to the reality that women in Cuba were (and still are) largely expected to take care of the family. But the last part of the commentary uses a language suggesting that women are incapable of enduring the same challenges as men (by living in tents) and that they are incapable of committing to the same schedules.

The realities within ICAIC did not seem conducive to women's work. Rebeca Valdéz, a laboratory technician who specialized in 35mm film, and who studied in Prague, was part of a group of technical personnel that, in 1963, included several women. By the end of the 1960s, the only woman who remained in that department was Valdéz. In reading about the way women were recruited by ICAIC, it is evident that sexism was common and was expressed by emphasizing the special hardships that a woman would have to endure to survive the job. For instance, Marta Planas, a young woman being trained by and for the film-printing laboratory of ICAIC, recalls that "From the first day they told us that the job at the lab was hard for a woman, and that we should think about it." Though she does not recall any blatant rejection by the rest of the (mostly male) lab workers, they expressed surprise at her involvement in the training and at her ambition to become a lab worker.[1]

Sara Gómez was one of the few women directors at ICAIC and one of the early products of ICAIC's training. She became involved with the institution in 1961 and throughout the 1960s worked as an assistant director for Tomás Gutiérrez Alea, Jorge Fraga, and Agnes Varda. Also during the 1960s, Gómez began directing her own projects. As was expected from all the trainees at ICAIC, she began working on documentaries and directed ten in roughly a decade. ICAIC's leaders believed that documentary training was essential to develop filmmakers' understanding of their social role, and also to develop the filmic and narrative techniques that could later be used to produce feature films.

Gómez's identity is key to understanding the themes and film aesthetics of *One Way* as well as the way her work was later commented upon. As an Afro-Cuban woman and as someone who repeatedly filmed issues of popular culture, Gómez brought a unique perspective to her first and only feature film. The film touched on the problems of gender, race, and class and did so using narrative devices that questioned the separation between fiction and nonfiction. In exploring these themes and the narrative potential of the fiction/nonfiction dialectic, she acted on her beliefs regarding the role of film in society. Gómez stated: "Cinema, for us, is inevitably partial, determined by a *toma de conciencia,* the result of a definite attitude in the face of the problems which confront us, of the necessity to decolonize ourselves politically and ideologically, and of breaking with radical values, be they economic, ethical, or aesthetic" (Gómez in Chanan 2004, 306).

If the critics' sex worked to differentiate interpretations of *Lucia,* cinema as an analytical tool and a decolonizing force became the aspects that catalyzed reviewers of *One Way.* Each of the reviews evaluated and valorized the film in terms of how it represented and explored reality, and how it investigated real contemporary social problems. Framing the film as a project aimed at producing knowledge fitted well with the changing role science and theory played in Cuban cultural communities during the 1970s. Heavily influenced by Althusser's work, Cuban discourses on culture and politics had changed from an emphasis on praxis to one on science and philosophy (Althusser 1971, 127–86, 171, 175). This accounted for the relationship between ideology and epistemology as proposed by Althusser. Given his unusual insights on the role Marxist theory should play in the analysis of ideology, and an increasing awareness of the difficulty in transforming certain ideologies common to Cubans (such as sexism and work attitudes), evaluating cultural work in terms of scientific discourse constituted a step forward in cultural criticism. In addition, this approach provided a bridge to past cultural policies that understood film as educational.

Although *Memories* and *Lucia* were accepted as examples of good, responsible revolutionary filmmaking (*Memories* a bit later than *Lucia*), they both were partially criticized by reviewers. This was not the case with *One Way or Another*. All of the reviews were positive and none mentioned any negative elements of the film. This is partly because Sara Gómez was an Afro-Cuban woman who had died in 1974, before the film was released. These factors were highlighted by reviewers and made it practically impossible to criticize the film or to criticize her decisions as a filmmaker. Additionally, the film could also be interpreted as a scientific endeavor. As such, *One Way* was seen less as an attempt to create reality than as an attempt to explain and problematize it.

I imagine that reviewers assigned Gómez's film might have known from the outset that they could not comment negatively. The reviewer's duty then became to find an interpretive framework that would allow her/him to compliment director and film. Because of its sparse, documentary-like aesthetics, its themes, and the tropes that denaturalized the film's fictive status, *One Way* could be interpreted as a successful application of science to filmmaking. For instance, Carlos Galiano (1977), reviewing in *Granma*, refers to the film as a "sociological analysis of marginalization and its manifestations in the psychological, moral, and cultural behavior of those who had been marginalized before the Revolution." Also, according to Gerardo Chijona, Gómez's film "reveals and analyzes in depth the conflict between old cultural habits found in marginalization."

Each review framed the film in terms of its relationship to reality, and this became central to its interpretation. I place an emphasis on this aspect of the reviews because the idea of science interpenetrated Cuban culture and institutions in such a way that it became one of the main means of organizing and presenting knowledge. For instance, in my research about cultural institutions, I found an overabundance of essays that spoke about cultural development in numeric terms. These reports would make culture into a quantifiable realm and, in so doing, would rely on citing the number of books published, the number of art schools, and so on. This emphasis on science was common in other New Latin American cinematic traditions and was patently at work in the classic films like *The Brickmakers (Chircales,* d. Marta Rodríguez and Jorge Silva, 1972) and *Pixote* (1982, d. Hector Babenco). *The Brickmakers,* like other films by Rodríguez and Silva, is an "anthropological investigation" in filmic format (West and West 1993). The documentary directly connects to Rodríguez's academic dissertation. In *Pixote,* Babenco, echoing Gómez, based his script on sociological investigations of homeless youth in Brazil.[2]

The reviewers inscribed the film into the scientific method, in particular as the method applied to sociology. The briefest of reviews, Galiano's, published October 22, 1977, two weeks after the film opened on Havana's new release circuits, interprets *One Way* through a revolutionary hermeneutic and the scientific method to give praise to "Sarita" and to the film. He argues that *One Way or Another* educates the viewer about the roots of social marginalization by providing an analysis of the effects of wide social structures on individuals. According to Galiano, the film uses documentary footage of the demolition of a poor Havana neighborhood as an allegory for the decolonization individuals must undergo in order to become true revolutionaries. Mario, one of the central characters, is presented as caught between two realities, one of which he must choose. The prerevolutionary macho and abusive past is represented through the character of Mario's friend Humberto, who tries to pull him back toward more traditional attitudes. Mario and Humberto are the products of similar poverty-stricken backgrounds where machismo is the rule and taking advantage of the revolution is common. The old self, Galiano continues, is destined "to be extinguished in the same way the old socioeconomic order was." Mario's motivation for this social and personal change is represented in the character of Yolanda, who has sacrificed her privileges for the revolution and now works, not without conflicts, in a poor neighborhood. Her romantic relationship with Mario gives moral support to his steps toward development and functions, Galiano observes, to establish a dialogue between both characters. Though the film's final resolution is ambiguous, Galiano believes that Gómez's sense of optimism in the process of social and personal transformation is evident precisely by ending the film with a dialogue between Yolanda and Mario. It is left open, suggesting that continuous dialogue is key to the processes of transformation.

The same scenes of building demolition that Galiano saw as allegories are, according to Chijona, explanatory devices used as specific kinds of argumentation. He is as interested as Galiano in explaining the film as science, but he sees the use of nonfictional and fictional footage as an analytic strategy aimed at explaining the personal and subjective experiences of the fictional characters resulting from general social structures such as urbanization (the demolition scenes), religion (Gómez uses footage of the Abakuá religion to illustrate points on traditional macho culture), poverty, and crime. Chijona explains: "Inserting documentary footage and testimonies in a fictional story, *One Way or Another* presents an interesting narration that, on the one hand, introduces us to a world authentically human, while at the same time it gives us the analytic elements to explain the behaviors—static and evolutive—of the different characters" (104). According to Chijona, Gómez uses these two narrative styles as complementary lines of argumentation that together better explain one reality. This reality is manifested at the general and particular levels where the general and particular are dialectically interrelated.

Chijona's rationalistic interpretation of the film's formal characteristics suggests a belief in a type of revolutionary aesthetic that is only marginally related to continental Marxist aesthetics and is a departure from the otherwise popular Brechtian aesthetics. At the time, Marxist aesthetics was heavily influenced by poststructuralism, and Screen theory was becoming popular in Europe and the North American continent. More in line with the Althusser of "A letter on Art to André Daspre" and with Lacanian psychoanalysis, Marxist aesthetics of the time was heir to a tradition that understood art's liberatory potential in terms of art's ability to exceed reason. Brecht belonged to this tradition. Thus understood, film had the potential to decolonize only when it went beyond the tradition that engendered it, and when it allowed for a reflection, as Althusser (1971) would state, "of the ideology to which [the film] allude[d]" (222).

Chijona (n.d.) clearly saw *One Way or Another* as a film that educated viewers. In his view, fiction and nonfiction are two ways of explaining reality that complement each other. Unlike Brechtian aesthetics, fiction and nonfiction were not used to show the ideology that engendered the film or to question the boundaries of fiction and of realism. As two types of arguments, mixing fiction and nonfiction gave the film a greater educational power than that of a straight documentary. "Because the cold documentary analysis is not enough to elicit a reflection on the theme of misery and ignorance of marginal people . . . what gives validity and efficacy to this operation [in the film] is the way in which these social factors insert themselves into the anecdote" (105). The success of the narrative relied on giving a human expression to those external factors, and in showing how difficult it was to eliminate the burden of the past. Chijona saw the film's biggest social and aesthetic values in its use of popular culture to show the difficulties of decolonization.

Decolonization was central also to Rigoberto López's essay on *One Way or Another* published in *Cine Cubano*. According to him, decolonization was necessary for Cuba's development and a necessary step toward socialism. He explained decolonization as "the organized violence of oppressed people to gain independence; the violence thereafter to transform society and to transform the individual" (No. 93, 107). Decolonization was an ideological struggle that depended for its success on analyzing "the particular of this fight in areas of our national reality." This is what, according to López, the film addressed.

When looked at in relation to the revolutionary hermeneutics, decolonization, as a discursive, theoretical, and ethical construct, became central to the discursive hermeneutic efficacy of the revolution. The concept (or discourse) of decolonization encompassed a cultural goal that is similar to the maxim "Revolutionary film and art must educate." It also aided the recognition that culture was political, film was transformative, and the vanguard should be exemplary through self-negation. It helped support the thesis that the proper aesthetics is transformative and that it should be an exploration of national culture that can generate *conciencia*. Thus, given the importance of the idea of decolonization, López was giving Gómez's film the highest honors in claiming that it decolonizes.

According to López, Gómez understood the problem of marginalization in contemporary Cuba because she had dealt with it personally (as a black woman) and professionally (by filming ten documentaries roughly dealing with the issue). Gómez was aware "of the conflict between the survival of inherited values" in marginal communities "and of the cultural and ideological values that socialism transforms and engenders" (109). Continuing his praise for Gómez's work, López elaborated on the aforementioned problem in great detail, and because of the weight he gave to this aspect of the film, I will briefly review his words.

The problem of marginalization is one that, for López, carries a huge weight in a neocolonial society such as Cuba. Marginalized groups are unique in that they have maintained strong traditions regardless of the cultural domination of Spain and the United States. Given the importance of these traditions for the identity of these groups, their traditions have become hardened over time and are particularly difficult to extricate. Thus, it is not surprising to find these traditional values still surviving within socialism, even if they are deemed unethical or reactionary. Machismo is one of such sets of values that can be found in Abakuá society, which contradicts the revolutionary belief in the equality of men and women. All of this underscores the necessity to investigate marginal groups in Cuba, but to do it without rejection or ideological antipathy *a la petit bourgeois* for those marginal people. Science, López argues, echoing Althusser, must guide these approaches.

One Way contributed to the goals of the revolution by investigating and challenging the ethical values of marginalization. It did so, López states, by abandoning "traditional aesthetic values." He observes the way Gómez used the camera, showing the conviction, care, and intellectual rigor of a documentarian. According to López, "The movie was developed from a documental concept as it was required by the objectives of reflection and analysis" (111). He observes that the film consisted of elements of fiction, documentary footage, and real people playing themselves and produced a distanciation and amplified the analytical aspect of film.

López places a great deal of importance on the film's ability to "reproduce" reality, not in a mimetic sense, but more in line with what Mirta Aguirre suggested socialist realism should do. According to her, realism should account for the most important characteristics of reality, even if this means using aesthetic tropes and fictive devices. Echoing Aguirre's concepts, Gómez used professional actors and fictional storylines to deepen her analysis of the Miraflores community in Havana. These tropes and aspects of fiction had to be shaped to make them authentic. With this in mind, López comments, Gómez's coaching of the professional actors, which included the actors interacting with inhabitants of Miraflores, was exceptional in giving them the opportunity to be authentic in their roles. Authenticity was also the goal of Gómez's use of 16mm black and white film, which she blew up to 35mm to give it the feeling of a documentary. And finally, in using real people playing themselves and real debates and situations, Gómez expressed a commitment to reality and to a realism sought out, not simply observed.

Sara Gómez's tragic and early death (asthma) required a tribute, and López wrote one. His words are clearly emotional and caring. Both belonged to the same community for roughly ten years, and during those years they discussed and shared professional and political goals. He finishes as follows: "Sara, her life in ICAIC, her questions and polemics and her oeuvre are . . . a dialectic homage to the authenticity of [*One Way or Another* as an answer to the politicization of culture]" (115).

Althusser's influence on the Cuban cultural and political landscape helped establish a hermeneutic tradition that interpreted cultural works using Marxism and historical materialism. This hermeneutics was displayed publicly through the language of science. Such was the case with the official reception of *One Way*. Marxist philosophy and science were used to review cultural work but they also became a representational technique. Though Cuban filmmakers were always trained first in documentary, and only later given the responsibility to produce works of fiction, the original impetus came from Italian neorealism and Marxist aesthetics (Brecht and others). That this impetus was born from the necessity to investigate Marxist aesthetics in film made the learning trajectory of the 1960s one of aesthetic exploration regarding the representational and tropical aspects of film. The results of this filmic pedagogy are evident in the work of Solás, who, in *Lucia*, used an array of filmic techniques to narrativize different historical times. His work, influenced by Neorealism, Mexican and Hollywood melodrama, nouvelle vague, and Visconti and Fellini, is daringly postmodern.

The later introduction of Althusser to the theoretical, aesthetic, and political mix shifted the focus from a pedagogy of aesthetics to a pedagogy of Marxist science. Gómez is quite interesting in this sense because though she was roughly the same age as Solás, she was professionally trained by Alea and by the ten documentaries she directed. Solás directed *Manuela* and *Lucia* in 1968, while Gómez directed *One Way or Another* until 1974. Those years allowed for the development of a different approach to film, one more in accordance with the principles of science and less as an elaboration of aesthetics. This is not to say that Gómez's approach was not influenced by Alea, Brecht, Aguirre, Espinosa, and even Solás, but rather to suggest that the options a filmmaker had during the 1970s regarding how to perform his/her job as a revolutionary vanguard were different and included the notion of science, the unicorn of Althusserian Marxism. This same cultural reality also served as a new parameter for reviewers, as it was just discussed.

One Way in the United States

The film was first shown in May 1978 at the New York Festival of Cuban Cinema and in Washington at the Key Theatre. Brief reviews in the *Washington*

Post and the *New York Times* previewed the film to readers and attempted to explain the revolutionary Cuban film tradition to American neophytes. Helped by the expertise of Santiago Álvarez, the famed documentarian and vice president of ICAIC, who was accompanying the film through the festivals, the writers Michael Kernan (1978) and Tom Buckley (1978) presented the case of a film industry that began from scratch in 1959 and that has followed at least some of the steps of Soviet cinema.

Using the framework of Marxist aesthetics, Kernan (1978) identified some of the formal and thematic characteristics that linked several Cuban films to other socialist and communist filmic traditions. *Cantata de Chile,* a film directed by Solás, was compared to Soviet and Maoist visual styles and immediately following *One Way or Another* was succinctly described as showing "the impact of the revolution on the marginally indigent of Havana." Like other reviewers before him, Kernan used communism to understand *One Way.* Also as other reviewers, he insisted that Goméz's work was indeed different from the run-of-the-mill propaganda cinema that, it is implied, most communist nations produce. Given the film's storyline, he states: "It could be a tract, but it is not." And later, he comments: "'Social consciousness' is an easy cliché, heard frequently in countries like Cuba. This picture makes the cant phrase into something real, the conflict between loyalty to a pal and loyalty to one's fellow workers." Such statements, that try to make specific Cuban films exceptional (in fact, each Cuban film is characterized as if it were the exception to the propaganda rule), evidenced the need to continue ideologically framing communism as a totalitarian machine that, as a rule, relies on dogma, and produces only clichéd culture. Kernan, however liberal or even leftist he may be, seems unable to see the pattern that the films from Cuba (he mentions eight) have produced and, instead, comfortably insists that each is an exception.

This way of understanding specific Cuban films as unusual cultural productions is more common in nonspecialized and mainstream press. Robert W. Butler's 1983 review for the *Kansas City Star* begins with the following: "Those who suspect that the Cuban film industry's sole output consists of documentaries about sugar-cane harvests and various Latin American liberation fronts may be somewhat comforted by *One Way or Another* . . ." Butler is either unaware of Cuban film cultural production or he is writing to a readership whose cultural expectations are predictably anti-Cuban. He is similar to Kernan when he criticizes the film for being "soft-core propaganda—in the sense that it toots the horn of the revolution and its role in knocking down cultural and class barriers." The mixing of sexual and political metaphors highlights the way morality structured the reception of the film's perceived political propositions. Presenting the revolution as something positive is an affront to Butler's sense of ethics, and thus the film is described as slightly ("soft-core") offensive. One imagines that had the film dealt with sugarcane, it would have been labeled "hard-core propaganda."

Butler also evaluated the aesthetics of the film with Western Hollywood-centric standards of image and sound quality. "Technically," he writes, "the film is fairly primitive, with grainy black-and-white photography and lots of incidental noises on the sound track."[3] In his assessment of aesthetic quality, Butler is correct in recognizing unusual visual and sound editing techniques, particularly if the norm is Hollywood. According to him, these characteristics mean that the film's aesthetics are "fairly primitive." However, the filmic qualities of *One Way or Another* are modeled after Third Cinema, which favors an aesthetics that García had called "imperfect cinema." Butler appears unaware of Third Cinema, and he is willing to value this Cuban film based on the hegemonic aesthetics of Hollywood fare that typically include crisp image definition and fairly calculated and controlled sound editing. Such cinematic conventions are what Butler implies modern filmmaking should be. In this example, the relationship between the perceived quality of the film is woven with intercultural competence, and such a relation translates in an ethnocentric commentary. The film, in its oddity, is labeled "primitive," not unprofessional, low budget, childish, gritty, rough, or even candid. These are all adjectives that Butler, for whatever reason, chose not to use, and he instead preferred the qualifier that more clearly described the difference between his modern standards and not-modern practices, the developed and the underdeveloped.

More specialized reviews of *One Way or Another* also picked up on these technical characteristics of the film. The difference is that for these commentators such aesthetics are precisely what placed the film among the most outstanding revolutionary films of all time. Dennis West (1985), a scholar who has written extensively on Cuban film, commented in 1985 that the Gómez's piece "represents a high point in ICAIC's efforts to decolonize Cuban cinema" (2287–88). The process of decolonization that West refers to is closely related to what Butler described as "primitive": as West points out, Gómez used 16mm film that was later blown up to 35mm. West informs us that such a technique was used for several reasons, all related to the aesthetic statement the director attempted to make. The technique tried to facilitate natural acting by providing an unobtrusive filming process (the size of a 35mm camera was smaller). That tactic was essential to invite good performances by the film's many nonprofessional actors. Nonprofessional actors were required because Gómez was interested in blending, and thus challenging, documentary and fictional cinematic forms. Moreover, because of its maneuverability, 16mm cameras were commonly used for documentaries, which meant that if the fictional story was to blend with documentary, it needed to look grainy (2287).

Continuing the tradition of interpreting a Cuban film based on ethnocentric and cold war stances, some of the mainstream reviewers used Westerncentric standards and Hollywood aesthetics to measure the quality and to interpret the political signification of *One Way or Another*. Deemed as exceptional and unique, this Cuban film served as a platform for enacting an anti-Cuba discourse in which Cuba is reduced to a totalitarian regime. Like others before, these cultural workers manifested an ambivalent relation to the film and to Cuba. For instance, they defended Cuba against some stereotypes (for example, Butler begins his review pointing out that Cuba does not produce only sugarcane harvest films), but did so in a way that denigrated the film (for example, Kernan's insistence that several Cuban films are quite good, yet not the common output of the Cuban film industry). Only more specialized reviewers in film journals like *Cineaste* and *Jump Cut* addressed the type of aesthetics the film used and the way political ideas were constructed. These writers used Third Cinema aesthetics as an interpretive framework.

Though the release of *One Way* in the United States came at a time when the issue of women's rights was part of the popular agenda, the reviewers saw it as a work dealing only marginally with the system of gender. This maybe was the result of the sex of the reviewers, all of whom were men. These sexed official responses to the film downplayed gender and instead saw it as a strong contribution to the issues of social marginalization and the use of documentary aesthetics in fictional film.

Gender and sex were arguably present throughout the film narratives, though often these discursive paradigms and social realities were invoked only in subtle fashion. Take, for instance, the following. There is a scene where Mario and Yolanda are conversing and he is complaining at having told his peer workers about the real reason Humberto had been absent from work. Previous to that, Humberto had claimed his mother's illness as the reason for his absence, but in reality he had spent those days with a woman. Mario was the only one who knew this and he eventually uncovered Humberto's lie. Yolanda was praising Mario for having acted honorably, but Mario, instead of accepting her praise, bitterly comments that what he did was womanly. None of the reviewers used this opportunity given by the text to talk about the constitution of masculinity and femininity that made Mario, Humberto, and Yolanda such realistic characters. Instead, the reviewers reduced this rich textuality to a succinct mention of the problems of machismo. But the word machismo in Cuba (as in other societies) is a term that has provided a disservice to discussions of gender, because it has been used to close off explorations on the nature of gender and sex (Amaya 2007). Once machismo is mentioned, the speaker seems to believe that everything has been said. Machismo, when ill used, can nullify the possibility of understanding gender, sex, feminism, and the speaker as belonging to the same system. The terms also connote a way between two clearly identifiable camps: old values versus new values, or patriarchy versus feminism, and sex inequality versus equality. When used to close off, the term becomes Manichean, and not a structural descriptor of reality.

Comparing the Critical Reception of *One Way*

Of the films analyzed in this book, *One Way* produced the smaller number of reviews, interpretations, and criticisms. Partly because it was exhibited only sporadically in the United States, and partly because it did not embrace a popular aesthetics like *Portrait of Teresa* (which uses drama), *One Way* was not the box-office success in Cuba that the other three films were, nor did it have enough crossover appeal for the American market. The film is perhaps too committed to embracing the proper filmic interpretations of Brechtian and Marxian aesthetics, too engaged with the idea that *conciencia* is not a ready-made identity that Cubans can just request and get, too aware of the interrelations of gender, labor, and political structures. Because of all these complexities, and its supposed limitations, *One Way* has continued to be a classic woman's film and prime example of Third Cinema.

However scant the evidence, the types of reviews the film elicited clearly illustrate the ways in which Cuban and American cultural workers applied quite different hermeneutic rules to interpret the film. For the Cubans, *One Way* was all about Marxist and Brechtian aesthetics, and about the possibility of decolonizing through film by objectively addressing the difficulty of having *conciencia* in a society with competing requests for identity. Mario, a poor mulatto, is hailed by the contradictory discourses of the revolution and sexism (through homosociality). Yolanda, a light-skinned upper-middle-class woman, is also hailed by the contradictory discourses of the revolution and her class and racial upbringings. To the Cuban reviewers, this plot is revolutionary gold—more so because the plot was delivered through what Cuban critics saw was a rigorous application of Brecht's distantiation techniques and Althusser's Marxist science.

Responding to the needs of the film festival circuit, some American reviewers wrote about *One Way* in a manner that would fulfill their corporate role (reporting on film in their cities), while also performing criticism in a political fashion. To them, the film was surprisingly good and even-handed and not the propaganda tool that they thought it was going to be. This reaction resembled earlier responses to *Memories*. The critics managed to praise the film while criticizing Cuban culture and Cuba's style of government. Although these reviews happened in the 1980s, the cultural embargo had the continuing effect of reproducing ignorance about Cuban culture, regardless of whether some Cuban films had been distributed and reviewed during the previous decade.

As importantly, these reviews also speak to the consistent pull of performing liberal identities through anticommunism. The cold war was still going strong. With the discourses of communism and antitotalitarianism, these American critics negotiated their own liberal political identities through their craft, marking themselves as citizens able to discern between national standards of filmic quality, political systems, and the relationship of socialism to culture. Each of these textual elements was treated through a hermeneutics of difference that assumed American ways of producing filmic quality, politics, and culture were superior to the Cuban way. The American hermeneutics was thus also clearly ethnocentric.

Chapter 8

Portrait of Teresa

Retrato de Teresa (*Portrait of Teresa,* 1979), directed by Pastor Vega, narrates the story of Teresa, a textile worker, wife, and mother of three, whose political and work commitments produce a rift between her and her husband, Ramón. He becomes increasingly resentful at Teresa's after-hours engagements that include leading a dance troupe organized by the union. Arguing that she is not fulfilling her roles as wife and mother, Ramón convinces Teresa to take a leave of absence from work. Pressured by the union leaders, who argue Teresa's skills as leader are required for the dance troupe to succeed at the national level, Teresa returns to her work and after-work duties. Ramón, unhappy about this turn of events, leaves Teresa, goes back to living with his mother, and takes a young lover. Her efforts paid off. The dance troupe wins a national competition, and Teresa and Tomás, the coleader of the troupe, are interviewed on television. After seeing them together in this way, Ramón, fearing Teresa's relationship with Tomás is more than professional, requests a meeting of reconciliation with her. At this meeting, Teresa confronts Ramón regarding his affair, which he claims is over. She challenges him to give her reasons why she should forgive him and, as argument, she points out that Ramón would never forgive her had she had an affair. He, agreeing, claims that the situation is not the same for men as it is for women. The film ends with Teresa walking away from Ramón.

Portrait in Cuba

Vega began his career in ICAIC in 1960. By 1979, he had directed thirteen documentaries and a fictional feature, *De la Guerra Americana* (1969). As Carlos

Galiano (1979a) comments, in this work Vega attempted to make a portrait of real life in Cuban society (4). Similarly, *Portrait* owed some of its success to realism. Realism here refers to a set of contingent narrative and aesthetic techniques that are interpreted by viewers/readers as proper ways of depicting reality. In the case of *Portrait,* realism was conveyed through subject matter, point of view, and the director's reliance on scientific discourses to validate character development.

Portrait addressed an important social issue of the time: gender equity in the home. During the mid-1970s (see chapter 1), the "problem of women" had become central to the public agenda. The Federación de Mujeres Cubanas (FMC) had proposed the Family Code in 1974, and this was made into law in 1975. In addition to becoming official, the Family Code was debated across the nation in all the People's Organizations (Holt-Seeland 1982, 102). Though the Code included provisions regarding parenting, children born out of wedlock, and, importantly, divorce, the Code's regulation of life within the home was what caught the attention of people in general. These regulations were the subject of debates because they meant that men would have to contribute equally in child rearing and housework. The Family Code and the debates it originated became key frameworks for the interpretation of *Portrait* and central to understanding it as a realistic film.

Vega's commitment to realism was mediated by science, which provided the basis for the script. He became interested in making a film on the subject of gender equity after reading a work produced by the Advanced Institute of Brain Research (Amaya 2000). This report described the emotional changes experienced by the adult population as a result of the transformations generated by the revolution. The most typical problems found in the interviewed subjects were conflicts generated among couples because of the new possibilities that the revolution offered to women (Holt-Seeland 1982, 102). After gaining access to some of the files, Vega brought the director of the institute, Dr. José A. Bustamante, to assist Ambrosio Fornet and himself in preparing a script that would draw from the fictionalized files. With Dr. Bustamante's expertise, the script began to take shape as a psychological, subtle melodrama dealing with the extensive pressures placed on women by the revolution and by the system of gender (Amaya 2000). Actors Daisy Granados (Teresa) and Adolfo Llauradó (Ramón) did their part for bringing realism to the film. They enrolled in the actual jobs that their characters performed for weeks, and in this way they gained precious understanding of the way these workers' lives developed. Granados became a staffer in a textile factory; Llauradó worked as a technician in an electronics shop. Without a full technical script, the filming began, and during it, actors were given the opportunity to improvise lines and acting details. Authenticity was the goal and Vega, like Sara Gómez before him, believed that well-prepared actors were those actors who had been immersed in the role they played, and that the director's responsibility was to let the actors improvise in front of the camera.

Portrait opened on July 25, 1979, as a celebration of the anniversary of the 26th of July movement. It succeeded at the box office and won numerous international awards. More important for this research, the film elicited strong public reactions (Vega confided that several fights began after film screenings) and these reactions were publicly discussed in *Granma* and the magazine *Bohemia* (Amaya 2000). In what follows, I analyze the reception in terms of both official reports and printed audience reactions.

The official reception came before the movie was released. *Revolución y Cultura* published in February 1979 a brief review, in which the film was described as having the objective to investigate the problems women face (A.R. 1979, 83). After its opening, *Granma* published an interview with Vega on July 26, 1979, and a formal review on July 30. Carlos Galiano, the same reviewer of *One Way or Another,* created both review and interview. Galiano's review of the film centers on the issues of sex and gender inequality (Galiano 1979b). He tries to convey the way society would speak to Teresa by recalling how the phrase "It's not the same" was repeated over and again by the husband Ramón, her cousin Charo, and her mother. These characters represent different ways in which tradition held back Teresa from self-fulfillment at work. Each of these voices also represents different aspects of the system of gender and sex. The mother corresponds to the subjection that is accomplished via family morals and the bond of blood and flesh that exists between mother and daughter. Ramón's corresponds to the passing of tradition via the conduit of love, romance, and marriage, and to the prohibition of breaking the conditions of love.

According to Galiano, Teresa's refusal to respond to the pressures of tradition is an attempt to defend her right to "create" something and in the process become the New Man. At work, Teresa's job consists of pushing yards and yards of fabric through the dulling machinery. She gains the opportunity to go beyond this routine by becoming involved in the union's dance organization. At this, she is quite successful and becomes the leader of her troupe, a contender in the national competition of folkloric dance. In a move of Marxist idealism, Galiano associates self-fulfillment with artistic creation, vindicating at once the movement of aficionados so popular during the decade and after and the idea of the total self and the New Man. According to the educational paradigm of the time (formal and informal), the New Man needed to be more than perfect; she needed to be complete, and this completeness was the result of a multifaceted development that included work, art, physical education, and Marxist philosophy. Teresa was a compromise of sorts, for her character incorporated some of the aspects that would make her the New Man, except that she lived in a Cuba where she could not become the New Man as a woman. "It is not enough, therefore, that women enjoy the same social rights that men do, or that men share the familial duties that before were her responsibility." These rights, at the time supported by law in the Family Code, were only the beginning. "Absolute freedom can only be reached if both give each other the possibility to develop their individual personalities and to widen their horizons of existence, without subjection or dependencies." For Galiano, the possibility of becoming a more developed individual, a better revolutionary, a whole self, a woman, was a possibility born out of subjective interdependence. A radical conclusion, the New Man is at once called upon as a symbol of the dream of self-fulfillment, only to be proved a community-offering to the future. Because of this interdependence, Teresa cannot be that which Ramón cannot be himself. His ways of embodying the past, which lead him to label all Teresa does as inappropriate and subject to contention, weigh him down, dragging Teresa down in the process. According to Galiano, the film's ending is a clear reference to sexual inequality. That Ramón can take a lover and expect to be forgiven, but that Teresa cannot expect the same, is evidence of outdated traditional sexual moral codes. These codes exist to protect men's freedom and to secure women's subjection and cannot be part of a revolutionary society.

By mid-August the film was so successful that *Granma* printed another review. In it, Santiago Cardosa Arias (1979) pointed out that *Portrait* had been viewed in two weeks by 250,000 people and "has awoken no few hot discussions, debates and controversies at homes, and workplaces . . ." His review, like Galiano's, sides with Teresa and dismisses those criticizing the film as "caveman." Talking about the film's conflict as a struggle in which only one of the parties was right became a common feature in reviews. To justify these opinions, reviewers talked about machismo, but Galiano and later Lourdes

Prieto (1980), reviewing for *Cine Cubano,* based their opinions on the fact that the films had constructed a script that used science to prove gender and sexual inequalities.

Prieto points out that Teresa's success at the box office and in the streets is because the film communicates with the general Cuban public (127). Putting aside the film's reliance on melodrama, a popular filmic form, Prieto argues that the film's communicative power comes from its content, which was based on scientific research and thus reflected the lives of many Cubans. Prieto dedicates most of her review to describing how the theme came about from research carried on at the Advanced Institute of Brain Research. She complimented the fact that a psychiatrist was part of the production staff, and that actors Llauradó and Granados worked at jobs that their characters had in the film.

Vega's approach to the making of the film, and the way it was narrativized by Prieto, speaks of the process of artistic creation in ways consistent with a scientific approach to aesthetics partly influenced by Althusser. Moreover, this "method" is what, according to Prieto, guaranteed the communication of *Portrait* with the Cuban people. An artful narrative, it is implied, results from a commitment to reality and its examination through methods of science. It is necessary to remark that for my argument, Vega's approach to the script's construction is a relevant as Prieto's recognition of the importance of science and realism to the film's communicative intent. That such a script could be generated in such a way fulfilled Prieto's expectations regarding representation. The film, instead being produced by the subjective reactions to reality of the director and writer, resulted from the objective examination of reality through science and Marxist philosophy.

Prieto and Galiano displayed their public personas and selves using key aspects of the revolutionary hermeneutics. Galiano interpreted and evaluated the film in relation to its social and political potential. Pietro centered hers on issues of realism and science. They both used political lexicon (for example, rights, duties, equality, realism) and measured the diagetic world created by *Portrait* as one would measure an anthropologic narrative. The realism is not questioned.

Portrait's type of aesthetics corresponds with *One Way or Another* in that both rely on scientific information to produce the narratives. They differ from each other in that the reviewers recognized Sara Gómez's film as an attempt to educate using the power of dialectics, which is the power of Marxist philosophy and historiography (historical materialism). These educational goals were made evident to viewers through the inclusion of documentary techniques and traditional ways of presenting knowledge with authority (such as using an adult male voice-over to present most of the knowledge). Reality was made multidimensional via different types of fictional and nonfictional narratives; each type of narrative corresponded to a different dimension. The subjective and personal were presented in the fictionalized story. The historic and scientific were presented with documentary techniques. Viewers had little difficulty understanding the pedagogic goal of the film and in broadly understanding the educational techniques utilized.

Portrait reached realism through the traditional genre of drama. Although the film used science, this fact was hidden from viewers, and only knowledgeable reviewers were able to speak to this. Moreover, the technique for script development used by Vega and the actors, which included consultations with psychologists and an ethnographic approach to acting, improved the realism of the drama, but the film did not question drama as a genre. In fact, though *One Way or Another* is almost essayistic, *Portrait* better fits the description of socialist realism as forwarded by Mirta Aguirre. Aguirre (1980 [1987]) argued that the best socialist art would use a realism that would dig into reality, re-create it, and perfect it (108). To produce socialist realist art, one may use an array of artistic techniques and genres, but these uses should always be informed by Marxist philosophy and science. Truly useful art is an elaboration of reality—not of artistic techniques. These aesthetic insights guided Vega to the movie and the actors to their characters.

Because the film was publicly discussed for months after its release, *Portrait*'s context of reception continued changing during the summer of 1979. This context was particularly affected by printed interviews with director, actors, scriptwriter, viewers' letters to the editor, and interviews of viewers. These interviews, notably Granados's, are particularly telling of the type of public self that ought to be performed in order to accommodate the period's political and cultural requirements (France 1987, 90; Goffman 1959, 2).

Interviews are unusual reception evidence: the interviewee is given a chance to present information about themselves, their past and future, in their chosen way. For this reason, interviews function similarly to autobiographies. In both cases, the interviewee is engaged in the construction and presentation of their self, which has to be presented and performed in a way consistent across time and dimensions (by dimensions I mean what we would call economic life, spiritual life, political life, and so on) (Giddens 1991, 53; France 1987, 29).

All interviews with Granados touched on roughly the same topics, which included her career, her opinions of Teresa, and her experiences during filming. Her answers showed the preferred way in which she wanted to present herself. In two of the interviews she was by her three kids (who played her three sons in the film). On one of those occasions, the interview took place at home, foregrounding the actress's normalcy. She was presented as a housewife, a mother of three (incidentally, Granados is married to Pastor Vega, the director of the film), and a cultural worker. Granados was presenting herself in this way to gain credibility as an actress by highlighting the similarities between Teresa and herself, and, in a sense, proving her qualifications to portray the character. She mentioned the way that she trained herself to play Teresa. At the textile factory Ariguanabo, she performed the same job as Teresa's character, and she had the chance to interview other women who worked there ("Una Visita en Compañia de Ramón a Teresa, Detras del Retrato" 1979; Paz 1979, 27). By interviewing these women, Granados learned of the challenges they faced as wives, mothers, and workers, and she incorporated this information into her character and into the script. In foregrounding the way she prepared herself, she declared herself aware of the requirements imposed on her as a member of the community of cultural workers. Granados showed that she knew that "the people," as Castro had requested almost two decades before, were a key source of learning for the vanguard. Moreover, she was also expected to reflect on her work and on the lives of those workers she was ultimately working with, the same lives she was trying to improve. Her opinions about Teresa showed her awareness of how she needed to be seen by others. Because the film hailed Teresa as a revolutionary character, Granados had to align herself with Teresa's plights for justice and equality. Granados assured *Granma*, "What Teresa does is not because of her stubbornness, like Ramón says, but because of her needs as a human being for self-realization." ("Una Visita en Compañia" 1979) She reminds the readers that it would have been more comfortable for Teresa to leave things unchanged, but that to become a revolutionary one must push for change, even if the process is arduous (Paz 1979, 27).

In talking about the character Ramón, Granados declared politely that he "is a good man, struggling with himself." "He is," she even proclaimed, "a revolutionary man," and yet still incapable of fully embracing the revolution (González Acosta 1980, 115). Llauradó, in a different interview, also politely stated that Ramón has evolved in some ways; after all, he said, Ramón lets

Teresa work (Galiano 1979c, 4). These gestures on behalf of Ramón by both actors signal the need to avoid alienating all the (mostly men) viewers who have been vocally and forcefully complaining about the wisdom of the film's gender and sexual proposals.

In reflecting on the many debates that the film originated among the audience, some of which ended in altercations and fistfights, *Bohemia* published a piece in which Enrique Valdéz Pérez and Manuel López Alistoy interviewed the factory workers at Ariguanabo, the one where Granados and Teresa worked. The debates and differences of opinion among this group of workers was intense, and of the points of view published in the article, it would seemed that most men disagreed with Teresa's claims and that most (but not all) women agreed with her. A point of particular relevance in the discussions was the double standard regarding, on the one hand, the infidelity of Ramón, and on the other, that Teresa fraternized with her coworker Tomás. The men, simply speaking, interpreted Teresa's friendship with Tomás as infidelity, though Teresa never was sexually involved with Tomás. The women saw the friendship between the two characters as innocent and Ramón's reactions as irrational and unfair.

Two letters to the editor published in *Granma,* written by experts, further illustrate these contrasting positions. The first letter was written by Dr. Elsa Gutiérrez Baró, director of the Clinic for Adolescence and the president of the Cuban Society of Psychiatry. Dr. Gutiérrez argued that *Portrait* framed the issues of inequality badly. In her opinion, the physiological fact that women can procreate precludes talking about equality. To prove her point, she suggested that the conflicts portrayed in the film were the result of Teresa's ineptitude as a wife and mother. As a wife, she lacked the ability to administer her time and commitments. As a mother, she has failed to raise her children correctly. For example, Teresa's kids drank milk from the bottle at the ages of four and six. She also observed that Teresa dressed the oldest boy as if the "boy were an invalid." Dr. Gutiérrez argued that the children were on their way to becoming machos. Finally, in a drastic rewriting of the plotline, Dr. Gutiérrez suggested that Teresa's complaints were sexual and had to do with whether she should have the right to cheat on her husband. Her opinion on this matter was, of course, that the Family Code forbade her from doing such a thing.

Professor Magaly Ramos Vera, affiliated with the Pedagogical Institute of Technical and Professional Education, responded to Dr. Gutiérrez. Ramos defended Teresa by pointing out that she was a very normal mother, one who had to take care of her kids alongside her work and other household duties. Given this, and as it is common, Teresa had been forced to be permissive with her children in some aspects, such as the bottle issue. Professor Ramos emphatically made her point by calling Teresa, and all women like her, heroes who have managed to care and educate their children while contributing to a nation that needed their work. She also pointed out that the movie does not center around the question of whether Teresa should have the right to commit adultery but, rather, that the issue is the existence of a double standard that forgives men who commit adultery and viciously attacks women who do the same.

What the letters and the audience interviews show is a society deeply divided on the issues of gender and sexual (in)equality. They also show how definitions of femininity and masculinity were becoming partly redefined by the idea of the New Man, or the ideal revolutionary citizen. These definitions were not equally important to everybody, and their impact was unequal. The evidence shows the ways these ideals were more uniformly embraced by the community of cultural workers as part of their vanguard position. All of the reviews and commentaries by cultural workers sided with the film's gender and sex proposals, no doubt partly because embracing gender and sexual equality in public was a way of properly defining their public selves.

Portrait in the United States

Portrait, which so squarely tackled some of the problems of the gender and sex systems in Cuba, most importantly the double shift and the double standard, invited reviewers to use gender and sex as a fundamental interpretive framework. From pro-feminist to pro-Cuba, the different ways in which *Portrait* was seen and understood signal hermeneutic and theoretical divisions among feminisms.

The only mainstream review that gave total praise to the film was a short piece in the *New York Post* ("Universal 'Portrait' " 1981). It has no byline and begins by stating: "An extraordinary cinema winner." Yet, in general, mainstream writers disliked or gave qualified praise to the film. As in the critical reception of the previous films, discourses regarding the political system of Cuba and gender were often used as hermeneutic frameworks, with gender being the most consistently present. Significantly, interpretations differed based on the sex of the reviewer, much in the same way it had happened in

Cuba regarding *Lucia* and *Portrait*. Male reviewers adopted, more or less consistently, several identifiable traits. They used genre as a way of criticizing the film. They believed the plotline was predictable. They interpreted narrative facts in ways that questioned Teresa's ethical position. And they gendered their descriptions of characters by referring to the female characters' physical appearance. The reviews by women in mainstream media showed a general empathy toward Teresa's character and were more likely to comment positively on the film's narrative and political features.

Variety, in their coverage of the Moscow Film Festival and the Chicago Film Festival in September and November 1979, respectively, first reviewed *Portrait of Teresa* (Mosk 1979, 26; Sege 1979, 18). These two early and brief commentaries on *Portrait* (the film was released the same year) continued evincing the importance of festivals to the distribution and exhibition of film from Cuba. Like *Memories, Lucia,* and *One Way or Another,* this film relied on its ability to impress at least some festival organizers and audiences. These two early reviewers, however, were not very impressed.

Mosk, a longtime reviewer for *Variety*, gave the film a questionable introduction by commenting in the first line of his review that *Portrait* "has the earmarks of a tv [sic] sitcom in its evasiveness of the more dramatic sides of female liberation coming to the Cuba of today." Given *Portrait*'s dramatic realism, that it is compared to a sitcom is a heavy criticism that implies a level of banality contrary to the filmmaker's goals (Peyton and Broullon 1979/1980, 24). Mosk was not claiming that the film was funny or the issues laughable; rather, his enjoyment of this drama was made difficult by the acting and directing of the female character: "But Teresa is played in a too martyred way by Daysy Grandados [sic] and robs the film of a more discerning insight into this problem . . ."

Mosk's unwillingness to consider Granados's acting as realistic may be more related to the genre of melodrama itself than to Granados's histrionics. Melodrama, a genre quite popular in Latin America, is perceived as a genre targeted toward women (López 1985, 4–5). Sege's review of *Portrait,* also in *Variety* (1979), confirms this. Like Mosk (or because of Mosk, his coworker), Sege first described the genre that the film seemed to fit and used genre expectations to dismiss the narrative style and realism of the film. "Except for a handful of scenes of telling verisimilitude . . . it would be easy to dismiss Cuban director Pastor Vega's offering as a soap-opera melodrama with a feminist slant." Though Sege tried to recuperate some of the film, by qualifying some elements of the narrative as "meticulously realistic," like Mosk, Sege used a lexicon that left little doubt as to where he stood. This is not to say that women reviewers enjoyed the film. Janet Maslin (1981), writing for the *New York Times,* commented that "the story of [Teresa and Ramón's] marriage is meandering and often slack" (15). Her criticisms, however, were far less virulent and without the language that Sege and Mosk used to try to diminish the film (for example, soap opera, martyred, sitcom).

Using genre to describe a film is a way of asserting that the film's narrative movements, characters, and events have a predictable feeling. Most of the time, even when genre is invoked within a film review, the reviewer does not feel compelled to state that the film is predictable. Sege (1979) found it necessary to state this: "Director Vega and coscripter Ambrosio Fornet, unfortunately, unfold the domestic scrapping in exhaustive detail and without a proper sense of pacing." The adjective "predictable" is in this case closely related to the expression "exhaustive detail" and "sense of pacing." The three are ways of describing a narrative that is, fundamentally, of little interest to the viewer. They are different ways of saying, "Just get it over with." Sege suggested that he knew what was going to happen, that the narrative did not need such details (which ultimately were "exhausting"), and that the pace was slow. The descriptions of "exhaustive" and the feeling that the pace was slow was likely a reaction to a nine-minute sequence of scenes that depicts Teresa waking up before everybody and beginning her work cooking, doing the laundry, and preparing the evening's dinner. When everything is ready, she wakes up Ramón and her kids so that they can begin their day. I often teach these scenes, and my students marvel at the degree of meticulous detail achieved by the film, but they also get bored, no doubt because their own sense of pace is now influenced by the action-film's and the music-video's faster editing. Sege, like my students, struggled with the film, calling it a "soap-opera melodrama" that simply did not hold his attention. Although Sege had earlier praised the narrative's careful detail, at this point in the review, details became a hindrance. Robert Hatch (1980) had a more subtle way of suggesting the film was predictable. He wrote for *The Nation:* "For all its excellence, *Portrait of Teresa* must be appreciated in context. Sexism has been in the North American consciousness for some time, and the film's discovery and sometimes didactic explanation of the problem may seem naïve to viewers here. We are far from resolving the issue, but we know by heart how the argument goes" (389).

Another sexed perspective is the interpretation of the film's ending (did Teresa have an affair?) and the ensuing moral dilemma or lesson that the viewer is left pondering. The film is quite ambiguous about this issue, but interpretation does not rely only on textual matters. Sex matters too. In the Cuban reviews, men typically believed that the couple had an illicit relationship. Similarly, Mosk and Hatch believed Teresa had an affair and that the ending was ambiguous. Other reviewers did not mention the final scene at all or, if they mentioned it, they believed that the film was addressing the double ethical standard (that the same sexual exploits by women and men will be judged differently) (Haskell 1980, 17–21; Shakur and Downing 1983, 65; and Imeson 1981, 160–61). In contrast, Hatch and Mosk believed the ending was quite complex and assumed that an easy moral resolution was impossible. For those who believed that Teresa had an affair but that the scene showed the double standard, the ethical resolution was clear: Teresa and Ramón may be wrong in their actions, but only Ramón was guilty of applying and expecting the double standard. Optionally, to those who believed an affair between Tomás and Teresa did not happen, Ramón is simply mistaken, and his suggestion that a double standard should exist proves that Teresa's rejection of his request was right. Ramón is clearly wrong and morally inferior, for not only is he unable to remain faithful, but he still expects Teresa to take him back, even when he is incapable of hypothetically treating Teresa's infidelity in the way he is requesting to be treated.

Finally, another glimpse into the gendered point of view is Mosk's comment that the film's theme is "by now universal enough for the lingo circuit usage abroad." That is, *Portrait,* despite its shortcomings (namely, over-the-top acting and banality) is nonetheless good enough for a feminist or women's film festival circuit. Implied are sexist issues of quality and stereotypical ideas about women as audiences. In assuming that the film is proper for a type of exhibition that targets (mostly) women or feminists, Mosk implied that such viewers may overlook overall film quality if the theme of the film uses the correct "lingo."

Sege went beyond Mosk at hinting his gendering by embracing a sexed voyeurism. In his review, Sege commented on the physical attributes of two of the female characters but failed to address the physical presence of male characters. About Teresa, he stated: "Grandados [sic] beautifully combines a housewifely frumpishness with sullen sensuality." About Llaurado, he wrote: "Llaurado is solid as a confused husband genuinely in love but without the slightest idea of what drives his mate." While the description of Granados (Sege, like Mosk, misspelled the actress's name) attempted to give the reader a mental picture describing her attractiveness as a housewife, Llauradó was described in relation to the intellectual space that the actor is able to portray through his acting. Hatch, in a similar vein, described Teresa as "handsome" and Ramón as an "exemplary young man." Sege also made a point of describing the appearance and sexual appeal of Ramón's mistress: "the husband takes up with a full-thighed young beauty (portrayed with appealing zest by Alina Sánchez)." Though Tomás, Teresa's friend and coworker, is more important to the plotline than Sánchez, the reader is left wondering whether his thighs are full or skinny. Teresa's gendering in these mainstream pieces is not only evidenced in Sege's interest in Teresa's physical appearance but also in his description of her social role as a housewife. For, though it is true that Teresa is often within her home, for at least half of her time onscreen she is presented at work or on the streets. This does not stop Sege from describing her as a housewife.

Compare this to Judith Crist's comments on both protagonists' physicality: "Daisy Granados is, at 37, a dark beauty, full-figured, with huge-eyed intelligence. Her Teresa is memorable. The virile, attractive Adolfo Llaurado as Ramón helps complete a portrait of the world . . ." (Crist 1980, 71). Crist's description has several details that make it more equitable. She mentioned Granados's age, and instead of "housewifely frumpishness," she is a "dark beauty, full-figured." Finally, Ramón is not only a mind working his way through life but is also a sexualizable being that Crist recognized as "virile and attractive."

Mainstream reviews, including those in *Variety* and *The Nation*, also tended to be anticommunist or, at least, negative toward Cuba's political system. Like other Cuban films before, that *Portrait* originated in a communist nation meant that some reviewers would place certain political expectations on the film. Sege, for instance, used the discourse of communism in addition to gender as a way of interpreting the film text. A scene in which a coworker of Teresa comments on the hope that the revolution will eventually succeed in erasing machismo is described by Sege as "agit-prop." According to him, Tomás "mouth[s] lines like, 'the revolution makes the impossible possible.' " Using "mouth" as a verb describing someone's speech is a way of disqualifying the value or truthfulness of what is being stated.

Judy Stone (1980), writing for the *San Francisco Chronicle*, contributed to normalizing the use of communism/totalitarianism as an interpretive framework for *Portrait*. She achieved this by opening her piece with the following anecdote: "There's an old 'joke' that needs a new punch line. A soapbox orator assures the crowd that 'comes the revolution, you'll eat strawberries and cream' and a little voice pipes up, 'But I don't like strawberries and cream.' The orator replies, 'Comes the revolution, you'll eat strawberries and cream.'" Though Stone was sympathetic to the film, both as a cinematic work and as a women's picture, she used a joke about communism as a way of introducing to the reader the strange reality regarding sex and gender in Cuba. In the rest of the piece, she implied that men in Cuba are put in a situation in which they must do that which displeases them, namely, stop taking advantage of women's work. In Stone's ethical system, freedom from state regulation is more important than women's oppression, which she acknowledged. The joke suggests that a revolutionary (communist) government that tries to do a social good by decree continues being totalitarian.

Like other mainstream reviews about Cuban films dealing with gender (*Lucia* and *One Way or Another*), Stone applied both antitotalitarian and feminist frameworks to the film. Her feminism is evidenced in several ways: First, she contextualized the film by commenting on its social success in Cuba at raising controversy, thus giving merit to the film. That is, the film retains the value of a social document about gender and sex in Cuba. Moreover, Stone interpreted narrative developments in a sexed way, and this is particularly evident in that she did not believe that Tomás and Teresa are having an affair or that Teresa is at all attracted to Tomás. Lastly, in the narrative, Ramón takes a lover. Stone described the lover in a very unsympathetic way: she is a woman "who has nothing better to do with her time than lie around reading magazines and waiting to be escorted to the beach." Clearly, Teresa is a better human being and citizen than Ramón's mistress, which makes Ramón's betrayal deplorable.

More politically specialized commentaries also used gender and Cuba's political system as ways of interpreting the narrative and as providers of standards of value and aesthetic quality. These writings were longer than a review, and several fit the essay format. The most significant difference between these and mainstream reviews were the degree of theoretical sophistication and the ways in which they stated their political goals.

Patricia Peyton and Carlos Broullon interviewed Pastor Vega and Daisy Granados in San Francisco, during the Telluride Film Festival. Published in *Cineaste* in the 1979/1980 issue, the interview shows in a concise manner the interviewers' set of expectations regarding the film and outlines its perceived social value. The first question was to Vega: *"Would you elaborate on your political objectives with* Portrait of Teresa*?"* (1979/1980, 24). Each question afterward related to issues of politics and gender in Cuba. The interviewers asked about women's reactions to the film, and about men's reactions, assuming correctly that each would be different. But perhaps the most typically feminist question was: *"The film's script was written by two men. Should a film that deals with a problem of major concern to women be written by men?"* (25). This question directly addressed issues that have been fundamental to the constitution of feminist criticism and feminist epistemology. Feminist criticism has, at the very least, suspected the way men have represented women—if not outright criticized it. From standpoint theory to Screen theory, the critiques maintain that men's subject constitutions are structured around the oppression of women, and that their subject positioning opens up vantage points from which women (not a socially constructed definition, but real beings) cannot be seen. Consistent with these ideas, Peyton, Broullon, and also Burton and, previously, Rosen (she reviewed *Lucia,* another film about women directed and written by a man) brought up the issue of sex and authoring. Vega's response was a functional way of addressing the issue. He stated: "Well, if you follow this logic, then carpenters have to make movies about carpenters" and so on. Peyton and Broullon, assuming this logic, followed Vega's answer with an inquiry on the participation of Granados (or other women) in the construction of the script. Though Granados had some impact on the script, Vega's legitimacy, he believed, came from the fact that investigations conducted by the Academy of Sciences of Cuba inspired the initial script idea. Though he had already mentioned the role science had played in assisting him in the script, Peyton and Broullon had, perhaps, "forgotten." In their frame of reference, which had been constructed through the recognition of alternative epistemologies (not only alternative aesthetics), science, like filmmaking, was also guilty of gendered and sexed bias. Vega's appeals to science were not compelling evidence that the script was built on truthful women's experiences.

Concerns regarding sex and authoring belong to a community that acknowledges the epistemological and representational shortcomings of narratives and representations of women. In her 1981 essay in *Portrait,* Burton, one of the foremost scholars on Cuban cinema, shared these concerns and wrote them in the form of a paradox: Modern cinema is engaged in the constitution of women as men's possession through sexist iconization (Burton 1981, 57; Burton 1985, 2547). *Portrait* belongs to modern cinema yet it also seems to belong to the "women-centered" genre, which often has the goal of challenging sexist iconization (Burton 1981, 52). Because both possibilities cannot simultaneously come to fruition, Burton first found exceptions that questioned the idea that modern cinema is only engaged in sexism. Using John Berger's now classic *Ways of Seeing,* Burton suggested that just as painters who painted their lovers sometimes produced artwork that transcended sexism, Vega, directing his wife Granados, was also able to go beyond some of the typical limitations of his sexism. Regardless, *Portrait* still belonged to modern cinema, and Burton continued her essay showing, with careful textual analysis, how the film betrays its own premise. Applying psychoanalysis and Pierre Macherey's theory of structural absence, Burton observed that the film portrays Ramón's infidelity, yet the nature of Teresa's relationships with Tomás is left out. "It is not inconsequential that this ellipsis replicates the social attitude which the film purportedly criticizes: that extra-marital sexual intimacy is tolerable, even encouraged, for men but inconceivable for women" (55). Also absent from the narrative, Burton continued, are any pleasures that Teresa may find in her extracurricular activities and any evidence "to the growth of Teresa's self-esteem." The final tally is mixed, with Burton praising and criticizing different aspects of *Portrait* and problematizing any easy resolution to the original paradox of male-created, women-centered film.

Defining what constituted women's films was important in the early 1980s when Burton, Peyton and Broullon, and Haskell reviewed *Portrait.* The 1970s had given way to a solid tradition of feminist film criticism, yet the commercial viability of women's movies in the United States, Hollywood claimed, had hampered the development of women-centered film. Already Rosen, reviewing *Lucia* in 1980 for *Ms.,* criticized Hollywood's sluggish response to the need of producing pictures for women. To emphasize her view, she reviewed commendable film works from Cuba, Italy (*Love and Anarchy,* d. Lina Wertmuller, 1973), and France (*The Mother and the Whore,* d. Jean Eustache, 1973). In the same issue of *Ms.,* Haskell (1980) also wrote reviews of other foreign films in an article subheaded by the following: "What Germany, Cuba, Hungary, France, and Australia Know About Women that Hollywood Doesn't" (17). For Rosen, the quality and diversity of this selection of foreign films about women proved the growing complexity of the genre and the eventual impossibility of using the label "woman's picture." She placed *Portrait* alongside *Angi Vera,*

The Marriage of Maria Braun, A Simple Story, and *My Brilliant Career,* showing the complexity of films that use women antiheroes as their protagonists.

Haskell (1980) embraced the film's theme, treatment, and place of origin and used these to give praise to the film: "But this film requires no apologies or special dispensations in the name of Third World 'development' or feminist good intentions: it is simply an artistic and dramatic success" (20). She saw Teresa as an admirable character because she is shown battling "against domestic slavery . . . without benefit of grass-roots Marxist or feminist support" (20). In both instances, Haskell hinted at a conception of selfhood that is quite liberal: a true social agent acts independent of or even against institutions or social structures. In this view of the self, Teresa's actions are true to herself in direct proportion to Teresa's perceived independence: "In Theresa's [sic] struggle to find the strength, the words, we see nothing less than the evolution of the Women's Movement from its most primitive urgings" (20). Imagining the women's movement represented in Teresa's struggle is a reference to feminism's 1960s mantra, "The personal is political." It also references the idea that for women to become truly independent, they must first transform their selves, and struggle with their ways of being, acting, and speaking. Though feminism was Haskell's hermeneutic framework, she used a particular version of feminism. According to it, Teresa did not have "Marxist or feminist support." This view is puzzling when considering that Teresa existed in an institutional environment where her labor and her participation in the public sphere were valued, albeit within relatively sexist frameworks. This feminism was in relative disuse in America by the 1970s, although it was the anchor of NOW's feminism, an organization that has understood that labor equity and legal equity are central to the project of gender equity, much like Marxist feminism.

While Haskell used language and interpretive tactics mostly associated with feminism, Judith Crist and Jo Imeson, writing for the *Saturday Review* and for *Monthly Film Bulletin* in 1980–81, respectively, mixed leftist and feminist language and frameworks in their reviews and assessments of *Portrait.* Crist (1980), informed by the interview published in *Cineaste,* the contexts of which she referred to repeatedly, reproduced Vega's opinions and wrote a quite positive review that highlighted Teresa's class background and her desires to go beyond class and gender limitations. Similar to Imeson's review (1981, 160), Crist began hers with class: "*Portrait of Teresa* sums up the situation of working women in Cuba and, to a large extent, our country" (72). This initial paragraph, as Imeson's, is quite significant in that it constructs the basis for a theory of society in which class and gender are interlinked and sets an interpretative ground on which the rest of the piece will build. Thus, later, the film is about the "Cuban working class," and Teresa is a "textile factory" worker who is also the "union's chairperson." Teresa's quest, instead of being reduced to a matter of personal freedom and gender equality, is also constructed as an attempt to become a better citizen. In this way, gender equality, personal freedom, and civic duties become interlinked and mutually dependent. Ramón's role at impeding Teresa's wishes risks obstructing the civic, professional, and personal development of Teresa and those around her.

Imeson wrote a compelling short essay-review that referenced Julio García Espinosa's ideas on imperfect cinema and that understood that Vega's use of drama was aimed precisely at making the film accessible to as many Cubans as possible. Like Crist, Imeson linked class to gender mores by suggesting that *Portrait* explores "the discrepancy between social practice and revolutionary ideology with regard to the position of women." Given that the working class has been linked in Cuba (as in the United States), perhaps unjustly, to more archaic notions of gender and sex, and because most Cubans belong to this class, Vega's selection of a plotline based on a specific social milieu is a way of addressing the mutually constitutive formation of gender and class. Imeson also examined some of the benefits the revolution has brought to women and the challenges to women's equality even within the revolution. In her assessment, mass media, including Cuban telenovelas, talk shows, and magazines, were primary challenges to women's status in society.

Comparing the Critical Reception of *Portrait of Teresa*

The critical reception of *Portrait* in Cuba showed a remarkable uniformity. Critics understood that the film was speaking to some of the most important political issues of the time: how to be and become a properly gendered revolutionary. In *Portrait* converged the discourses of the New Man, equality, citizenship, and gendered and sexed behavior, an array that could bring, head-to-head, prerevolutionary behaviors against the political and social goals of the revolution. These prerevolutionary behaviors included the old sexisms of capitalist patriarchy, which placed different values on labor associated with women and men and which organized the economy in such way that valued work would be culturally proper for men and devalued work for women. This system of economic difference was not the only reason capitalist patriarchy existed. Capitalist patriarchy also relied on a complex set of social rewards for individuals of any gender willing to follow traditional gender rules, and on a set of punishments that would be levied on those breaking them. Because the official position of the revolution was that capitalism and sexism ought to end, and this position was, by 1978, the traditional position of the vanguard, of the intellectuals, and of most public cultural and political figures, critics were heavily disposed to embrace the same positions. Their jobs were, after all, to be political, vanguard, and intellectual, qualifiers that were ascribed only to those performing their cultural tasks in ways fitting to revolutionary goals. The critics' disposition was further strengthened by the recognition that Vega, the director, had followed proper aesthetic practices, namely, realism and Marxist aesthetics. To his credit, Vega had approach the potentially dangerous topic of gender in a way perfectly suited to the legal, cultural, and aesthetic revolutionary parameters of the previous couple of decades. For these reasons, *Portrait* is perhaps the most pure example of revolutionary cinema, and whatever limitations the film has are partly reflections of broad social and political limitations. Perhaps the most glaring one is the film's and the critics' tendency to see sexist behavior as remnant of prerevolutionary society. In the film, Teresa's mother points out the benefits of abiding by traditional gender rules. For Ramón, sexual expectations ought to continue. For critics, Ramón's behavior is underdeveloped and those who sided with Ramón were called "cavemen" or "machos."

By contrast, the letters and the audience interviews are evidence that Cuban society was divided on issues of sex and gender and that public performances of sexism were still quite popular and accepted. On this, cultural workers at large, and critics in particular, were at odds with the rest of Cubans, for cultural workers were expected to perform their public identities in ways proper to their politicized locations.

In the United States, reviewers of *Portrait* used the hermeneutic frameworks of gender (and sex) and totalitarianism (or its opposition) to interpret the film. Mainstream reviewers were far more likely to criticize negatively some or most aspects of the film. Their criticisms were rationalized in the following ways. The critics placed the film in genres (TV sitcom, melodrama) that the reviewer disrespected. They commented that the plot was predictable and tiresome. They interpreted the ending in a way that diminished any possible moral clarity. Additionally, they described the characters in sexed ways, alluding to female bodies and not to male bodies. Some used antitotalitarian remarks as general framework presented to the reader.

Other reviews, published in film journals and women's magazines, also used gender and political framework expectations, but they did so in ways that reflected a feminist and/or Marxist perspective(s). These reviewers tended to make more explicit their political goals and to assume that the social value of the film was related to *Portrait*'s contribution to the discussion of gender inequality, the double shift, and the double standard. Though a couple of reviews isolated gender from class, the rest attempted to explain the constitution of gender in relationship to class, thus problematizing personal and/or isolated solutions to inequality.

Conclusion
Film Criticism in Cuba and the United States

The goal of this study has been to understand the politicized critical reception of *Memories of Underdevelopment, Lucia, One Way or Another,* and *Portrait of Teresa* in two national/cultural contexts (Cuba and the United States) and relate this reception to the performance of political identities. I have taken this approach because it allows me to tie together the cultural, epistemic, and institutional conditions of the production of criticism together with its actual textual traces: the review. The conditions for the production of criticism provide the staging cues to the social actor, the critic, to carry on her/his political role. I use the first half of the book to lay down these staging cues. These cues are found in the institutional contexts and in the discourses that explain the political role of the critic. These discourses, which circulate within cultural and political institutions, help explain why cultural work is political and how cultural work should be interpreted. Because of these discourses, criticism becomes a place for the performance of specific political identities. The performances are the actual reviews, writings, interpretations, and commentaries. I analyze these in the second half of the book. Together, staging cues and performances allows me to talk about criticism and its production as central to understanding specific citizenship practices in Cuba and the United States. In this book, political criticism is civics. In general, individuals engage in civic behavior in order to accomplish political tasks, but also to become proper political beings, proper citizens. Below, I bring together insights from the previous chapters to explain the relationship of criticism to proper citizenship in both national contexts. I begin reviewing institutional contexts, followed by commenting on how criticism becomes political. Finally, I argue for understanding criticism as a public performance of political selfhood.

Institutional Contexts

The 1959 Cuban Revolution produced the conditions for the institutionalization of Cuba's field of cultural production, including film and criticism. Perceived by the leadership as a necessary tool for securing the support of the population and for transforming the population into a revolutionary social force, culture and criticism became increasingly politicized, typically, in line with the government's ideological requirements. The close relationship between the field of culture and the field of power had profound implications for the lives of cultural workers, for it meant, among other things, that their professions (as sets of actions, expectations, and discursive legitimizations) would be often, if not always, shaped by politics. Culture was politicized and cultural workers became political actors.

This point was evident from the third issue of *Cine Cubano,* in 1960, which printed a short article written by the Cuban film director Julio García Espinosa entitled "Criticism and the Public" (12–13). In this article, Espinosa suggested that criticism had to play a strong and revolutionary role in the new Cuba. To do so, the critic ought to practice her/his craft in ways consistent with the needs of the revolution and with those of an increasingly aware and media-savvy public. The critic would have to forget the facile and formalist criticism that went hand in hand with North American movie fare. "Together, we will have to approach the more lively content and the most proper form. Criticism will profit the most by observing the progress of the artist in such direction" (13) (see also Kolker 1983, 279). In the following issue, the director of the Instituto Cubano de Artes e Industria Cinematográficos (ICAIC), Alfredo Guevara, expanded on Espinosa's ideas in an article titled "Culture and the Revolution" ("La Cultura y la Revolución") (45–47). Criticism, Guevara contended, must be harnessed in the struggle against imperialism and cultural decolonization. Criticism "must be the product of philosophic and aesthetic positions, the product of an analytical method, the product of the knowledge of reality and of reality's internal contradictions, reality's tendencies and character" (46). In short, criticism would use aesthetics, methodology, and epistemology for the betterment of the revolution.

In so quickly (only one year after the triumph of the revolution) recognizing the importance and necessity of cultural criticism for the constitution of the field of cultural production, Espinosa and Guevara placed criticism within a system of social relationships bound by the grid of power. Espinosa defined criticism as a social practice enacted "together," and in close relation to, the artist's work. Recognizing the systemic nature of criticism as a social practice, the critic would have to acknowledge the revolution's, the public's, and the artist's needs. Guevara, already a cultural leader, upped the ante and declared criticism to be subservient to the field of power, and practically declared criticism a revolutionary weapon against imperialism. Criticism would wage war with the weapons of philosophy, aesthetics, methodology, and epistemology; its target would be civics, ethics, and the constitution of a new "ethos." Substantial evidence shows that in Cuba, cultural criticism became part of the political policing of culture. That is, cultural critics took it upon themselves to evaluate work based on cultural and governmental policy, adding to their typical role as gatekeepers of the field. The Heberto Padilla and the *P.M.* cases, discussed in chapter 1, and the *Hoy* case, discussed in chapter 2, were problems involving criticism. In these cases, cultural critics addressed political issues in such manner as to help the Cuban government make a case against other cultural workers, who ended up marginalized, censored, or jailed. Cultural criticism played a role in structuring the field of cultural production and its relationship to the field of power. Cultural criticism was a way of performing citizenship.

Unlike in Cuba, where cultural policy had largely normalized a growing cultural field through a process of state institutionalization, the American cultural field had been relatively unregulated (though specific industries like film and television had been self-regulated), decentralized (though Hollywood and New York City have historically constituted two strong cultural poles), highly heterogeneous, capitalist, and ambiguous in its relation to the field of power. All of these factors complicate the understanding of any given section of the field at any given time. However, the contingent conditions of critical reception surrounding Cuban film in the United States allow me to section off an area of the cultural field characterized by modes of exhibition, critical expectations, and some of the audiences' (including critics') ideological, cultural, and political leanings. Cuban film has been exhibited mostly through art houses, film festivals, and universities. This has meant that it has shared a cultural space with art cinema from Europe, political film from Third Cinema traditions, cult and classic film, and independent cinema from the United States. Although quite diverse, these exhibition sites influence modes of reception and criticism, creating specific expectations, including assumptions about the film's aesthetic quality and political and/or ideological complexity. Given these assumed textual characteristics, the spaces invite educated, intellectual, urban, and cosmopolitan viewers and critics looking for the film's intellectual and aesthetic stimulation and for the identity branding that the films and exhibition venues bring. Borrowing from Bourdieu, I have called this branding distinction. Unlike Bourdieu's distinction, this distinction is experienced politically because it relates to dissenting practices and the viewers' desire to engage nonhegemonic culture.

These institutional spaces, which gave shape to specific identities, were constructed through a complex relation between the field of power (the economic hegemonic system and the political system) and the field of culture. Contrary to Cuba's public way of recognizing that culture and politics are codependent, culture and politics in the United States often act as if they are independent. Americans and media consumers are told that their cultural systems are not regulated by politics; if anything, they are regulated by the market. In the discourse of American capitalism, the market serves as evidence of independence and the possibility of freedom. Thus, the purported independence of the cultural field need only be based on the assumption of the market as regulator. From the MPAA and the ratings system to patriotic self-censorship after 9/11, industry self-regulation has become a norm, and, at least publicly, cultural institutions claim their independence by establishing their own limits for action. The field of culture is not the only one prone to this public performance of independence through claiming market regulation. This discursive strategy is common in other fields (for example, the demise of the union system and affirmative action attest to the fact that labor markets are today, again, mostly under the spell of "market freedom") because this strategy originates, ironically, in the field of politics through the theoretical and discursive constitution of American liberalism. In this way of seeing politics and politicized identities, human organizations and individuals ought to strive for independence from broad social pressures. Markets, we are told, function better when competition serves as an evolutionary standard that selects between the companies, ideas, and corporations that ought to survive and those that ought to perish. With individuals, we are also told, it is the same. Large segments of American capitalism seem to rely on the idea that neoliberalism is to the economy what liberalism is to individual development. In both, the practices interpreted or discursively constructed as unregulated competition and individualistic development equal freedom. To me, it is clear that contrary to claims of independence, institutions and individuals who fit their identities into narratives of unbridled action are simply enacting a dis-position to see their identities defined by a politicized notion of worth, which links the promises of liberalism (as a political theory that attempts to set the basis for human development) to the right to exist. If citizenship in Cuba is often marred by obtrusive policies that reduce the scope of individual rights, citizenship in America is mangled with liberal discourses that overstress the possibility of freedom and that are naïvely blind to the significant ways in which legal frameworks and corporatism affect individual activities.

Seeing oneself through the eyes of liberalism is a widespread disposition in American society, where the product of liberal individualism is assumed to be freedom, while the product of societal norms is assumed to be constraint. As Thomas Streeter (1996) commented in relationship to U.S. broadcasting, "a result of this individual/social opposition is that debates about broadcast structure are regularly framed in terms of reconciling individual freedom with social constraint, of reconciling the competing self-interests of individual (or stakeholders or consumers) with one another and with social stability and progress—the famous Hobbesian problem of order" (29). He also showed that contrary to claims of independence, law and regulation have played a key role in the way radio and television are structured.

Transposing Streeter's arguments to film exhibition and criticism means emphasizing the different interrelations between the American field of power and the cultural field. These include, at the very least, the following. Changes to the structure of exhibition were partly the result of governmental policy, chiefly the Paramount decision in 1948, which was based on the principle of antitrust. Antitrust regulations, in turn, are designed to increase competi-tion (the decision was an application of the Sherman Anti-trust Act of 1890) and secure the "free" and "unbridled" economic behavior of movie exhibitors and producers. Changes to the middle class were partly the result of the G.I. Bill, a piece of legislation signed into law by Franklin Delano Roosevelt (FDR) that gave extraordinary benefits to war veterans, including unemployment insurance, aid for college and university education, and home loan guaran-ties (benefits that were not equally available to whites and nonwhites). The university system also grew because of governmental decree and intervention. For instance, spending for scientific research multiplied to accommodate FDR's goal of securing technological military hegemony (the report "Science, the Endless Frontier" includes some of FDR's views on the matter) and, later, to keep the Soviet threat at bay. The federal government's ability to finance the

G.I. Bill and the expansion of the university system, in turn, was the result of America's World War II victory, which gave the United States the extraordinary privilege of being the supplier of "goods" for ravaged Europe during the following decades, strengthening America's role as economic world leader. The economic benefits of the war were huge, more than doubling the American Gross National Product (GNP) in the short span between 1940 and 1960 (200 to 500 billion dollars). Throughout these decades, classical Hollywood and, later, television, consistently upheld the virtues of liberal individualism and the "American way."

Echoing structural relations in Cuba, the sixties and post-sixties U.S. institutional context for cultural criticism was deeply influenced by the U.S. field of power (politics and economics). Simply put, the American sixties are unimaginable without post–World War II corporate and government wealth, and federal interventions in the educational and real estate systems. These factors provided the material basis for the constitution of 1960s political identities, affecting film exhibition and the types of subjectivities that exhibition could, and would, encourage. Art film and foreign film distribution, partly the result of the Paramount decision, and partly a reaction to massification and the rise of suburbia, was nurtured by the university system and became a popular way of gaining distinction and expressing dissention from the masses. Not surprisingly, the readership of *The New Yorker, The Nation,* and *Ms.* (evidence considered here) were (and are) wealthier and more educated than most Americans; they were also mostly white, and urban. The price of (liberal) freedom could be afforded, at least by some.

Politicized Cultural Work

Cultural forms, or at least some cultural expressions, are considered political in most societies. In Cuba, however, the closeness between fields (culture and power) and their ideological alignment made politicization different from the ways it has occurred in most capitalist, Western societies. Take for instance France, where, as Bourdieu (1993) noted, the field of culture and the field of power are interlinked but function on an assumption of relative independence (39). This notion is particularly important to the cultural field. To support this assumption, the field relies on aesthetic theories and conceptions of freedom and individuality that give an ethical, epistemological, and experiential validity to its status. The field is thus partly dependent, but this reality is sublimated.

The rewards for being dependent on the field of power but sublimating this knowledge are that the cultural field can grant "distinction," a characteristic that favorably distinguishes those who participate in the cultural field and that has been commonly associated in France, as in the United States, with moral, intellectual, and spiritual superiority. The cultural field's appearance of independence is constituted through the circulation and canonization of common aesthetic "theories," such as the idea that art is its own goal ("art for art's sake") or that the proper way of engaging art is through disinterested contemplation. These and other tactics preserve the aura of independence, while granting art (and other high-brow cultural forms, including art film) an antihegemonic patina.

Because in Cuba many cultural workers and government officials openly recognized this interdependence of culture and power (see chapter 1), the field of cultural production had to rely on different legitimating tactics. The value of cultural work and cultural production could not depend only on granting those involved in it a certain intellectual and "spiritual" distinction (though Cubans often expressed their value judgments based on the "greatness" of the work or of the cultural worker, indicating a significant reliance of liberal individualism as central to aesthetics). That politics came to constitute the field's boundary (Fidel Castro's famous dictum illustrates this point: "Within the revolution, anything; against the revolution, nothing"), this distinction would have to come, at least partly, from culture's political role, which had been outlined in Cuba's cultural policies. The kernel of these policies—that art, including film, should educate the new citizenry—gave the cultural realm a social value and distinctive political function. It also provided rationales that could explain the dependent relationship culture had with power. These rationales were developed over time and took the form of aesthetic theories that recognized the ideological nature of culture and that rejected the idealist bases of Western formalism.

Distinction, both in the United States and in Cuba, is based on material reality and discourse. If Bourdieu originally linked it to museums, I have linked it, in the United States, to art houses, film festivals, and university screenings, and in Cuba to post-Batista exhibition models and national cinema. Each structure politicized differently. The period covered in my investigation roughly spans from 1972 to 1985. During this time, the discursive remnants or dispersions of the 1960s political struggles still politicized significant areas of the American cultural field. The civil rights, antiwar, and countercultural movements and, later, the women's and gay rights movements normalized the public display of political identities and normalized the political interpretation of film in an ideologically diverse media system.

This normalization was particularly true regarding films coming from Cuba, a nation that since the 1950s was represented in U.S. media in quite political terms. In the 1950s, a few but popular representations of the Cuban revolutionary army in literature, print, and media provided a romantic aura to Cuba's political struggle and a heroic tint to Fidel Castro. During the 1960s, the military and political animosity of both nations and mainstream "antiauthoritarianism" gave a cold war hue to most representations of Cuba in the United States. Antiauthoritarianism continued influencing much of the critical reception of Cuban films in the 1970s and 1980s.

Other factors shaping the political interpretation of the Cuban films had to do with the ambiguous relation the American cultural field has had with the field of power. Supporting Bourdieu's idea that the cultural field relies on the assumption of independence (an idea better suited to the United States and France than to Cuba), some reviewers asserted their opposition to the field of power through sympathy to Cuba, in opposition to the U.S. State Department's anti-Cuban stance. Particularly when reviewing *Lucia* and *Memories,* critics placed a wedge between themselves and the government by implying that the government's cultural embargo on Cuba had become the basis for censorship-like activities. Those government actions resulted in a threat to cultural freedoms, an idea central to the field of culture, one as central to the mediated American cultural field as the idea of "art for art's sake" among the highbrow elite. Nevertheless, just as disinterestedness was a way of constituting a field of distinction invested in the reproduction of established power hierarchies, critics defending expression did so from positions of gender, class, cultural, ethnic, and racial privilege. In addition, these critics re-created a cultural space where the consumption of foreign film was a social activity that granted cultural and intellectual distinction and that likely participated in the stratification of American society.

A field of cultural production (and exhibition) is a social system that gives meaning and structure to cultural transactions, but because of the different ways in which the fields of power are structured in Cuba and the United States, each field has constituted a different habitus, held together by different rules, practices, discourses, and manifestations of their relations to power. In postrevolutionary Cuba, the field of cultural production had an overt relation of dependence to the field of power and, accordingly, the habitus structured dispositions that aided the reconstitution of the field of power. The cultural field, including the cinema world and criticism, engendered these dispositions by very narrowly defining culture. As a whole, the field of culture in Cuba followed Castro's request in "Palabras a los Intelectuales" for discovering what is "noble, useful, and beautiful." Seeking nobility in cultural production gave the field an ethical character, a type of socialist "distinction" that cultural workers could make a reality only if they embodied nobility, only if they embodied the revolution. Understanding cultural work as useful gave the field a functionalist epistemology and aesthetics in which the definitions of truth, reality, and artistry depended on whether they facilitated the coming of socialism and/or communism. An ethos of function dominated the habitus and set dispositions for evaluating work based on the work's prospective usefulness to broad social/political goals. Cultural policing abided by the same dispositions. In this habitus, as in all, aesthetics became subject to politics, and useful, noble work was deemed beautiful. Beauty was as beauty did.

Criticism, like Espinosa and Guevara argued, was a political craft that required the application of a revolutionary hermeneutics. Besides regulating the activity of criticism, these hermeneutical templates became the theoretical basis for institutional activities and important criteria in evaluating general aspects of cultural works. As discussed earlier, revolutionary hermeneutics were based on socialist aesthetics that promoted moral over economic rewards, voluntarism, anti-imperialism, and the nation over the individual. The central axioms were that the revolution is equivalent to the nation, and that socialism and communism could redeem the people and make them proper subjects of a developed Cuba. More specifically, the revolutionary hermeneutic was centered on the notion that culture could transform political ideas. Thus, culture became political.

This revolutionary hermeneutics was applied to other areas besides culture. It was, in fact, the basis for discursive constructions of history. The idea that the revolution was the only logical result of Cuba's past, a sort of Manifest Destiny, was a call for a reevaluation of all Cuban histories written before 1959. This category of principles was (and is) eminently historiographical in that it constituted principles to historicize Cuba's past and present. At an individual level, these principles enticed those Cubans born before the revolution to renarrativize their past to fit a new set of valuable histories. To see this, one need only read the many books and publications that use biography (via autobiography, interview, or self-histories), implicitly or explicitly focusing on the question "How have you changed?"[1] This question was an invitation to reevaluate Cuba's past using current values. Using Foucault's idea of technologies of self, it is possible to see how these values and axioms made historiography (including autobiography) one of the areas that needed to be ethically modified, and helped locate criticism on the map of self-identities. These values and axioms invited a renarrativization of selfhood, with the revolution at the center of the narrative.

The American habitus also included normative ideas of interpretation. Critics often used communism as a key framework to interpret the Cuban films. However, as the cases show, most liberal, leftist, and feminist writers did not use straight-out anticommunism to interpret these films. Instead, they used the discourse of antitotalitarianism; this was manifested by multiple references to cultural freedoms and propaganda in Cuba. In addition, the Cuban films were seen through the prisms of leftist and feminist politics, and these prisms were hermeneutical in nature. When applied to specific films, these interpretive tactics helped highlight issues of class oppression, history, gender oppression, and the ideological character of filmmaking. Moreover, these tactics also led critics to use extratextual information to complement or shape the meaning of the text, giving weight to what the critic knew about the contexts of production: the Cuban fields of culture and power.

The habitus also structures the way an individual makes sense of herself/ himself as a member of a community, nation, and/or society. In the case of American critics, this was shown in the ways in which reviews hit double registers that at once claimed independence from and subjection to the field of power. Some reviewers asserted their independence from power by criticizing governmental actions (for instance, when reviewers framed *Lucia* and *Memories* in relation to the U.S. State Department's actions against the first Cuban Film Festival) or hegemonic ideologies (as when reviewers of *Portrait of Teresa* complained about the lack of "women's films" in Hollywood). Reviewers showed their subjection to the field of power and to overarching ideologies of domination by reference to ethnocentric discourses (such as the discourse of cinematic quality brought up in relation to *Memories*), gender discourses (like the ones used by reviewers of *Portrait of Teresa,* who used genre to criticize it), and political discourses that implied the inferiority of the Cuban cultural system (likely based on Cuba's single-party system) and its lack of freedom.

That reviewers performed their identities through this dual register suggests that the American critical reception of these Cuban films often relied on a hermeneutics of ambivalence, a hermeneutics embracing both consent to power and political dissent. Moreover, it also suggests that this hermeneutics of ambivalence reenacted, at the level of the subject and the self, the dual position the cultural field has in relation to the field of power. Using antiauthoritarian rhetoric, many reviewers expressed the idea that their own cultural field was and should be independent from the field of power, but did so while ideologically echoing some of the U.S. government's claims about Cuba and the Cuban system of freedoms.

Criticism as Public Performance of Selfhood and Citizenship

The revolutionary hermeneutics found in official Cuban writings and the hermeneutics of ambivalence found in American reviews are two textual tactics partly constructed on different discourses of selfhood and citizenship. The Cuban institutional contexts invited the application of nonliberal theories of selfhood, while the U.S. cultural field relied on liberal theories of the self. Each obeyed the rules of the habitus, which, Bourdieu theorizes, marks the lifestyle of a community and is thus key to understanding identity. Besides suggesting which hermeneutical procedures should be used to interpret cultural work, the discourses of selfhood and citizenship provide cultural workers in general, and critics in particular, other types of ideas to help them make sense of themselves vis-à-vis their institutional location. In the moment of politicized reception, criticism becomes a means to perform citizenship and thus becomes circumscribed by the notions of political duty, political goals, and public performance of political identity. Political criticism, thus, became entwined in Cuba with the idea of the vanguard and revolutionary citizen. For the critics examined in the United States, political criticism became part of liberal/leftist performances of citizenship. I began this book with the question of whether these public performances of civics could be understood also as technologies of self, and the answer is positive.

To Michel Foucault (1988), technologies of self allow individuals to shape themselves (for example, behavior, body, mind, soul) into the type of individuals they ought to be in order to obtain a specific state of positive being (for example, salvation, happiness, wisdom) (18). Technologies of self are not created by individuals, but exist in specific habitus, which provide the proper techniques (*technes*) to shape the self and the utopian form that the self ought to replicate (*telos*). Although these technologies come from the habitus, the individual typically understands the actions needed to achieve the desired self (the *telos*) as acts of contingent freedom. In the United States and in Cuba, political criticism is part of different technologies of self, which are modulated through the contingent discourses of politics, aesthetics, and citizenship. Although the definition of good citizenship was different in each nation, and although the rules for properly interpreting the political world were different, each set of critics showed remarkable consistencies that point to two technologies and two ways of performing contingent freedom to criticism.

In Cuba, the gravitational pull of the revolution changed the whole map of Cuban political self-identities. To understand oneself as a political self in Cuba in 1970 was a different thing than understanding oneself as a political self in 1958. The map had changed. This change was not the result of randomness but the partial product of practices that, over time, became technologies of self. The revolution provided the framework. *Technes* and *telos* related to ideals that individuals should aspire to become or be. Self-negation was perhaps the clearest of these ideals. It requested from the vanguard, and anyone aspiring to occupy a vanguard position, a constant vigilance over their actions. Self-negation was one element of a procedural hermeneutics that helped monitor behavior and that helped discriminate among future actions. Also belonging to this procedural hermeneutics were the axioms of *conciencia,* decolonization, and the idea that film must educate. These procedural hermeneutics encouraged individuals to evaluate the present, and give it meaning in reference to an idea of a desirable future. Procedural hermeneutics provided *technes* (ways of doing things in the present), and *telos* (goals for self-formation), helping the Cuban vanguard understand present activities and how these would shape the future. The ways people incorporated them into their lives were, no doubt, varied, but always through action. Either individuals would declare their desire to be better revolutionaries, or they would make this declaration through their work and the decisions that directed their futures. Filmmakers and artists, for instance, constructed narratives, images, or sounds that would evoke how good it was to gain *conciencia;* how important it was to decolonize oneself; how valuable it was to produce cultural work that would engender an active audience. Demonstrating these processes meant recognizing their importance and a way of testifying as to one's desire to embrace them. Historiographical (placing the revolution at the center of your personal history, as commented above) and procedural hermeneutic (for example, self-negation) tactics assisted the interpretational and evaluative tasks that cultural workers had to perform to create and evaluate film and other cultural works.

Cuban criticism depended on specific *technes* that related to its institutional identity and habitus. Because of the type of task associated with their labor, critics (and other members of the cultural field) used the discourse of aesthetics to negotiate self-understanding. This is so because aesthetics provided tools for comprehending, evaluating, and interpreting cultural work. Given that cultural fields are always in flux, and that members are in constant struggles over position, aesthetics can become a most useful tool for self-definition, advancement, and, when needed, for defending a position in the system.

In the case of Cuba, aesthetic discourses were used to displace people from the field, to censure, to praise, to explain the nature of good (socially valuable) cultural work and, thus, the proper definition of the cultural worker. Critics and other cultural workers needed to learn how to interpret cultural work using at least some elements of the revolutionary hermeneutics and aesthetics. My case studies show the application of such interpretive techniques. Though methods of interpretation varied depending on the cultural worker and on the film being reviewed, writings consistently measured the text against its political/social value; this is evidence of how important it was to perform, publicly, civically responsible work. These displays of selfhood fitted the official discourse of the intellectual and the cultural vanguard and suggest that cultural workers existed in institutions and communities where technologies of public selfhood circulated as attractive options to better answer the call of culture and the call of power.

The Cuban revolutionary hermeneutics and aesthetics provide a counterpoint to Western "avant-garde" aesthetics and to liberal theories of the individual, which were central to the American practice of criticism and technology of self. That is, in most Western societies, the artist who abides by the rule of "art for art's sake" is often an archetype of freedom and individuality, a maverick, an explorer of the unruly territories of abstractionism, of the personal and social unconscious, of nonart, or of the unthinkable. Thought of in this way, the artist is, together with the intellectual, and the (honest) politician, a liberal archetype for whom liberal freedoms are constructed. Indeed, the artist's value as human archetype is one of the key discourses that support the idea of "freedom of expression," of action, and of belief. Yet, as Bourdieu and several Cuban cultural workers have observed, these ideas about artists and art are ideological and support already established hegemonic structures.

That Cubans often challenged liberal ideas of self and freedom (at least within cultural institutions) meant that a different idea of the self would have to come to prominence. This idea of self, which I argue is also an idea of citizenship, was modeled after the New Man, which was and is an archetype of the socialist self. To pursue the *telos* of becoming a New Man, Cuban cultural workers often used Marxist aesthetics and the revolutionary hermeneutics. With these tools, cultural workers were able to perform their work in a socially responsible way and did so while making themselves more in the image of the New Man. Practicing their professions in this way was (defined as) a liberatory practice, for it challenged the capitalist and liberal past, and it placed the social over the private good. More important, practicing their professions in this way meant subjecting themselves to ethical self-evaluation and modeling. "To be like the Che" (a common slogan in Cuba) was something that could be achieved only through the disciplining of the self. Interpreting filmic works in ways that showed this disciplining was one way of abiding by ethical standards and a way of applying a technology of self to cultural work.

That Cubans issued sometimes-timely criticism of Western aesthetics and ideas of the self did not mean that Cuban aesthetics and cultural practices were intrinsically progressive or socially responsible. As I have commented since the introduction, things are much more complex. The advent of a new hegemonic structure in Cuba, a new economic system and political establishment, benefited from this functional aesthetics and from the redefinition of core social concepts such as freedom and individuality. As I showed in chapter 2, in official cultural publications, freedom was weighed against the standard of civic duty and social responsibility. These last two concepts also became central requirements for acquiring full citizenship and became arguments used against cultural work and workers. As seen in the case of *P.M.*, Heberto Padilla, Reynaldo Arenas, and others had to endure censorship and cultural and legal repression; this can be seen as the ironic result of the application of otherwise progressive Marxist aesthetics.

Contrary to the closeness between official culture and power found in Cuba, the habitus of the American cultural workers manifested an attractive pluralism and also a discursive ambivalence toward the field of power, an ambivalence that resembled the agonistic relation between cultural systems and political structures. Cultural fields are always in a position of subordination in relation to power. However, their cogency depends, Bourdieu argues, on being able to sustain the belief of independence from power.

The idea of independence, which is a central *techne* in the American cultural field, is supported through different discursive means depending on specific cultural locations. "Entertainment," for instance, is commonly thought of as a discursive and symbolic cultural realm quite apart from politics. It is "apolitical," an idea that cultural studies has exposed as faulty. Foreign film, by contrast, corresponds to a set of social and discursive practices that depend on politicized notions of the world. However, the political here relates to politics of dissention and the antihegemonic practices of cosmopolitanism and antimassification. These are practices that separate critics and viewers from "them," where "them" refers to the traditionally defined field of politics and power and "they" are also the masses fooled by power and ideology. At the center of this proposal are aesthetics and elitism. Ideas regarding taste, genre, narrative competence, and auteuristic knowledge (which reviewers used to "contextualize" the films and, typically, to compare them to European art film) legitimated the "quality" of each film in reference to noneconomic, nonhegemonic terms, something that separated these reviewers and the films from the field of power. Critics commonly used two *technes* to demarcate the boundary between their cultural location and the field of power: They "objectified" hegemonic ideologies, such as patriarchy and capitalism, and they used extratextual knowledge to interpret the films. American reviewers, particularly the ones writing for better-educated readers, resorted to feminist and leftist theories to do this performance of self and civics, drawing a fragmented political field where they often occupied the margins. Yet, insofar as these discursive and interpretive practices draw the separation between power and culture based on practices that give "distinction" to the reviewer (through dissention), they simultaneously reconstitute certain aspects of hegemony and thus participate in subjection. Speaking against power, as Stanley Kauffmann, Marjorie Rosen, and Julianne Burton did, required power, the power gained by belonging to highly regarded institutions, being educated, and having a dissenting political identity.

Although my cases show a broad array of interpretive techniques by American critics and reviewers, they also show consistencies that support the notion that these critics were using, like the Cubans, specific technologies of self that were validated through broad social discourses of citizenship and selfhood. This technology of self, a type of cultural and institutional discipline, is evident in the ongoing efforts by American cultural workers to produce hermeneutics that allowed the critics to couch their hermeneutic practices in terms of dissention and on the side of liberalism. To this end, members of the cultural field reproduced an ambivalence rooted in the sublimation of culture's dependence on power. The *technes* used were film theories that allowed some evidence to be used and other evidence to be left out. Moreover, if *techne* is understood as a disciplining of physical experiences, the senses, and the mental processes used to interpret information from the physical world, then, the *techne* used by these reviewers required the selective use of historical evidence (for example, cold war versus colonialism), the imposition of an ethnocentric definition of liberal freedoms, and the assumption that form in and of itself had value (for example, commentaries about genre and lack of production quality of the Cuban films). These three aspects of this hermeneutics are in contrast to the hermeneutics used by Cuban reviewers, and they are made more evident when interpreted in relation to the structural role they played. Because the Cuban cultural field members could not, in good faith, claim independence from the field of power, they produced aesthetic theories that would make sense of their dependence on politics. These theories went as far as criticizing any theory that claimed or sought out independence. To claim independence was reactionary. The U.S. reviewers, by contrast, used theories that allowed them to reconstitute their dependency on the field of power while negating it. Auteur theory, formalism, and certain strands of liberal feminism reconstituted the supposed independence of the critic from the power, however varied this position was (university, leftist liberalism, feminism).

I am not suggesting here that the American critics were wrong. Although I very much disagree with some of the comments issued, I agree with others. My goal is to underline the profound pull that "identity through dissention" has in these U.S. critics and the curious cultural effect that this may be having. What political world is structured when political dissention is performed through economically and political sanctioned practices such as criticism? I wonder whether this is a thinning down of the realm of civics and citizenship or just another way of being modern. What is clear is that the citizenship practices that I have reviewed relied on narrow definitions of belonging, on officialisms, and, at times, on elitisms. In Cuba, the critics used ideas of citizenship that reproduced the government's limited definitions, thus reconstituting the, at the time, revolutionary practices of denying full citizenship rights to dissidents, homosexuals, and other sexual and racial minorities. In the United States, critics relied on practices of dissent that disqualified the majority from being able to embody ideal liberal citizenship. These cases suggest that citizenship, whether it is sketched after the ideal New Man or the ideal liberal individual, is a category of belonging that relies, at its very core, on the possibility of exclusion.

Closing Remarks

In *Internationalizing Media Theory,* John Downing (1996) observed the lack of international media studies that use comparative methodologies (xi). The bulk of our knowledge on media, he noted, is based on either American or British media, and so are the range of theories, concepts, and methodologies that help us think about media (including film). Because of this, comparative media studies are always at risk of theoretical and methodological biases. Trying to avoid the pitfalls of using political economy approaches designed to illuminate the connections between economic and political power proper to capitalism, Downing relied heavily on old-fashioned political theory and political history. After all, he was researching Russia, Poland, and Hungary during the Soviet and post-Soviet eras, and his methods had to account for socialist and postsocialist realities.

This book tries to fill some of the gap on comparative studies that Downing identified. Following Downing, I take methodological and theoretical precautions for comparing Cuban and U.S. realities. Typical political economic methods and issues, for instance, would be incomparable in these nations. For instance, the yearly funding for ICAIC has always been a fraction of the cost of one single Hollywood production. The primary goal of ICAIC is not to seek out profit but to fit the cultural necessities of the revolution. Lastly, ICAIC is a state monopoly and yet does not behave as an economic monopoly. Antitrust logic does not apply. What is applicable is the concern that having one institution dominate film production, exhibition, and distribution will produce an ideologically monolithic film world. So, what is relevant is ideology, not money.

Given this, I brought forward criticism, citizenship, and film reception as categories of analysis that are at play both in Cuba and in the United States. These comparative categories speak to the ideatic and political worlds that Cuban films inhabit in both nations. To illuminate these worlds, however, I did not use a straightforward ideological analysis. Instead, relying on Staiger, Foucault, and Bourdieu, I offer an account of cultural institutions as they are organized around sets of knowledge and aesthetic propositions. By using these comparative parameters, this book provides a glimpse into the cultural and political effects of the cold war and some of the radical differences between American and Cuban ways of understanding civics. Though not the only ones, these ways of understanding civics were quite common in each nation. Both speak to the official ways of defining good politics: liberalism in the United States and socialism in Cuba. As importantly, both speak to the official ways of defining good political film. Using the words of critics, I show the liberal parameters of quality in the American contexts and the socialist parameters of cultural quality in Cuba.

Although the cold war made Cuban films political to both American and Cuban critics, the local contexts of reception and the styles of civics the films elicited remained quite different. The practices of reception by each set of cultural workers were shaped by discrete social, institutional, and national realities. Because of these, Cuban film was experienced differently by Cuban and American writers and critics. The films' power to signify was, for Cuban critics, an expansion of the social promises of the Cuban Revolution. For liberal and leftist American citizens, the same films were rendered meaningful by cold war discourses and by socialist, revolutionary, and antiestablishment values common among progressive Americans. For both sets of viewers, Cuban films were political and to view them, to enjoy them, or to hate them was a way of being political, a way for citizens to perform their respective political identities.

Notes

Introduction

1. Before 1971, American Documentary Films distributed 16mm copies of Cuban documentaries to schools, religious organizations, and community groups (Myerson 1973, 28).

2. There is a diversity of methodologies used to investigate reception. In television studies, sociological and ethnographic methods are common. Classic studies of reception in this tradition include the work of Ien Ang (1989, 1991), Henry Jenkins (1992), and Janice Radway (1984). For a compelling review of reception methodologies that include television, films, and literature, see Goldstein and Machor (2008). For a study that evaluates this diversity of methods, see Staiger (2005).

Chapter 1. Cuban Culture, Institutions, Policies, and Citizens

1. For an overview of the material published by *Cine Cubano,* see the *Índice de la Revista Cine Cubano 1960–1974,* published by Biblioteca Nacional José Martí in 1975.

2. For more detailed accounts, see Chanan (2004, 122–43), Paul J. Smith (1996, 65–67), Cabrera Infante (1994, 66–67), Reed (1991, 55–58), Carlos Ripoll (1985), and Thomas Anderson (2006, 100–103).

3. *P.M.* can be found through Miami-based vendors at the end of the film *Before Night Falls* (d. Julian Schnabel, 2000), and, at the moment of this publication, even on youtube.com.

4. From here on, I will use "Palabras."

5. Chanan reports that Castro was aware of this tension. In 1967, Castro mentioned to K. S. Karol in an interview the following: "Ideally, revolutions should be made when the object and subjective conditions are perfectly balanced. Unfortunately, this happens too rarely" (Karol in Chanan 2004, 391).

6. In 1986 Lisandro Otero became acting president of UNEAC because of Guillén's bad health. And from 1988, Abel Prieto became president (Azicri 1988, 186).

7. Cuba also exasperated Latin American leaders, which exacerbated internal problems during the 1960s (Padula 1993, 20–21).

Chapter 2. The Cuban Revolutionary Hermeneutics: Criticism and Citizenship

1. Casa de las Américas is both an institution (Casa) and a publication (*Casa*).

2. As commented before, the early 1960s cultural publications offered a wide array of work on aesthetics and the philosophy of culture that included the works of Sartre, Althusser, and Sánchez, to mention three that could hardly be used as theoretical support of Soviet realism.

3. Documentary, on the other hand, was immediately involved in recording the exciting first years of the revolution (Chanan 1997, 201, 219; Burton 1997).

Chapter 3. The U.S. Field of Culture

1. There are many histories written about the 1960s in the United States. Works about 1970s are less common. However, for two compelling approaches that match the goals of this book, go to Carol Fairbanks Myers's *More Women in Literature: Criticism of the Seventies* (1979) and, for a political and cultural history, Edward Berkowitz's *Something Happened: A Political and Cultural Overview of the Seventies* (2006). In film, the 1970s coincided with the rise of New Hollywood. Though New Hollywood is not the immediate context to the reception of Cuban films in the United States, it works as a cultural context worth keeping in mind. See, for instance, Horwath, Elsaessser, and King (2004).

Chapter 4. U.S. Criticism, Dissent, and Hermeneutics

1. In 1995, directors Francis Ford Coppola and Martin Scorsese helped the release of the Soviet-Cuban film *Soy Cuba* (*I am Cuba,* 1964) to American audiences (Johnson 2005). That same year, Robert Redford was instrumental in bringing *Fresa y Chocolate* (*Strawberry and Chocolate,* 1994) to American audiences.

Chapter 5. *Memories of Underdevelopment*

1. *The New Republic* is one of the most prestigious liberal magazines in the United States. Its readership is highly educated (99 percent attended college) and wealthy (the average household income in 2001 exceeded $150,000).

2. Among those that, like Kauffmann, mentioned censorship regarding *Memories* are Peter Schjeldahl (1973) of the *New York Times,* Horacio Lofredo (1973) of *Film Quarterly,* and Julia Lesage (1974) of *Jump Cut.*

3. Similarly, John Mraz (1995, 108) points out the difficulty reviewers like Andrew Sarris had with allocating the proper political value to the separation between documentary and fiction. Like others, Sarris saw *Memories* as critical of the Cuban regime.

Chapter 7. *One Way or Another*

1. For more on the issue, see chapter 2. To learn more about women's lives in Cuba, look at the important strand of feminist scholarship that has used interviews and personal narratives to represent/learn about Cuban women. In particular, see the work of Margaret Randall (1974) and Inger Holt-Seeland (1982).

2. See interviews with directors using this filmic methodology in Julianne Burton's *The Social Documentary in Latin America* (1990).

3. Ibid.

Conclusion

1. A good example of this tendency to ask this question is found in the issue of *Casa de las Américas* that celebrated the revolution's tenth anniversary. The issue included interviews with dozens of intellectuals, writers, and artists, including Juan Marinello, Alejo Carpentier, Mirta Aguirre, Cintio Vitier, Edmundo Desnoes, Miguel Barnet, and Belkis Cuza Malé, to new a few. These cultural workers were asked four questions: 1) Which cultural form has best expressed the revolution? 2) Is your literary production linked to the revolution? 3) What prerevolutionary literary tradition remains valid? and 4) What fundamental change in relation to the revolution have you experienced between 1959 and today? "Literatura y Revolución (Encuestas): Los Autores" 1968–69.

Bibliography

"1st. Congreso del Partido Comunista de Cuba: Tesis 'Sobre la Cultura Artística y Literaria.'" In *La Lucha Ideológica y la Cultura Artística Literaria,* edited by Nora Madan, 69–100. Havana: Editora Política, 1982.

A. R. "*Retrato de Teresa.*" *Revolución y Cultura* no. 78 (February 1979): 83–84.

Adler, Kenneth P. "Art Films and Eggheads." *Studies in Public Communication* 2 (Summer 1959): 7–15.

Adorno, Theodor W., and Max Horkheimer. *Dialectic of Enlightenment.* New York: Verso, 1944 [1979].

Aguirre, Mirta. "Apuntes Sobre la Literatura y el Arte" [1980]. In *Pensamiento y Política Cultural Cubanos: Tomo II,* edited by Nuria Nuiry Sánchez and Graciela Fernández Mayo, 108–21. Havana: Editorial Pueblo Educación, 1987.

"Al Pie de la Letra." *Casa de las Américas* 10, no. 57 (November–December 1969): 142.

Alexander, William. "Class, Film Language, and Popular Cinema: Jorge Sanjines and Tomás Gutiérrez Alea." *Jump Cut* no. 30 (March 1985): 45–48.

Althusser, Louis. *For Marx.* London: Allen Lane, Penguin Press, 1969.

———. *Lenin and Philosophy and other Essays,* trans. Ben Brewster. London: Monthly Review Press, 1971.

Álvarez, Santiago. "Medios Masivos de Comunicación: Cine." In *Literatura y Arte Nuevo en Cuba,* 47–52. Barcelona: Editorial Estela, 1971.

Amaya, Hector. "Unpublished interview with Pastor Vega," July 2000.

Anderson, Terry H. *The Movement and the Sixties: Protest in America from Greensboro to Wounded Knee.* New York: Oxford University Press, 1994.

Anderson, Thomas F. *Everything in its Place: The Life and Works of Virgilio Piñera.* Lewisburg, Pa.: Bucknell University Press, 2006.

Anderson, Kelly, and Tamy Gold. "Can We Talk? Cuba Mediamakers Size Up Their Future." *The Independent* 15, no. 1 (January–February 1992): 18–22.

Ang, Ien. *Watching Dallas: Soap Opera and the Melodramatic Imagination.* New York: Routledge, 1989.

————. *Desperately Seeking the Audience.* New York: Routledge, 1991.

Aranowitz, Stanley. *Roll Over Beethoven: The Return of the Cultural Strife.* Hanover, N.H.: Wesleyan / University Press of New England, 1990.

Arnold, Matthew. *Culture and Anarchy and Other Writings* [1861–1878]. New York: Cambridge University Press, 1993.

Aspinall, Sue. "*One Way Or Another:* Sue Aspinall Reports on a Recent Weekend School on Cuban Cinema." *Screen* 24, no. 2 (1983): 74–77.

Aufderheide, Pat. "Red Harvest." *American Film* 9 (March 1984): 28–34.

Azicri, Max. *Cuba: Politics, Economics and Society.* New York: Pinter Publishers, 1988.

Baran, Paul. "El Compromiso del Intelectual." *Casa de las Américas* 2, no. 7 (July–August 1961): 14–21.

Barnard, Timothy. "Death is Not True: Form and History in Cuban Film." In *New Latin American Cinema: Vol. 2. Studies of National Cinemas,* edited by Michael T. Martin, 143–54. Detroit: Wayne State University Press, 1993.

Behar, Ruth. "Post-Utopia: The Erotics of Power and Cuba's Revolutionary." In *Cuba, the Elusive Nation: Interpretations of National Identity,* edited by Damián J. Fernández and Madeline Cámara Betancourt, 134–54. Gainesville: University Press of Florida, 2000.

Belton, John. *Widescreen Cinema.* Cambridge, Mass.: Harvard University Press, 1992.

Bengelsdorf, Carollee. *The Problem of Democracy in Cuba: Between Vision and Reality.* New York: Oxford University Press, 1994.

Bennedeti, Mario. "Situación Actual de la Cultural Cubana." In *Literatura y Arte Nuevo en Cuba,* 7–32. Barcelona: Editorial Estela, 1971.

Berkowitz, Edward D. *Something Happened: A Political and Cultural Overview of the Seventies.* New York: Columbia University Press, 2006.

Biskind, Peter. "Struggles with History." *Jump Cut,* no. 2 (July–August 1974): 7–8.

Blades, Joseph Dalton, Jr. *A Comparative Study of Selected American Film Critics: 1958–1974.* New York: Arno Press, 1976.

Bordwell, David. *Making Meaning: Inference and Rhetoric in the Interpretation of Cinema.* Cambridge, Mass.: Harvard University Press, 1989.

Boudet, Rosa Ileana. "Socialización del Teatro." *Revolución y Cultura* no. 33 (May 1975): 72–83.

Bourdieu, Pierre. *Distinction: A Social Critique of the Judgment of Taste.* Cambridge, Mass.: Harvard University Press, 1988.

————. "The Field of Cultural Production." In *The Field of Cultural Production,* edited by Randal Johnson, 29–73. New York: Columbia University Press, 1993.

————. "The Historical Genesis of a Pure Aesthetics." *Journal of Aesthetics and Art Criticism,* no. 46 (1987): 201–10.

————. *The Logic of Practice.* Stanford, Calif.: Stanford University Press, 1990.

Brodkin, Karen. *How Jews Became White Folks and What that Says about Race in America.* New Brunswick, N.J.: Rutgers University Press, 1998.

Buckley, Tom. "At the Movies." *New York Times,* May 12, 1978: n.p.

Burton, Julianne. "Film and Revolution in Cuba: The First 25 Years" [1985]. In *New Latin American Cinema: Volume 2, Studies of National Cinemas,* edited by Michael T. Martin, 123–42. Detroit: Wayne State University Press, 1997.

———. "*Memories of Underdevelopment* in the Land of Overdevelopment." *Cineaste* 8, no. 1 (1977): 16–21.

———. "*Portrait of Teresa.*" *Film Quarterly* 34, no. 3 (1981): 51–58.

———. "*Retrato de Teresa.*" In *Magill's Survey of Cinema: Foreign Language Films, Vol. VI,* edited by Frank Magill, 2547–52. Englewood Cliffs, N.J.: Salem Press, 1985.

———. *The Social Documentary in Latin America,* Pitt Latin American Series. Pittsburgh: University of Pittsburgh Press, 1990.

Cabrera Infante, Guillermo. *Mea Cuba.* New York: Plaza & Janes Editors, 1994.

Canby, Vincent. "Alea's '*Certain Point,*' From Cuba." *New York Times,* March 13, 1985: n.p.

———. "Memories of Underdevelopment." *New York Times,* May 18, 1973: n.p.

Cardosa Arias, Santiago. "'Retrato,' Retrata." *Granma,* August 11, 1979: n.p.

"Cartelera," *Granma,* October 12, 1968.

Castro Ruz, Fidel. "Palabras a los Intelectuales" [1961]. In *Pensamiento y Política Cultural Cubanos: Tomo I,* edited by Nuria Nuiry Sánchez and Graciela Fernández Mayo, 23–42. Havana: Editorial Pueblo Educación, 1987.

———. "Castro Radio and TV Interview." *Revolución,* July 6, 1961: n.p.

Chadwick, Whitney. *Women, Art, and Society.* London: Thames & Hudson, 1990.

Chanan, Michael. *The Cuban Image: Cinema and Cultural Politics in Cuba.* Bloomington: Indiana University Press, 1985.

———. *Cuban Cinema.* Minneapolis: University of Minnesota Press, 2004.

———. "Rediscovering Documentary: Cultural Context and Intentionality." In *New Latin American Cinema,* edited by Michael T. Martin, 201–19. Detroit: Wayne State University Press, 1997.

———. "Cuban and Civil Society or Why Cuban Intellectuals are Talking about Gramsci." *Nepantla: Views from South* 2, Issue 2 (2001): 387–406.

Chijona, Gerardo. "*De Cierta Manera.*" *Cine Cubano* no. 93 (n.d.): 103–5.

Citron, Michelle, Julia Lesage, Judith Mayne, B. Ruby Rich, Anna Marie Taylor, and the editors of *New German Critique.* "Women and Film: A Discussion of Feminist Aesthetics" [1978]. In *Feminist Film Theory: A Reader,* edited by Sue Thornham, 115–21. New York: New York University Press, 1999.

Clecak, Peter. *America's Quest For the Ideal Self: Dissent and Fulfillment in the 60s and 70s.* New York: Oxford University Press, 1983.

Colina, Enrique. "24 x Seg." *Cine Cubano* no. 73–74–75: 102–4.

"Como Haremos." *Casa de las Américas* 1, no. 1 (June–July 1960): 3.

Cook, Pam, and Claire Johnston. "The Place of Woman in the Cinema of Raoul Walsh" [1974]. In *Movies and Methods: Volume II,* edited by Bill Nichols, 379–87. Berkeley: University of California Press, 1985.

Cooper, Arthur. "Critic as Superstar." *Newsweek,* December 24, 1973: 96.

Cossio, Nicolas. "TGA Desarrolla el Subdesarrollo." *Bohemia* 60, no. 35 (August 30, 1968): 74–75.

Cowie, Elizabeth. "The Popular Film as Progressive Text—a Discussion of *Coma*" [1979]. In *Feminism and Film Theory,* edited by Constance Penley, 104–40. New York: Routledge, 1988.

"Creación del Instituto Cubano del Arte e Industria Cinematográfica (ICAIC)" [1959]. In *Pensamiento y Política Cultural Cubanos: Tomo IV,* edited by Matilde del Rosario Sánchez, 7–10. Havana: Editorial Pueblo y Educación, 1987.

Crist, Judith. "Mazursky's Clear-Eyed Vision." *Saturday Review* 7 (August 1980): 70–71.

Cuban Cultural Workers. "A los Firmantes de la Carta al Primer Ministro." *Casa de las Américas* 11, no. 67 (July–August 1971): 146–47.

Damovsky, Marcy, Barbara Epstein, and Dick Flacks, eds. *Cultural Politics and Social Movements.* Philadelphia: Temple University Press, 1995.

Daniels, Robert V. *A Documentary History of Communism and the World: From Revolution to Collapse.* Hanover, N.H.: University Press of New England, 1994.

Davies, Catherine. "Modernity, Masculinity and Imperfect Cinema in Cuba." *Screen* 38, no. 4 (Winter 1997): 345–59.

"Declaración de la Casa de las Américas." *Casa de las Américas* 11, no. 67 (July–August 1971): 147–49.

"Declaración de la Unión de Escritores y Artistas de Cuba." *Casa de las Américas* 11, no. 67 (July–August 1971): 153–54.

"Declaración de los Cineastas Cubanos." *Casa de las Américas* 11, no. 67 (July–August 1971): 149–52.

"Declaración del Primer Congreso de Educación y Cultura" [1971]. In *Pensamiento y Política Cultural Cubanos: Tomo II,* edited by Matilde del Rosario Sánchez, 211–15. Havana: Editorial Pueblo y Educación, 1987.

"Del Estilo Epico de Bertolt Brecht," *Cine Cubano* 4, no. 21, (n.d.): 38–42.

Denning, Michael. *The Cultural Front: The Laboring of American Culture in the Twentieth Century.* New York: Verso, 1997.

———. *Culture in the Age of the Three Worlds.* New York: Verso, 2005.

Díaz, Daniel. "*Lucía* (I)." *Granma,* October 15, 1968: n.p.

Díaz, Elena. "*Memorias del Subdesarrollo.*" *Cine Cubano* 9, nos. 52–53 (January–February 1970): 79–84.

"Dirigentes de Organismos Hablan Sobre el Movimiento de Aficionados." *Revolución y Cultura* no. 1 (March 1972): 24–32.

Doane, Mary Ann. "Film and the Masquerade: Theorizing the Female Spectator." In *The Sexual Subject: A Screen Reader in Sexuality,* edited by *Screen* Editorial Board, 227–43. London: Routledge, 1992.

Dopico Black, Georgina. "The Limits of Expression: Intellectual Freedom in Postrevolutionary Cuba." *Cuban Studies* 19 (1989): 107–42.

Dorticós Torrado, Osvaldo. "Apertura del Primer Congreso de Escritores y Artistas de Cuba" [1961]. In *Pensamiento y Política Cultural Cubanos: Tomo II,* edited by Nuria Nuiry Sánchez and Graciela Fernández Mayo, 43–49. Havana: Editorial Pueblo Educación, 1987.

Downing, John. "Four Films of Tomás Gutiérrez Alea." In *Film & Politics in the Third World,* edited by John Downing, 279–301 (New York: Praeger, 1987).

———. *Internationalizing Media Theory: Transition, Power, Culture: Reflections on Media in Russia, Poland and Hungary, 1980–95.* London; Thousand Oaks, Calif.: Sage Publications, 1996.

Du Bois, W. E. B. "Of Mr. Booker T. Washington and Others." In *The Souls of Black Folk.* (1903). Retrieved on April 2, 2007, from http://www.swarthmore.edu/SocSci/rbannis1/Progs/Dubois.html.

Duberman, Martin. "An Experiment in Education." In *Left Out: The Politics of Exclusion/Essays/1964–1999,* edited by Martin Duberman, 217–28. New York: Basic Books, 1999.

———. "The Shifting Mood on Campus in the Seventies." In *Left Out: The Politics of Exclusion/Essays/1964–1999,* edited by Martin Duberman, 237–53. New York: Basic Books, 1999.

Dyer, Richard. *Stars.* London: BFI, 1998.

D'Lugo, Marvin. "'Transparent Women': Gender and Nation and Cuban Cinema." In *New Latin American Cinema: Vol. 2. Studies of National Cinemas,* edited by Michael T. Martin, 155–66. Detroit: Wayne State University Press, 1993.

Eisenmann, Linda. *Higher Education for Women in Postwar America, 1945–1965.* Baltimore: John Hopkins University Press, 2006.

"El Cine las Decidió." *Mujeres* (1974): 46–47.

Elliott, David. "'Memories of Underdevelopment' Stuns with Its Delicacy." *Chicago Sun-Times,* October 20, 1978: n.p.

"Ellos Habrian Sido Como Nosotros." *Unión, Revista de la Unión de Escritors, Artistas de Cuba* 6, no. 4 (December 1968): 236–37.

Evans, Sara. *Personal Politics: The Roots of Women's Liberation in the Civil Rights Movement and the New Left.* New York: Vintage Books, 1980.

Fagen, Richard R. *The Transformation of Political Culture in Cuba.* Stanford, Calif.: Stanford University Press, 1969.

Fairbanks, Carol. 1979. *More Women in Literature: Criticism of the Seventies.* Metuchen, N.J.: Scarecrow Press.

Fernández, Enrique. *Cuba and the Politics of Passion.* Austin: University of Texas Press, 2000.

———. "Proper Conduct." *Village Voice,* March 19, 1985, 58.

"The Film Daily Year Book of Motion Pictures." New York: Arno Press, 1950.

"The Film Daily Year Book of Motion Pictures." New York: Arno Press, 1964.

Fornet, Ambrosio. "El Intelectual en la Revolución." In *Literatura y Arte Nuevo en Cuba,* 33–39. Barcelona: Editorial Estela, 1971.

Foucault, Michel. *Language, Counter-Memory, Practice: Selected Essays and Interviews,* Cornell Paperbacks. Ithaca, N.Y.: Cornell University Press, 1980.

———. "Technologies of the Self." In *Technologies of the Self,* edited by Luther H. Martin, Huck Gutman, and Patrick H. Hutton, 16–49. Amherst, Mass.: University of Massachusetts Press, 1988.

————. *The Use of Pleasure* [1984]. Translated by Robert Hurley. *The History of Sexuality 2*. New York: Pantheon Books, 1985.

Fox-Genovese, Elizabeth. "The Personal is Not Political Enough." *Marxist Perspectives* 8 (Winter 1979–80): 94–113.

France, Peter, *Rousseau Confessions*. New York: Cambridge University Press, 1987.

Frank, David, and John Meyer. "The Profusion of Individual Roles and Identities in the Postwar Period." *Sociological Theory* 20, no. 1 (March 2002): 86–106.

Gadamer, Hans-Georg. *Truth and Method* [1960]. New York: Continuum Publishing Co., 1989.

Galiano, Carlos. "Adolfo Llauradó, o el Retrato de un Actor." *Granma*, August 8, 1979a, 4.

————. "*Retrato de Teresa*," *Granma*, July 30, 1979b, 5.

————. "*De Cierta Manera*." *Granma*, October 22, 1977, 5.

————. "*Retrato de Teresa*: 'Hacer por Medio de la Ficción, un Reportaje de la Vida Actual en Nuestra Sociedad.' " *Granma*, July 26, 1979c, 4.

García Espinosa, Julio. "La Crítica y el Público." *Cine Cubano* 1, no. 3 (n.d.): 12–13.

————. "For an Imperfect Cinema." In *New Latin American Cinema: Vol. 1. Theories, Practices and Transcontinental Articulations,* edited by Michael T. Martin, 71–82. Detroit: Wayne State University Press, 1993.

García Mesa, Héctor. "El Nuevo Cine Cubano: Con Motive del Veinticuatro Aniversario del Instituto Cubano del Arte Industria Cinematográficos." In *Revolución y Cultura,* no. 126 (February 1983): 35.

Gelbspan, Ross. *Break-ins, Death Threats and the FBI: The Covert War against the Central America Movement.* Boston: South End Press, 1991.

Giddens, Anthony. *Modernity and Self-Identity: Self and Society and in the Late Modern Age.* Stanford, Calif.: Stanford University Press, 1991.

Gilliat, Penelope. "The Current Cinema." *The New Yorker,* April 8, 1974.

Gitlin, Todd. *The Sixties: Years of Hope, Days of Rage.* New York: Bantam Books, 1987.

Goffman, Erving. *The Presentation of the Self in Everyday Life.* Garden City, N.Y.: Doubleday, 1959.

Goldstein, Philip, and James L. Machor. *New Directions in American Reception Study.* New York: Oxford University Press, 2008.

González Acosta, Alejandro. "Con Teresa, Punto y Seguido." *Cine Cubano,* no. 98 (1980): 113–27.

Gosse, Van. *Where the Boys Are: Cuba, Cold War America and the Making of a New Left.* New York: Verso, 1993.

Gregg, Kathleen Mary. "Film as a Cultural Industry: Is It Art or is It Commodity?: The Case of Film Festivals." Master's thesis, University of Texas at Austin, 1995.

Guevara, Alfredo. "La Cultural y la Revolución." *Cine Cubano* 1, no. 4 (n.d.): 45–47.

Guevara, Ernesto. *El Hombre Nuevo* [1965]. Mexico City: Universidad Nacional Autonoma de México, Coordinación de Humanidades, Centro de Estudios Latinoamericanos, Facultad de Filosofia y Letras, 1978.

———. "Notas para el Estudio de la Ideología de la Revolución Cubana" [1960]. In *Pensamiento y Política Cultural Cubanos: Tomo II,* 14–20. Havana: Editorial Pueblo Educación, 1987.

———. *El Socialismo y el Hombre Nuevo.* Mexico City: Siglo XXI, 1988.

Guillén, Nicolás. "Informe al Congreso" [1961]. In *Pensamiento y Política Cultural Cubanos: Tomo II,* edited by Nuria Nuiry Sánchez and Graciela Fernández Mayo, 66–79. Havana: Editorial Pueblo Educación, 1987.

Gunn, Giles. *The Culture of Criticism and the Criticism of Culture.* New York: Oxford University Press, 1987.

———. "*Memorias del Subdesarrollo:* Notas de Trabajo." *Cine Cubano* 7, no. 45–46 (August–October 1967): 18–25.

———. "The Viewer's Dialectic." In *New Latin American Cinema,* edited by Michael T. Martin, 108–30. Detroit: Wayne State University Press, 1997.

Gutiérrez Vera, Elsa. "Asunto: Teresa." *Granma,* August 15, 1979, 2.

Hall, Stuart. "The Rediscovery of 'Ideology': Return of the Repressed in Media Studies." In *Culture, Society, and the Media,* edited by Michael Gurevitch, Tony Bennett, James Curran, and Janet Woollacott. London: Methuen, 1982.

Halperin, Maurice. "Culture and the Revolution." In *The New Cuba: Paradoxes and Potentials,* edited by Ronald Radosh, 190–210. New York: William Morrow and Co., 1976.

Hamilton, Richard F., and Lowell Hargens. "The Politics of the Professors: Self Identification, 1969–1985." *Social Forces* 71, no. 3 (March 1993): 603–25.

Hart Dávalos, Armando. *Las Cartas Sobre la Mesa: Cuba Aclara Posiciones.* México City: Siglo XXI Editores, 1984.

———. "Trabajo Cultural con las Masas" [1981]. In *Pensamiento y Política Cultural Cubanos: Tomo III,* edited by Nuria Nuiry Sánchez and Graciela Fernández Mayo, 113–27. Havana: Editorial Pueblo Educación, 1987.

Hartl, John. "Relationships at the Heart of Cuban Oppression Film." *Seattle Times,* February 10, 1995, n.p.

———. "'Memories' Lingers on." *Seattle Times,* November 18, 1978.

Haskell, Molly. "Seeing: What Germany, Cuba, Hungary, France, and Australia Know About Women That Hollywood Doesn't." *Ms.,* June 1980, 17–21.

———. *From Reverence to Rape: The Treatment of Women in the Movies.* Chicago: University of Chicago Press, 1987.

———. "'Three Sisters,' Cuban Style." *Village Voice,* March 7, 1974, n.p.

Hatch, Robert. "Films." *The Nation,* June 11, 1973, 764–65.

———. "Films." *The Nation,* March 16, 1980, 349–50.

Henríquez Ureña, Camila. "Lucía, 1895." *Cine Cubano* 9, nos. 52–53 (January–February 1969): 3–7.

Hernandez, Andres R. "Filmmaking and Politics: The Cuban Experience." In *Conflict and Control in the Cinema,* edited by John Tulloch, 468–80. Melbourne: Macmillan, 1977.

Hess, John, and Catherine Davies. "No Mas Habermas, or Rethinking Cuban Cinema in the 1990s." *Screen* 40, no. 2 (Summer 1999): 203–11.

Hogner, Steve. *"Memories of Underdevelopment."* Austin (Tex.) *American Statesman,* June 8, 1975, n.p.

Holt-Seeland, Inger. *Women of Cuba.* Westport, Conn.: Lawrence Hill & Co., 1982.

Horwath, Alexander, Noel King, and Thomas Elsaesser. *The Last Great American Picture Show: New Hollywood Cinema in the 1970s.* Amsterdam: Amsterdam University Press, 2004.

Humm, Maggie. *Feminism and Film.* Bloomington: Indiana University Press, 1997.

Hunter, Allen. 1995. "Rethinking Revolution in Light of the New Social Movements." In *Cultural Politics and Social Movements,* edited by Marcy Damovky, Barbara Epstein, and Richard Flacks, 320–43. Philadelphia: Temple University Press, 1995.

Imeson, Jo. "Retrato de Teresa (Portrait of Teresa)." *Monthly Film Bulletin* 48 (August 1981): 160–61.

Índice de la Revista Cine Cubano 1960–1974. Havana: Biblioteca Nacional José Martí, 1975.

"Informe Central al I Congreso del Partido Comunista de Cuba." In *La Lucha Ideológica y la Cultura Artística Literaria,* edited by Nora Madan, 59–65. Havana: Editora Política, 1982.

Jauss, Hans Robert. *Aesthetic Experience and Literary Hermeneutics, Theory and History of Literature, Vol. 3.* Minneapolis: University of Minnesota Press, 1982.

Jenkins, Henry. *Textual Poachers: Television Fans & Participatory Culture.* New York: Routledge, 1992.

Johnson, Brian D. "Havana Fantasia." *Maclean's* 48, no. 2 (January 10, 2005).

Johnson, Randal. "Editor's Introduction: Pierre Bourdieu on Art, Literature and Culture." In *The Field of Cultural Production,* edited by Randal Johnson, 1–25. New York: Columbia University Press, 1993.

Johnston, Claire. "Women's Cinema As Counter-Cinema." In *Notes on Women's Cinema,* edited by Claire Johnston, 24–31. London: Society for Education in Film and Television, 1973.

———. "Women's Cinema As Counter-Cinema" [1973]. In *Feminism and Film,* edited by E. Ann Kaplan, 22–34. New York: Oxford University Press, 2000 [1973].

Kauffmann, Stanley. "Stanley Kauffmann on Films: Communist Films, Two Kinds." *New Republic,* June 10, 1978, 18–19.

———. "Stanley Kauffmann on Films: A Journal of the Plague Years by Stefan Kanfer. *Memories of Underdevelopment." New Republic,* May 19, 1973, 22,

Kearney, Mary C. E-mail to Hector Amaya. August 14, 2003.

Kenyon, Amy Maria. *Dreaming Suburbia: Detroit and the Production of Postwar Space and Culture.* Detroit: Wayne State University Press, 2004.

Kernan, Michael. "Festival Showcases the Films of Cuba." *Washington Post,* May 3, 1978, n.p.

Kim, Jun. "Regarding Film. Author: Stanley Kauffmann." *PopMatters,* May 2001. Retrieved November 11, 2001, from www.popmatters.com.

Klatch, Rebecca. "The Counterculture, the New Left, and the New Right." In *Cultural Politics and Social Movements,* edited by Marcy Damovky, Barbara Epstein, and Richard Flacks, 74–89. Philadelphia: Temple University Press, 1995.

———. "The Underside of Social Movements: The Effects of Destructive Affective Ties." *Qualitative Sociology* 27, no. 4 (Winter 2004): 487–509.

Kolker, Robert P. *The Altering Eye: Contemporary International Cinema.* New York: Oxford University Press, 1983.

Kopkind, Andrew. "Memories of Underdevelopment." *The Nation,* March 30, 1985, 377.

Kuhn, Annette. *Women's Pictures: Feminism and Cinema.* New York: Verso, 1993.

Ladd, Everett Carll. *The Ladd Report.* New York: Free Press, 1999.

Larguia, Isabel, and John Dumoulin. "Hacia una Ciencia de la Liberación de la Mujer." *Casa de las Américas* 9, nos. 65–66 (March–June 1971): 37–53.

Laverde, Cecilia. "Anotaciones Sobre Brecht en Cuba." *Casa de las Américas* 2, nos.15–16 (November–February 1963): 77–90.

Lears, Jackson. "A Matter of Taste: Corporate Cultural Hegemony in a Mass Culture Society." In *Recasting America: Culture and Politics in the Age of the Cold War,* edited by Lary May, 38–57. Chicago: University of Chicago Press, 1989.

Leiner, Marvin. *Sexual Politics in Cuba: Machismo, Homosexuality, and AIDS.* Boulder, Colo.: Westview Press, 1994.

Lesage, Julia. "*De Cierta Manera,* de Sara Gómez: Pelicula Dialéctica, Revolucionaria y Feminista." In *Discurso Femenino Actual,* edited by Adelaida López de Martinez, 269–94. San Juan: Universidad de Puerto Rico, 1995.

———. "Images of Underdevelopment." *Jump Cut,* no. 1 (May 1974): 9–11.

Levy, Yagil, Edna Mosky-Feder, and Noa Harel. "From 'Obligatory Militarism' to 'Contractual Militarism'—Competing Models of Citizenship." *Israel Studies* 12, no. 1 (Spring 2007): 127–48.

"Literatura y Revolución (Encuestas): Los Autores." *Casa de las Américas* 9, nos. 151- 52 (November–February 1968–69): 119–74.

Lofredo, Horacio D. "Short Notices." *Film Quarterly* 26, no. 2 (1972–73): 56–57.

López, Ana M. "The Melodrama in Latin America: Films, Telenovelas and the Currency of a Popular Form." *Wide Angle* 7, no. 3 (1985): 4–13.

———. "Cuban Cinema in Exile: The 'Other Island.'" *Jump Cut* 38 (June 1993b): 51–59.

López, Rigoberto. "*De Cierta Manera.*" *Cine Cubano* no. 93 (n.d.): 106–15.

López Cámara, Francisco. "Ideología y Filosofía." *Casa de las Américas* 3, no. 19 (July–August 1963): 29–32.

Lukács, György. *History and Class Consciousness: Studies in Marxist Dialectics.* Cambridge, Mass: MIT Press, 1920 [1979].

———. "Realism in the Balance." In *Aesthetics and Politics: Debates Between Ernst Bloch, Georg Lukács, Bertolt Brecht, Walter Benjamin, and Theodor Adorno,* edited by Ronald Taylor, 28–59. London: NLB, 1979.

Lutjens, Sheryl L. "Remaking the Public Sphere: Women and Revolution in Cuba." In *Women and Revolution in Africa, Asia, and the New World,* edited by Mary Ann Tètreault. Columbia: University of South Carolina Press, 1994.

Marchese, Theodore. "U.S. Higher Education in the Postwar Era: Expansion and Growth." *U.S. Society & Values, USIA Electronic Journal* 2, no. 4 (December 1997).

Retrieved November 12, 2003, from http://usinfo.state.gov/journals/itsv/1297/ijse/marchese.htm.

Marcuse, Herbert. *One Dimensional Man; Studies in the Ideology of Advanced Industrial Society*. Boston: Beacon Press, 1964.

Marinello, Juan. "Despues del Congreso" [1971]. In *Pensamiento y Política Cultural Cubanos: Tomo II*, edited by Nuria Nuiry Sánchez and Graciela Fernández Mayo, 216–17. Havana: Editorial Pueblo Educación, 1987.

Martin-Lipset, Seymour. "Coalition Politics: Causes and Consequences." In *Emerging Coalitions in American Politics*, edited by Seymour Martin-Lipset, 445–46. New Brunswick, N.J.: Transaction Books, 1978.

Martínez Heredia, Fernando. "Gramsci in 1980s Cuba." *Nepantla: Views from South* 2, no. 2 (2001): 373–85.

Marwick, Arthur. *The Sixties: Cultural Revolution in Britain, France, Italy, and the United States, c. 1958–1974*. New York: Oxford University Press, 1998.

Marx, Karl. "On the Jewish Question" [1843]. In *The Marx-Engels Reader*, edited by Robert C. Tucker, 26–52. New York: W.W. Norton & Company, 1978.

Maslin, Janet. "Film: 'Portrait of Teresa' at the Modern." *New York Times*, April 27, 1981, n.p.

Matthews, Herbert L. *Revolution in Cuba: An Essay in Understanding*. New York: Charles Scribner's Sons, 1975.

Matthews, Meg. *"Lucia." Films in Review* 25 (May 1974): 310.

Mayer, Michael F. *Foreign Film on American Screens*. New York: Garland Publishing, 1985.

McNay, Lois. *Foucault and Feminism: Power, Gender and the Self*. Cambridge, U.K.: Polity Press, 1992.

Medin, Tzvi. *Cuba: The Shape of Revolutionary Consciousness*. Boulder, Colo.: L. Rienner Publishers, 1990.

"Memorias del Subdesarrollo: Film Cubano / con Sergio Corrieri y Daisy Granados / Foto Ramón F. Suárez / Dir. Tomás G. Alea." *Cine Cubano* 8, nos. 49–51 (August–December 1968): 152–55.

Méndez Capote, Renee. "Lucia, 1932." *Cine Cubano* 9, nos. 52–53 (January–February 1969): 8–12.

Menton, Seymour. *Prose Fiction of the Cuban Revolution*. Austin: University of Texas Press, 1975.

Mesa-Lago, Carmelo. *Cuban in the 1970s: Pragmatism and Institutionalization*. Albuquerque: University of New Mexico Press, 1977.

Meyer, Robert, Jr. *Festivals U.S.A. and Canada*. New York: Ives Washburn, 1967.

Meyer, Roberto. *"Lucia:* Fastos Cubanos." *Cine Cubano* 10, nos. 63–65 (July–December 1970): 156–57.

Miller, Toby. *The Well Tempered Self: Citizenship, Culture, and the Postmodern Subject*. London: Johns Hopkins University Press, 1993.

Millet, Kate. *Sexual Politics*. New York: Avon, 1969.

Montejano, David. *Anglos and Mexicans in the Making of Texas, 1836–1986*. Austin: University of Texas Press, 1987.

Moore, Ryan. "Alternative to What? Subcultural Capital and the Commercialization of a Music Scene." *Deviant Behavior* 26, no. 3 (May–June 2005): 229–52.

Mosk. "*Retrato de Teresa.*" *Variety,* September 5, 1979, 26.

Mosquera, Gerardo. "Estética y Marxismo en Cuba." *Cuadernos Americanos* 5, no. 29 (September–October 1991): 169–86.

Mraz, John. "De Cierta Manera." In *International Dictionary of Films and Filmmakers,* edited by Nicolet V. Elert and Aruna Vasudevan, 256–58. New York: St. James Press, 1997.

———. "*Memories of Underdevelopment:* Bourgeois Consciousness/ Revolutionary Context." In *Revisioning History: Film and the Construction of a New Past,* edited by Robert Rosenstone, 102–14. Princeton, N.J.: Princeton University Press, 1995.

———. "Visual Style and Historical Portrayal." *Jump Cut* no. 19 (December 1978): 21–27.

Muguercia, Magaly. "Un Teatro Popular Masivo y Partidario." *Revolución y Cultura,* no. 32 (April 1975).

Mulvey, Laura. "Visual Pleasure and Narrative Cinema." In *The Sexual Subject : A Screen Reader in Sexuality,* edited by *Screen* Editorial Board, 22–34. London: Routledge, 1992.

Muncy, Robyn. "Cooperative Motherhood and Democratic Civic Culture in Postwar Suburbia, 1940–1965." *Journal of Social History* 38, no. 2 (Winter 2004): 285–310.

Myerson, Michael. *Memories of Underdevelopment: The Revolutionary Films of Cuba.* New York: Grossman, 1973.

Noriega, Chon A. *The Future of Latino Independent Media: A Nalip Sourcebook.* Los Angeles: UCLA Chicano Studies Research Center, 2000.

Ogan, Christine. "The Audience of Foreign Film in America." *Journal of Communication* 40 (Fall 1990): 58–77.

O'Guinn Thomas, and Andrew Hardy. "Art Films in the Suburbs: A Comparison of Popular and Art Film Audiences." In *Current Research in Film: Audiences Economics and Law,* edited by Bruce Austin, vol. 4, 45–53. Norword, N.J.: Ablex, 1988.

Otero, Lisandro. *Cultural Policy in Cuba.* Paris: UNESCO, 1972.

Padula, Alfred. "Cuban Socialism: Thirty Years of Controversy." In *Conflict and Change in Cuba,* edited by Enrique A. Baloyra and James A. Morris, 15–37. Albuquerque: University of New Mexico Press, 1993.

Paranaguá, Paulo Antonio. "Tomás Gutiérrez Alea (1928–1996) Tensión y Reconciliación." *Encuentro de la Cultural Cubana* no. 1 (Summer 1996): 77–89.

Paz, Senel. "Teresa en Dos Tiempos." *Bohemia* 71, no. 34 (August 24, 1979): 27.

Pérez, Louis A., Jr. "Toward a New Future, from a New Past: The Enterprise of History in Socialist Cuba." *Cuban Studies* 15, no. 1 (Winter 1985): 1–13.

Pérez-Stable, Marifeli. *The Cuban Revolution.* New York: Oxford University Press, 1993.

Pescosolido, Bernice A., and Beth A. Rubin. "The Web of Group Affiliations Revisited: Social Life, Postmodernism, and Sociology." *American Sociological Review* 65 (2000): 52–76.

Peyton, Patricia, and Carlos Broullon. "Portrait of Teresa." *Cineaste* 10, no. 1 (1979–80): 24–25.

Pogolotti, Graziella. "Lucia 196 . . ." *Cine Cubano* 9, nos. 52–53 (January–February 1969): 13–17.

Polletta, Francesca. "Culture and Its Discontents: Recent Theorizing on the Cultural Dimensions of Protest." *Sociological Inquiry* 67, no. 4 (Fall 1997): 431–50.

Prieto, Lourdes. "*Retrato de Teresa* de la Realidad a la Ficción." *Cine Cubano*, no. 98 (1980): 126–29.

Putnam, Robert D. "Bowling Alone: America's Declining Social Capital." *Journal of Democracy* 6, no. 1 (1995): 65–78.

"Puzzling Seizure by LA Customs of Cuba's 'Teresa.'" *Variety*, February 27, 1980, 5.

Radway, Janice. *Reading the Romance: Women, Patriarchy and Popular Literature.* Chapel Hill: University of North Carolina Press, 1984.

Ramos Vera, Magaly. "Teresa: Otra Carta." *Granma*, August 20, 1979, 2.

Randall, Margaret. *Cuban Women Now: Interviews with Cuban Women.* Toronto: Women's Press Publications, 1974.

Recio, Milena, et al. "Sociedad Civil en los 90: el Debate Cubano." *Temas*, no. 16–17 (November 1998 to June 1999): 155–75.

"Record Label Discographies." In *Wang Dang Dula! . . . It's Rock'n'rollah!* Retrieved February 21, 2003, from http://members.tripod.com/hoppula/.

Reed, Roger. *The Cultural Revolution in Cuba.* Geneva: Latin American Round Table, 1991.

Rich, B. Ruby. "In the Name of Feminist Film Criticism." In *Multiple Voices in Feminist Film Criticism*, edited by Diane Carson, Linda Dittmar, and Janice R. Welsch, 27–47. Minneapolis: University of Minnesota Press, 1994.

Ripoll, Carlos. *Harnessing the Intellectuals: Censoring Writers and Artists in Today's Cuba.* Washington, D.C.: Cuban American National Foundation, 1985.

Rist, Peter. "*Lucia*." In *Magill's Survey of Cinema: Foreign Language Films, Vol. IV*, edited by Frank Magill, 1858–63. Englewood Cliffs, N.J: Salem Press, 1985.

Rodnitzky, Jerome L. *Feminist Phoenix: The Rise and Fall of a Feminist Counterculture.* Westport, Conn.: Praeger, 1999.

Rosen, Marjorie. "The Return of the 'Women's Picture' Film." *Ms.*, June 1980: 29–34.

Ross, Andrew. *No Respect: The Intellectuals and Popular Culture.* New York: Routledge, 1989.

Sánchez Vázquez, Adolfo. "Ideas Estéticas en los Manuscritos Económico-Filososóficos de Marx." *Casa de las Américas* 2, nos. 13–14 (July–October 1962): 3–24.

Sayre, Nora. "Screen: Solas's '*Lucia*.'" *New York Times*, March 1, 1974, n.p.

Schiller, Friedrich. *On the Aesthetic Education of Man: In a Series of Letters English and German Facing.* New York: Oxford University Press, 1982.

Schjeldahl, Peter. "Cuban 'Memories' You Won't Soon Forget." *New York Times*, May 20, 1973, 13.

Schuck, Peter H. *Citizens, Strangers, and in-Betweens: Essays on Immigration and Citizenship, New Perspectives on Law, Culture, and Society.* Boulder, Colo.: Westview Press, 1998.

Schwartz, Richard. *Cold War Culture: Media and the Arts, 1945–1990*. New York: Checkmark Books, 2000.

Scott, Janny. "Stanley Kauffmann: A Steady Critical Eye on Film's Shifting Currents." *New York Times,* June 28, 1998, n.p.

Sege. "*Retrato de Teresa.*" *Variety,* November 7, 1979, 18.

Shakur, Nyisha Mbalia, and John Downing. "Selected Third World Classic Films." *Film Library Quarterly* 16, no. 4 (1983): 53–68.

Showalter, Elaine. *A Literature of Their Own: British Women Novelists from Bronte to Lessing*. Princeton, N.J.: Princeton University Press, 1977.

Smith, Paul J. *Vision Machines: Cinema, Literature, and Sexuality in Spain and Cuba, 1983–93*. New York: Verson, 1996.

Smith, Sharon. "The Image of Women in Film: Some Suggestions for Future Research" [1972]. In *Feminist Film Theory: A Reader,* edited by Sue Thornham, 14–20. New York: New York University Press, 1999.

"Sobre Un Debate Entre Cineastas Cubanos." *Cine Cubano* 3, nos. 14–15 (n.d.): 14–17.

Staiger, Janet. *Interpreting Films: Studies in the Historical Reception of American Cinema*. Princeton, N.J.: Princeton University Press, 1992.

———. *Perverse Spectators: The Practices of Film Reception*. New York: New York University Press, 2000.

———. "The Politics of Film Canons" [1985]. In *Multiple Voices in Feminist Film Criticism,* edited by Diane Carson, Linda Dittmar, and Janice R. Welsch, 191–209. Minneapolis: University of Minnesota Press, 1994.

———. *Media Reception Studies*. New York: New York University Press, 2005.

Stark, Susan. "A Trilogy of Love with a Cuban Accent." *Detroit Free Press,* May 23, 1975, n.p.

Stern, Jane, and Michael Stern. *Sixties People*. New York: Alfred A. Knopf, 1990.

Stone, Judy. "Machismo and the Revolution." *San Francisco Chronicle,* February 6, 1980, n.p.

Streeter, Thomas. *Selling the Air: A Critique of the Policy of Commercial Broadcasting in the United States*. Chicago: University of Chicago Press, 1996.

Stubbs, Jean. "Revolutionizing Women, Family, and Power." In *Women and Politics Worldwide,* edited by Barbara J. Nelson and Najma Chowdhury, 190–207. New Haven, Conn.: Yale University Press, 1994.

Taylor, Ann Marie. "*Lucia.*" *Film Quarterly* 28, no. 2 (1974–75): 53–55.

Tienda, Marta. "Demography and the Social Contract." *Demography* 39, no. 4 (2002): 587–616.

Thomson, Irene T. "The Theory that Won't Die: From Mass Society to the Decline of Social Capital." *Sociological Forum* 20, no. 3 (September 2005): 421–48.

Thornham, Sue. *Passionate Detachments: An Introduction to Feminist Film Theory*. New York: St. Martin's Press, 1997.

———. "Part I: Taking Up the Struggle." In *Feminist Film Theory : A Reader,* edited by Sue Thornham, 9–14. New York: New York University Press, 1999.

"The TNR Media Kit." In *The New Republic Online, The New Republic*. Retrieved February 3, 2003, from http://www.tnr.com/media_kit/.

Towmey, John. "Some Considerations in the Rise of the Art-Film Theatre." *Quarterly of Film, Radio and Television* 10 (Spring 1956): 239–47.

"Una Visita en Compañia de Ramón y Teresa, Detras del Retrato." *Granma,* August 1979, n.p.

"Universal 'Portrait.'" *New York Post,* May 1, 1981, n.p.

Vega, Pastor. "Cuba: El Cine, la Cultura Nacional." *Cine Cubano,* nos. 73–74–75 (n.d.): 80–92.

Vogel, Amos, et al. "Censoring Cuba." Letter. *New York Review of Books,* May 4, 1972, n.p.

Wandersee, Winifred D. *On the Move: American Women in the 1970s.* Boston: Twayne Publishers, 1988.

West, Dennis. "*One Way or Another (De Cierta Manera).*" In *Magill's Survey of Cinema: Foreign Language Films, Vol. IV,* edited by Frank Magill, 2286–90. Englewood Cliffs, N.J.: Salem Press, 1985.

West, Dennis, and Joan West. "Conversation with Marta Rodríguez." *Jump Cut: A Review of Contemporary Media* 38 (June 1993): 39–44.

Westerback, Colin L. "The Screen." *Commonweal,* July 27, 1973, 405–7.

———. "The Screen." *Commonweal,* April 5, 1974, 109–19.

Wilinsky, Barbara Jean. *Sure Seaters: The Emergence of Art House Cinema.* Minneapolis: University of Minnesota Press, 2001.

Wuthnow, Robert. *Acts of Compassion.* Princeton, N.J.: Princeton University Press, 1998.

Index

103, 188–89, 196. *See also* technologies of self

Frankin, Ricki, 84

Franqui, Carlos, 7, 12

freedom, xviii–xxi; aesthetics and freedom in Cuba, 36–38, 53; and criticism, xix, 184–95; cultural freedoms in Cuba, 11–15, 19–23, 30, 109, 127, 130–31, 161, 171, 175; culture and freedom in the U.S., 61, 70, 81, 101–3, 115–18, 123–24, 182–84; and field sociology, xvii

French New Wave, 17, 71, 115

French structuralism, 86

Friedan, Betty, 90

Fromm, Erich, 70

Fuentes, Carlos, 20

Fulbright, J. William, 83

Gaceta de Cuba, La, 16

Gadamer, Hans-Georg, 34

García Buchacha, Edith, 12

Garfield, John, 85

Gelber, Jack, 82, 84

gender. *See* feminism

Gilman, Richard, 84

Ginsberg, Allen, 81

Girón, 50

Gledhill, Christine, 98

globalization. *See* transnationalism

Godard, Jean-Luc, 76, 121, 142

Goffman, Ervin, xiv, 163

Goldmann, Lucien, 9

Goldwax records, 68

Gómez, Manuel Octavio, 49, 50

Gómez, Sara, xii, xxii, 25, 100, 108, 144–57, 160, 162

Gramsci, Antonio, 34–36, 39, 51–55, 57

Granma, xii, xxii, 7, 16, 18, 108, 127, 147, 161–65

"grunge" music, 69

Guevara, Alfredo, 3, 7, 9, 11, 12, 16, 17, 25, 27, 31, 57, 126, 180, 181, 187

Guevara, Ernesto "Che," 12, 17, 18, 38, 40, 51–54, 59, 83, 85, 108–12, 126, 130

Guillén, Nicolas, 7, 16, 28, 39–40, 48, 197

habitus, xvi–xviii, 4–8, 13–16, 26, 32–35, 115, 186–94

Hart, Armando, 7, 27, 28, 119

Haskell, Molly, 95, 135, 138, 139, 140, 173, 174

Hendrix, Jimmi, 67

Hentoff, Nat, 84

hermeneutics, xv–xxiii, 156, 186–94; hermeneutics of liberal dissent, 76–80, 88–103, 157, 166, 174–76; revolutionary hermeneutics, 4–5, 14–15, 27–32, 48, 62, 75, 110–12, 120–32, 137, 142, 148–52, 162

Holiday, Billie, 66

Hollywood film and studios, 70–72; blockbooking, 70; Paramount Decision of 1948, 70

Hoover, J. Edgar, 78

House for Swap (Se Permuta), 50

House Un-American Activitivies Committee (HUAC), 77, 115

Hoy, 31

Humm, Maggie, 90

ideology, xiii, xviii–xxii, 8, 14–16, 20–26, 29–30, 32, 35, 38–39, 41–42, 46, 47, 50–53, 55, 57, 59, 63, 64, 67, 74–75, 77, 80, 82, 84–103, 109, 110, 111, 113, 117, 123, 124, 128, 129, 132, 136, 139, 146, 149, 150, 151, 153, 175, 180–96

Instituto Cubano de Artes e Industrias Cinematográficas (ICAIC), xii, xiv, 8–17, 20–22, 25–44, 54, 57, 73, 108, 112, 131, 180, 195; women in ICAIC, 25, 131, 145–54

In these Times, 69

Italian neorealism. *See* realism

Ivens, Joris, 10

Jakobson, Roman, 86

Johnston, Claire, 95–96

Juarez, 85

Jump Cut, 77, 114, 136, 155, 198

Kael, Pauline, 76–77, 115

Kauffmann, Stanley, 76–79, 84, 114–23

Kearney, Mary C., 98
Kerouac, Jack, 82
Kissinger, Henry, 83
Koch, Stephen, 84
Kopkind, Andrew, vii–viii, 78–79
Kuhn, Annette, 97–101

labor, xxii; in Cuba, 8–13, 19, 22–23, 29, 32, 41–46, 54–55, 59, 131, 133, 134, 145, 156, 191; in the United States, 61, 65, 66, 75, 174, 175, 182
Ladd, Everett, 65
Last Supper, The (*La Última Cena*), 49
Lawrence, D. H., 92
Lears, Jackson, 72
leftism as political identity. *See* liberalism as political identity
leftist aesthetics. *See* aesthetics
Lenin, Vladimir, 22, 37, 44, 46
Lesage, Julia, 99, 198
liberal aesthetics. *See* aesthetics
liberalism as political identity, xv, xviii–xxiii, 15, 20–21, 51, 62, 65–69, 75, 79, 86–95, 109–15, 119–24, 134, 136, 142, 152, 157, 174, 182–96
Literacy Campaign of 1961, 10, 35
López, Ana, xiv, 17, 140, 167,
Lucía, xi, xii, 4, 22, 37, 40, 49, 109, 125–43, 145–47, 152, 167, 171–73, 179, 186, 188
Lukács, György, 9, 45, 86
Lunes de Revolución, 12, 13, 15–18, 57

MacDonald, Dwight, 84
Machado, Gerardo, 85, 125, 127, 130–31
machismo. *See* feminism
Mailer, Norman, 92
Man, a Woman, a City, A (*Una Mujer, un Hombre, una Ciudad*), 50
Marinello, Juan, 20, 131, 199
Marker, Chris, 10
Marwick, Arthur, 67
Marxism, xiii, xxi, 3, 12, 22, 34, 37, 51–57, 88, 89, 97, 134–39, 152; alienation, 14, 23, 40, 43–46, 53–56, 78, 107, 116, 119–22; historical material-

ism, 52, 152, 162; Mao, 3, 83; Maoism, 18, 35, 153; Marxism-Leninism, 37; Marxism of the Frankfurt School, 43, 86, 88; reification, xiii
Marxist aesthetics. *See* aesthetics
masses and massification: in American political thought, 70, 86–90, 184, 193; in Cuban political thought, 13, 17, 28, 29, 33, 38, 46, 53; mass media in Cuba, 10, 40–41, 175; mass media in the United States, 67, 70–74
Massip, José, 3, 7
Matthews, Herbert, 81
Mayne, Judith, 99
McNally, Terence, 82
Mekas, Jonas, 84
melodrama, 98, 99, 140, 143, 152, 159, 162, 167–68, 176
Memories of Underdevelopment, vii, xii, xxii, 4, 22, 37, 77–82, 106–24, 126, 127, 134, 142, 147, 157, 167, 179, 186, 188, 198
Metz, Christian, 96, 99
Michelson, Annette, 84
Military Units to Aid Production (UMAP), 11, 17
Miller, Henry, 92
Miller, Toby, xv, 33, 38
Millet, Kate, 94, 101, 136,
missile crisis, 18, 82, 85, 107
Mosquera, Gerardo, 44
Mother Jones, 69
Ms., xx, xxiii, 69, 75, 77, 173, 184
Muerte de Un Burócrata, 50
Mulvey, Laura, 96–99
Muni, Paul, 85
Murray, Pauli, 90
Myerson, Michael, vi, 83, 134–38, 197

national formation, xiii–xvi, xix, 67, 179, 195; American nationalism, 80, 83; American nationalism and criticism, 80, 83, 115–24, 153, 170, 185–88; Cuban nationalism, 4, 6, 7–14, 22, 35–38, 48, 56, 59; Cuban nationalism and criticism, 111, 112, 127, 128, 150, 166, 187; na-

tional cinemas, 111, 127, 141–43, 157, 185; nationalism, xi
National Organization for Women (NOW), 90–91
neoliberalism, xxi, 52, 182,
New Latin American Cinema (NLAC), 3–4, 46
New Left, xvii, 82, 83, 88, 138
New Man, xix, 5, 18, 35, 38, 44, 45, 51, 53–54, 59, 108, 110, 127, 160, 161, 166, 175, 192, 195
New Masses, 67
New Republic, The, xxiii, 69, 76, 77, 114–16, 119, 198
Newsweek, 76, 77
New York Book Review, 69
New York Times, xi, xii, xxiii, 75–77, 81, 84, 114–19, 153, 168
Nillson, Torre, 70
Nixon, Richard, 83–84, 114
Nordstrom, Kristina, 73
Nuestro Tiempo, 3, 7

Ogan, Christine, 71
One Way or Another, xii, xxii, 37, 40, 100, 144–57, 160–63, 167, 171, 179
Organs of Popular Power (OPP), 19
Otero, Lisandro, 18, 22, 197
Other Francisco, The (El Otro Francisco), 49

pachuco as aesthetics, 68. *See also* race
Padilla, Heberto, 12, 18–22, 26, 33, 56, 181, 192
"Palabras a los Intelectuales." *See* Cuban cultural policy
Paramount Decision of 1948. *See* Hollywood film and studios
Peck, Gregory, 82
performance and criticism, vii, xiv–xv, xx–xxiii, 189–93; American citizenship as performance, 62, 103; citizenship as performance, xiv, 179–82; Cuban citizenship as performance, 4, 58–60; political identity as performance, xiii, 176
Piñera, Virgilio, 25
Platt Amendment, 6

Playa Giron. *See* Bay of Pigs
P.M., 11–13, 17, 42, 57, 181, 192, 197
Polanski, Roman, 73
political criticism. *See* criticism
political economy, xxi, 195
political film, xii, xx, 62, 72, 74, 79, 86, 123, 181, 196
popular cinema, 47, 99, 162
Popular Front, 66
Portrait of Teresa, xii, xxii, 4, 37, 40, 156, 158–77, 179, 188
prejudice against Latin America. *See* race
Primera Carga del Machete, La, 49
Putnam, Robert, 64

race, 82, 84–86, 146; critical race theory, 88, 89, 102, 143; prejudice against Latin America, xx, 84–86, 167
radical feminism. *See* feminism
Radio Mambí, 7
Ray, Satyajit, 70
realism, 50, 95, 100, 112, 129; in Cuban criticism, 149–52, 159–67, 176; in feminism, 100; Italian neorealism, 3, 17, 50, 71; Socialist realism (also Soviet realism), 17, 34, 45–47, 151. *See also* aesthetics
reception theory, xii–xxiii, 4, 32, 46–48, 58, 61, 69, 74, 79, 90, 97–103, 122–24, 141–43, 156–57, 175–77, 179–86
Reisman, David, 70
Revolución y Cultura, xxii, 7, 12–13, 16, 22, 23, 31, 160
revolutionary citizenship. *See* citizenship, Cuban
revolutionary cultural field. *See* cultural field, Cuban
revolutionary hermeneutics. *See* hermeneutics
Rich, B. Ruby, 99
Richardson, Tony, 10
Rivera, Diego, 13
Roca, Blas, 24, 31
Rocha, Glauber, 4
rock music, 68, 69, 81,
Rosen, Marjorie, 95, 138–40, 172–73, 193

Viva Zapata!, 85
Vogel, Amos, 84

Wandersee, Winifred, 90
Washington, Booker T., 86
Washington, George, 82
Watergate Hotel, 83
Weathermen, 64, 82

We Were Strangers, 85
Wilinsky, Barbara, xiv, 70
Wilson, Sloan, 70
Wolf, William, 84
women in ICAIC. *See* Instituto Cubano
    de Artes e Industrias Cinematográficas
    (ICAIC)

Hector Amaya is an assistant
professor of media studies
at the University of Virginia.

The University of Illinois Press
is a founding member of the
Association of American University Presses.

Composed in 9.5/14 ITC Officina Serif
with ITC Officina Sans display
by Jim Proefrock
at the University of Illinois Press
Manufactured by Sheridan Books, Inc.

University of Illinois Press
1325 South Oak Street
Champaign, IL 61820-6903
www.press.uillinois.edu